D-DAY IN THE PACIFIC

Twentieth-Century Battles

Spencer C. Tucker, Editor

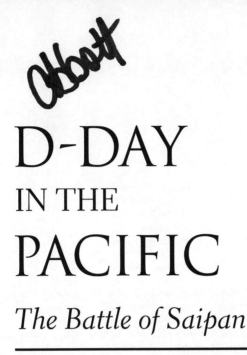

D-DAY
IN THE
PACIFIC
The Battle of Saipan

HAROLD J. GOLDBERG

INDIANA UNIVERSITY PRESS

BLOOMINGTON AND INDIANAPOLIS

This book is a publication of

Indiana University Press
601 North Morton Street
Bloomington, IN 47404-3797 USA

© 2007 by Harold J. Goldberg

Manufactured in the United States of America

ISBN 978-0-253-34869-2

For Nancy, Alex and Emily, and Zack and Alena
and
the courageous marines and soldiers whose
presence honors these pages

The Marianas are the first line of defense of the homeland.

Admiral Nagumo Chuichi

I have always considered Saipan the decisive battle of the Pacific offensive.

General Holland M. Smith (USMC)

CONTENTS

ILLUSTRATIONS

MAPS

Abbreviations Used in Maps

Symbols within a rectangle indicate a military unit. An X within a rectangle indicates an infantry unit. A dot within a rectangle indicates artillery.

The number to the left of a rectangle indicates the unit, and the number to the right of the triangle is the parent unit to which the unit belongs.

Two vertical lines above a rectangle indicate a battalion.

Three vertical lines above a rectangle indicate a regiment.

Horizontal lines connecting two numbers indicate the boundary between two units.

Unit Division

Antiaircraft Artillery   AA

Artillery   •

Engineers   E

Infantry   ⊠

Tank Division   ⬦

Unit Size

Company   I

Battalion   II

Regiment   III

Brigade   X

Division   XX

Corps   XXX

Examples

3rd Battalion, 8th Marines   3⊠8

14th Marines (Artillery)   ⊡14

Boundary between 6th Marines (Regiment)   6
    and 8th Marines (Regiment)   –|||–
                                                     8

Source for maps: National Archives or Marine Corps Reproduction Department.

ACKNOWLEDGMENTS

I am grateful to the following marines of the 2nd Division: John "Mitch" Alcorn, John Armstrong, Dick Bailey, Ed Bale, Bill Ball, Gene Brenner, Ralph L. Browner, Arnold Cook, Watson Crumbie, Sammy Davis, Joseph De Leo, Gene Douglas, Dave Dowdakin, Ed J. Driscoll, Reginald H. Dunbar, John Einarson, Fayette Ellis, James Evans, Robert E. Everett, Arthur C. Faquin, Frank Farmer, Alvin D. Ferry, John Geary, Sal "Sam" Giordano, Jerry G. Goforth, Robert L. Groves, Chuck Haffner, Raymond "Chick" Hill, Douglas P. Hopkins, Clyde Hughes, Dale W. Husemoller, William L. Jefferies, Steve Judd, Robert A. Kane, David E. Kinder, Donald Kirkman, William Krenke, M. F. Leggett, George F. Mead, James H. Monroe, James A. Montgomery, Robert R. Montgomery, Preston "Pres" Newman, Harry H. Niehoff, Wayne Lamar Owen, Robert D. Parker, Dick "Pete" Peterson, Harry Phillips, Charles D. Porter, Albert C. Rainey, Dock Riddle, Ralph Roden, Bill Rogal, Roy William Roush, Rod Sandburg, Robert Schultz, W. M. Scott, David V. Sebern, Joseph L. Shimek, Ed Skrabacz, Dodson Smith, Ken Stinson, John "Jack" Stone, Ralph Stratton, Chester Szech, Bob Thatcher, George Van Houten, Jerry Wachsmuth, Larry H. Wade, Arthur Wells, Robert Winters, and Robert Zurn.

I am grateful to the following marines of the 4th Division: William B. Allen, Walter Bailey, Jerome "Jerry" Baron, Paul B. Beverly, Bill Bouthiette, Enzo I. Brandolini, Frank Britt, Clair C. Chaffin, E. M. Cook, Julian Cusey, Leo E. "Pete" Cypher, John A. Dickinson, Jim Disney, Basil Duncan, Joseph C. Epperson, Norm Gertz, Christie Goudas, Earl P. Guy, Everett "Bud" Hampton, Howard Haury, Richard A. Hertensteiner, Willie Higgs, Bill Holden, Orvel E. Johnson, Gerald G. Kelleher, Rich-

ard S. Kelly, Charles W. Koehl, Charles A. Kubicek, John E. Lane, Dick
Lehr, Herbert Levinson, Rowland Lewis, Don MacDonald, Clint Martin,
George L. Mazarakos, William W. "Mac" McConnell, Mike "Iron Mike"
Mervosh, William L. More, John Murach, Robert H. Nicks, Joe E. Ojeda,
Alva R. Perry, David Ragan, Wallace Ralston, Jim Reed, John R. "Jack"
Rempke, Keith Renstrom, Byron Reppert, Joe R. Risener, R. B. Roberts,
Paul S. Schwartz, Marvin C. Scott, Walter H. Shiplee, Jasper Smith, Ar-
nold Stanek, Edgar E. "Earl" Steffen, William A. Stephenson, Donald
Swindle, Joe Tamulis, Alan Ian Taylor, B. G. "Bill" Taylor, Eugene V. Tay-
lor, John Teuchert, J. Edward Tincher, William Tosline, Victor L. Varanay,
Robert Verna, Peter Vogliano, R. P. Willson, and Glen E. Young.

I am grateful to the following soldiers of the 27th Infantry Division:
John F. Armstrong, Steve Behil, Frank Cimaszewski, Jack Cotton, Joseph
E. Diamond, John P. Earley, Wiliam W. Ellsworth, Luther "Luke" Ham-
mond, Charles Roy Hilbert, Clifford W. Howe, Daniel Koshansky, Julius
F. Kovalski, Erwin W. "Mark" Marquardt, Joseph Meighan, Cliff Me-
lim, John A. Munka, Liam Murphy, Eli Nicosia, Martin E. Nolan, Roy
Nyquist, Emmett Scott "Scotty" Prothero, Harold Smith, Vince Walsh,
Casimer Wilk, and J. William Winter.

Others who provided assistance include John "Jack" Armstrong, son of
army veteran John Armstrong; Stephen Bird, son of Byron Bird, USMC;
Brian Blodgett, U.S. Army warrant officer, who teaches at American Mili-
tary University in Manassas Park, Virginia; Dale Cook, Fourth Marine
Division Association; Major Charles Crosby, executive officer of the 2-
108th Infantry Battalion; Erin E. Day, granddaughter of Robert Williams,
USMC; Alan Diskin, son of army veteran Edward Diskin; Lieutenant
Colonel David Evangelista, commander of the 2-108th Infantry Battalion;
John Faquin, son of Arthur Faquin, USMC; Jeff Fought, nephew of Major
Lester S. Fought, USMC; Ann Fuhrman, coordinator, University Archives,
Oklahoma State University; Austin Geiling, Fourth Marine Division As-
sociation; Charles David Hall, son of army veteran Charles Joseph Hall;
Jack Hitt; Colonel Chuck Van Horne, executive secretary for the Second
Marine Division Association; G. Allen Meighen Jr., attorney at law; Na-
tional Archives in College Park, Maryland; Victor Olney, New York Army
National Guard; Barbara Owen, wife of Wayne Lamar Owen, USMC; Bob
"Doc" Pecce, Fourth Marine Division Association; Pat Quinn, Stillwater
News Press; Tammy Scissom in Print Services at the University of the
South, who worked on maps and photos; Beret Strong, producer of Iwo
Jima: Memories in Sand; Ben Swan, nephew of Lieutenant Harry Blaine;

University of the South Research Grants Committee; Brigadier General David Wilkinson (Ret.), former deputy commander of the 27th Brigade; and Major Gary S. Yaple, assistant operations officer for the 27th Brigade and editor of *Orion Gallivanter.*

Colonel Joseph H. Alexander, USMC (Ret.), read two chapters of the manuscript dealing with the amphibious landing. I greatly appreciate his corrections and comments. He remains the leading authority on amphibious landings, and he is certainly not responsible for any errors in this book.

My friend and colleague Dan Backlund, scenic designer and professor of theatre arts at the University of the South, traveled with me to Saipan in June 2004 for the sixtieth commemoration of the battle. Using old maps and guidebooks, we searched the island for Japanese guns, caves, and other remnants of the battle. While I drove our rental car, Dan read the map and directed me onto small roads and forgotten trails. We then hiked to our final destinations, through jungle or thick underbrush or over coral fields or up hills. We successfully found every abandoned battle site we sought, and in all these endeavors Dan's assistance and companionship were invaluable.

From the beginning of this project, Bruce M. Petty, author of *Saipan: Oral Histories of the Pacific War* and *Voices from the Pacific War,* has been generous in sharing materials and knowledge. He read the manuscript more than once and provided extremely useful comments and suggestions. I am grateful for his help and encouragement.

Professor Emeritus Spencer Tucker, holder of the John Biggs Chair of Military History at Virginia Military Institute, read the manuscript and provided detailed corrections and suggestions. I appreciate his assistance on this project as well as his many contributions to World War II studies.

Despite all of the assistance I have received, I am fully responsible for the contents of this book. I hope it will make a contribution to our understanding of World War II. I again want to thank the brave marines and soldiers for speaking with me as well as for their sacrifices in the Pacific war.

D-DAY IN THE PACIFIC

INTRODUCTION

Take all the Pacific battles that had gone before, from the fall of Corregidor to Eniwetok. Take Tulagi and Guadalcanal, and Tarawa and Attu, and Los Negros and Buna and Gona. Stir them all together, and add a little European seasoning—perhaps from Sicily—and pour them out on a flat blue sea under a blue bowl of sky, and you'll have something that looks and smells and feels and hurts like Saipan. For Saipan had everything: caves like Tulagi; mountains and ridges like the 'Canal; a reef nearly as treacherous as Betio's; a swamp like Buna; a city to be conquered, like those on Sicily; and death-minded Japs like the defenders of Attu. A lot, for so small an island.[1]

As indicated by this official history of the 2nd Marine Division, the Battle of Saipan in June 1944 included elements that made it one of the most dramatic and fascinating encounters of the war. One factor was the presence of an entrenched and dedicated enemy force, prepared to fight for victory or die in the process. The Japanese were dug into the island in numbers far greater than the Americans expected at the time of the invasion. While Japanese tenacity was not unusual in the Pacific war, the finale of the Saipan battle included mass suicides on a scale previously unknown. For Japanese soldiers and civilians, devotion to Japan's Asiatic mission and to the emperor remained primary, and many considered it their duty to die for these causes. When faced with likely defeat or the prospect of surrender, most Japanese soldiers chose death.

An equally resolute invading force of U.S. marines and army soldiers confronted these Japanese troops, with the Americans sure of victory and willing to make extraordinary sacrifices for their own cause as well. As a result the battle was bloody from its first day to its last; even with American victory assured, the fighting ended only when one side had been totally destroyed. American plans for a three-day commitment on Saipan turned into a three-week struggle. In the light of the intensity of Japanese resistance on Saipan, the resulting carnage was predictable—on Saipan, and subsequently on Peleliu, Iwo Jima, and Okinawa.

This book explores all of the factors that made the Battle of Saipan both strategically important at the time and ultimately fascinating for history. Chapter 1 introduces the reader to some of the most important American commanders, including General Douglas MacArthur and Admiral Ernest King, who clashed with each other over the best way to proceed with the war against Japan. While MacArthur pressed for a commitment to retake the Philippines, King favored a naval campaign across the central Pacific. In the end the Joint Chiefs compromised and allowed both drives to advance simultaneously. As a result, while MacArthur moved across New Guinea toward the Philippines, the U.S. Navy pressed forward relentlessly from island to island.

Chapter 2 looks at the history of the island of Saipan. The topography of this former Spanish, then German, and finally Japanese possession provided perfect cover for the Japanese defenders. The terrain included beaches, jungles, swamps, hills, mountains, valleys, and caves, and everywhere thick vegetation and dense growth. The variety of natural environments on the island confronted the Americans with constant yet ever-changing challenges, and at the same time provided the defenders with caves, hills, coral outcroppings, and other easily defensible locations.

Nevertheless, the reader learns why the island's natural defenses did not help the Japanese as much as they might have. Japanese military strategy called for constant attacks against the enemy. As a result, the defenders, committed to stopping the Americans on the beach, emerged from their caves and protective strongholds to pursue an offensive battle plan that allowed the marines and soldiers to destroy the Japanese soldiers, tanks, and equipment. This strategic and tactical error by the Japanese meant that the defenders wasted one of their best resources—the terrain of the island—and Japanese commanders exposed their soldiers to overwhelming and devastating American firepower. One of these Japanese officers was Vice Admiral Nagumo Chuichi, commander of the Japanese aircraft carrier force that had attacked Pearl Harbor in December 1941. Nagumo's death on Saipan provided American officers an additional reason to celebrate their victory.

Chapter 3 examines the training of American military personnel in Hawaii. Both marines and soldiers worked hard for the difficult battle ahead, and they left Hawaii as well-prepared combat troops. Unfortunately, one flaw in their preparation would emerge soon after the invasion began. While in Hawaii, the marines and army did not train together and did not harmonize their battle plans. During the ensuing battle it became clear that marines and soldiers, employing different battle tactics, had not carefully coordinated their views of how the battle might proceed. It was evident that the marines and the army approached the coming events from different perspectives, and this discrepancy led to an eventual clash between the service commanders during the battle.

Chapter 4 describes the morning of 15 June, D-Day for the Americans. The marines of the 2nd and 4th Divisions awoke early, were served an elaborate breakfast, collected their equipment, and said their prayers. Many knew that they or their closest friends would become casualties of the invasion. An amphibious landing is always dangerous and difficult, and the Japanese had all their guns trained on the landing beaches. Nevertheless, the marines moved on schedule toward their landing vehicles—amphibious tractors, or amtracs—for the run to the beach. For the admirals and generals the invasion was a total success, as twenty thousand Americans were ashore by the end of the first day. For the marines caught in Japanese cross fire, success was tempered by sadness that had no time to be expressed over lost buddies.

Chapter 5 focuses on the landing of the 2nd Marine Division on beaches designated Red and Green. As amtracs crossed the reef for their final approach, intense Japanese fire drove several companies away from their designated landing zones. The result was unplanned crowding in one area, providing a target for Japanese artillery and mortars. The marines took their casualties, held their ground, and pressed forward. That first night, the Japanese, intent on driving the marines off the beach and back into the ocean, attacked in force with infantry and tanks. The marines withstood the attack and destroyed most of the Japanese tanks used in the offensive. The 2nd Division accomplished its goal of holding the west coast of the island in order to allow the 4th Division to land just to its south and then swing around them, like a gate on a hinge, first toward the east coast of Saipan and then northward.

The landing of the 4th Division on Blue and Yellow beaches, explored in chapter 6, did not include the crowding and difficulties that the 2nd Division had encountered. Nevertheless, the Japanese defenders also had those beaches well in sight, and the marines suffered heavy casualties during the landing. These marines had two immediate objectives: seizing control of the airport and then crossing to the east coast, in effect cutting off the bottom third of the island and isolating the Japanese defenders at the southern tip. Within a couple of days the first task had been turned over to the army, and the second objective, traversing the island, was achieved.

With twenty thousand Americans on Saipan by the end of the first night, the Japanese position had become desperate. Tokyo had been planning for such an eventuality and was ready to commit a major portion of its navy to this battle; in fact, the Japanese had been anticipating another major sea confrontation with the Americans ever since the Battle of Midway in June 1942. With a large part of the American fleet anchored near the Marianas, the Japanese military saw an opportunity for a decisive battle that would turn the war's momentum in their favor. The Japanese plan, called Operation A-Go, had been designed for just this moment, and a huge naval force moved out from the Philippines in the direction of Saipan. Chapter 7 analyzes the disastrous result for Japan as the Imperial Navy lost more than four hundred airplanes. The overwhelming American victory, dubbed the Great Marianas Turkey Shoot, left Japan without the pilots and planes necessary for success in the war.

Chapters 8 and 9 examine the advances by the 2nd and 4th Divisions, respectively, during the succeeding two weeks. While some units of the 2nd Division moved up the west coast in the direction of the capital city of Garapan, other assault battalions were assigned the crucial task of taking the highest peaks on the island, Mt. Tapotchau and Mt. Tipo Pale. While in control of those mountaintops, the Japanese had been able to target the marines on the beaches and other areas of the island. The marines had to take those summits, and they did so only after brutal and bloody campaigns. When the Americans had achieved their objectives, the Japanese lost the advantage provided by control of the strategic highlands and were pushed toward the island's northern tip. While elements of the 2nd Division completed their mission, the 4th Division moved north along the east coast of the island. This phase of the battle also proved to be long and difficult, whether it involved crossing sugarcane fields that gave the Japanese a clear line of sight or cleaning out caves and hills that provided the defenders with good protection and shelter.

Chapter 10 departs briefly from the narrative to look at the life of a marine involved in this battle. Marines operated in a world of brutality, in which, in addition to normal combat, they attempted to navigate through Japanese traps, tricks, and ambushes. Day after day they fought in the same clothes, ate the same food, fought off the ubiquitous flies, and hoped for a few hours of sleep. The focus was on survival.

Marines were not the only American combat personnel in this battle. The army played a large role in the fight for Saipan and in the ultimate victory, and chapters 11 and 12 look at its role on the southern end and in the center of the island. In the south, elements of the 27th Infantry Division held the airfield and cut off the remaining Japanese defenders in the rocky, coral-laden fields of Nafutan Point. At the same time, the main army force moved north between the 2nd and 4th Marine Divisions. The soldiers encountered major Japanese defensive positions as they dealt with some of the most difficult terrain on Saipan. The army made slow progress, and as a result an impatient General Holland Smith, in command of all American land forces, blamed and removed General Ralph Smith, the army commander.

On Saipan the desperate Japanese soldiers were determined to kill as many Americans as possible before their inevitable defeat. During the night of July 6–7, as chapter 13 describes, several thousand Japanese moved against the American lines and nearly destroyed two army battalions. Despite heroic efforts by their officers and enlisted men, the 1st and 2nd Battalions of the 105th Regiment were decimated. Elements of Headquarters Company of the 105th as well as the 3rd Battalion, 10th Marines, also fought valiantly to stop the Japanese advance. In the end the Japanese lost thousands of troops while American sacrifices led to the awarding of well-deserved medals of honor to a few fallen soldiers and marines.

Chapter 14 describes what should have been a routine mopping up, but nothing about the Battle of Saipan was routine. Instead, Japanese soldiers performed their final act of resistance. With the battle over and American victory assured, hundreds of Japanese soldiers threw themselves, and in some cases their wives and children, off the appropriately nicknamed Suicide Cliff or Banzai Cliff. These gruesome suicides provided a horrific end to a fierce struggle in which neither side recoiled from the slaughter of close battle. For many years thereafter, this grisly scene on the northern end of the island haunted the marines, soldiers, and sailors who had witnessed it.

Chapter 15 and the Conclusion look briefly at the consequences of the Battle of Saipan—the resignation of Premier Tōjō Hideki, the American invasion of Tinian, and the larger implications of the American conquest of the Marianas. Clearly, June 1944 was the decisive month of the war.

Appendix A revisits in greater detail the dispute between the marine and army generals. While no one questioned Holland Smith's authority over Ralph Smith in the chain of command, army officers resented the way in which Holland Smith handled the situation. When certain partisan newspapers in the United States picked up the story for their own political purposes, the controversy exploded and threatened to undermine interservice cooperation in the midst of the war. While Ralph Smith lost command of the 27th Division, Holland Smith, after Saipan, was not allowed to lead army troops into battle again.

Appendix B continues the story beyond Saipan, examining the lives and thoughts of some of the marines and soldiers who fought in that battle. All participants were affected by the memory of a struggle that was both brutal and bloody, and some carried physical or psychological scars after the war. Nevertheless, most adjusted well to civilian life.

Despite all of the dramatic elements involved in the Battle of Saipan, most Americans remain unfamiliar with it. This crucial and bloody battle in the war against Japan has been largely forgotten, eclipsed by better-known events in Europe and by other struggles in the Pacific. Guadalcanal achieved fame as the first major amphibious assault by the United States against Japanese forces. Tarawa, at the end of 1943, became notorious for its high casualty count in only three days. The struggle for the Philippines in the fall of 1944 featured the gigantic personality of General MacArthur, and in 1945 Iwo Jima and Okinawa received vast coverage and recognition as American forces moved inexorably toward the Japanese home islands.

Sandwiched between these battles, the Battle of Saipan took place in the shadow of the landing in Normandy in June 1944. While the U.S. Navy crossed the Pacific Ocean from Hawaii to Saipan—in many ways a more difficult journey than its English Channel counterpart—the American public watched the situation in France more closely. Just as the European war demanded the preponderance of American resources during World War II, so too the fighting against Germany received the greatest press attention. Throughout June 1944 newspapers in the United States closely followed American progress in France, with Saipan appearing as a secondary feature. It is ironic that while events in the Pacific brought the United States into the conflict, the resources of the U.S. government and the focus of the American people remained centered on Europe throughout the war.

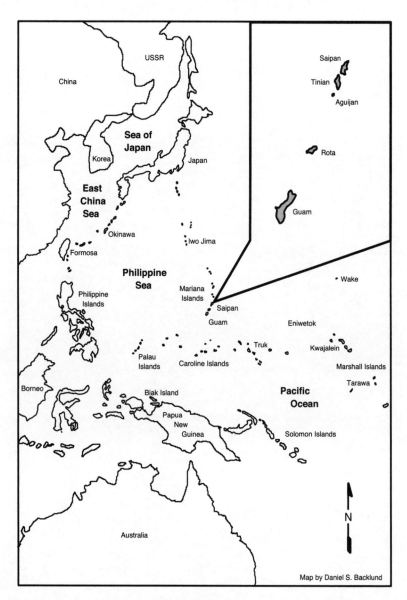

Map 1. Western Pacific with Mariana Islands inset

CHAPTER ONE

ADMIRAL KING AND GENERAL MacARTHUR

By 1943 the United States knew that the road to Berlin ran through France. Although the exact timing of the Normandy invasion would not be set until late that year at the Teheran Conference, there was no doubt that an invasion of France was a necessary component of eventual victory in Europe. Such certainty was not at all the case for the war in the Pacific. In fact, American military strategists had not decided which route would lead to Tokyo. Different services proposed alternative invasion plans: the army favored a land route across New Guinea aimed at the Philippines, while the navy supported a water route across the central Pacific. The rivalry between the services was intense.

Already subjugated to a policy of "Europe first" and the commitment to a cross-channel landing in France as a priority, American forces in the Pacific had to battle for their fair share of men and materiel. In general, the European theater received about 85 percent of the American war allocation, leaving the remainder for the war in the Pacific. This allotment of resources reflected the American view that Germany's defeat would inevitably result in the defeat of Japan, while Japan's surrender would not necessarily bring about the end of the war with Germany. At the same time, the United States and Britain had to placate Soviet leader Joseph Stalin in order to keep the USSR in the war, and that also mandated the commitment of more resources to Europe. Basically, the United States and Britain agreed that Germany was the more dangerous of the two enemies and that the Pacific war effort would receive resources as quickly as practicable. Ultimately, given the productive power of the United States, American forces in the Pacific were able to obtain materiel sooner than originally anticipated. Nevertheless, given the unequal division of resources, American accomplishments in the war against Japan should be viewed as remarkable and ranked with the world's greatest military accomplishments.

Forced to divide the 15 percent dedicated to the Pacific, the army and the navy jockeyed for position and prominence throughout the Pacific theaters. This interservice strife erupted in planning meetings as the two branches argued over future targets. Personal rivalries and ego clashes exacerbated these conflicts, with General Douglas MacArthur confronting Admiral Ernest King in a struggle for supplies and ascendancy. The perpetually enraged King was a good match for the imperious MacArthur.

MacArthur was one of the most famous American commanders of the period, and despite his lackluster performance in the Philippines early in the war he retained his position and reputation. His goal subsequently was to return to the Philippines, an obsession that was based on both strategic and personal reasons. In staff meetings in 1943 he argued that resources should be funneled to his command for use in New Guinea, the first step in the drive back to Manila. In this regard, MacArthur lobbied the American Joint Chiefs for additional military equipment for his personal road to Tokyo—from New Guinea through the Philippines and then on to Japan itself. MacArthur was a brave and perhaps even brilliant soldier, but he also swaggered with an arrogance and sense of self-importance that often annoyed his colleagues and overshadowed his talents.[1]

Despite his constant attempts to seek maximum support for his own operations at the expense of others, MacArthur did not always get his way in staff and planning meetings. He met his match in Admiral Ernest J. King, chief of naval operations during the war. In the immediate aftermath of Pearl Harbor the U.S. Navy was reorganized, with King appointed commander in chief, U.S. Fleet (CINCUS, soon changed to COMINCH; King did not like the implication of the acronym CINCUS, which could be pronounced "sink us"). He was also a member of the Joint Chiefs of Staff.

E. B. Potter, biographer of Admiral Chester Nimitz, described King as "imperious, often caustic . . . hard-nosed . . . rough, tough," and *Time* magazine reporter Robert Sherrod repeated the legend that King shaved with a blowtorch. At the same time, General Holland Smith praised King as "a brilliant man . . . dynamic, energetic."[2] He was impatient and often angry with those who did not perform up to his standards, but he was

Figure 1. Admiral Ernest J. King, commander in chief, U.S. Fleet, chief of naval operations during World War II; photo from 1945; U.S. Naval Historical Center photo.

straightforward and would tell a colleague to his face what he thought. Most importantly, if King believed he was right on an important point, he was willing to defend his position even against solid opposition. He held his ground against MacArthur.

At the Casablanca Conference in Morocco in January 1943, King argued in general for greater resources for the Pacific war and specifically in favor of a campaign in the central Pacific, with the Mariana Islands as the eventual target. At that meeting he asked the Combined Chiefs of Staff (American and British Joint Chiefs together) to establish a formula for dividing materiel between Europe and the Pacific. King considered the 15 percent of Allied resources devoted to the war against Japan insufficient to prevent the Japanese from reinforcing and consolidating their positions. He claimed that allowing this trend to continue would give Japan the time to strengthen its defenses and would only make the eventual assault against Japanese targets more difficult as the war progressed. In subsequent discussions with the Combined Chiefs, King reiterated his call for moving toward the Marianas and aiding China in its struggle against Japan. In contrast,

MacArthur's aides (the general did not attend the conference) insisted that all resources in the Pacific should be concentrated in the army's drive through New Guinea toward the Philippines. King clearly did not support MacArthur's demands; he argued that an advance across the Dutch East Indies aimed at the Philippines would be too slow and difficult.[3]

King's opposition to a push toward the Philippines put the admiral in direct opposition with MacArthur and illustrated the interservice rivalries at work at the highest levels in the U.S. military. In the end, the Casablanca Conference's final report left all attack routes open as possible options. The Allies reiterated their "Europe first" strategy and committed themselves to an invasion of Sicily and Italy. As far as the Pacific was concerned, the communiqué contemplated movement across New Guinea toward the Philippines as well as naval action in the central Pacific in the direction of the Marianas. Neither King nor MacArthur had prevailed on this issue, but each had received some of what he wanted. Indeed, neither King nor MacArthur would ever be totally successful in this struggle.

In May 1943, in order to elaborate and give specificity to some of the discussions held at Casablanca, British prime minister Winston Churchill traveled to Washington, D.C., for the Trident Conference. Following talks among the Combined Chiefs on plans for Sicily, Russia, China, and Burma and the proposed invasion of northern France in 1944, Admiral King summarized the various options in the Pacific from his perspective. The recovery of the Philippines could be attempted from several different lines of attack, he said, but "the Marianas . . . were the key to the situation because of their location on the Japanese lines of communication."[4] While the Trident meeting is generally remembered for setting 1 May 1944 as the date for the cross-channel invasion of northern France (the invasion was later postponed until June 1944), it should also be recalled as one of the moments when King's personality and determination helped push the Pacific war to the forefront of Allied concerns.

Following the conclusion of the Trident Conference, King traveled to San Francisco at the end of July to confer with Admiral Chester Nimitz, commander in chief of the U.S. Pacific Fleet (CINCPAC). Unlike King, Nimitz was easygoing and amiable; like King, Nimitz was a competent leader. Despite occasional differences, the two admirals respected each other and worked well together. In this meeting they discussed various scenarios for future action, with King returning to the theme of the importance of the Marianas. He hoped to use an offensive in the central Pacific to cut Japanese communication lines, possibly force Japan into a major

Figure 2. Admiral Chester W. Nimitz, commander in chief, U.S. Pacific Forces during World War II; photo from December 1944; U.S. Naval Historical Center photo.

sea battle, and establish American bases for the bombing of Japan. King again described the Marianas as "the key to the western Pacific."[5] In all of this maneuvering, he was the primary advocate of an assault on the Marianas.

In mid-August 1943, President Franklin Roosevelt, Prime Minister Churchill, and the Combined Chiefs met in Quebec at the Quadrant Conference. Several of the themes from the Trident meeting were revisited, with the date of 1 May 1944 reiterated for the cross-channel invasion of Europe. King, as usual, used the opportunity to argue for greater investment in the Pacific war. In the end the meeting reaffirmed the Gilbert, Marshall, Palau, and Mariana islands as targets in the central Pacific during 1943 and 1944 and also accepted the two-pronged strategy that included MacArthur's advance in New Guinea.[6]

The Joint Chiefs' decision to advance in the Pacific with a two-pronged attack was a compromise intended to keep both the army and the navy happy. One prong, under the direction of MacArthur and the army, would originate in the southwest Pacific and drive through New Guinea toward the Philippines. The other, led by the navy, would push across the central Pacific and attack Japanese island bases in the Gilberts, Marshalls, and Carolines. This dual approach satisfied the conflicting demands of the military services, each of which desired to lead the offensive. Again, neither side received all that it wanted, but each won sufficient concessions to be satisfied for the moment.

In late September 1943 King met again with Nimitz, this time at Pearl Harbor, along with Vice Admiral Raymond A. Spruance and Admiral William "Bull" Halsey, the latter in command of U.S. naval forces in the South Pacific. They reaffirmed the Gilberts and Marshalls as their next objectives and reviewed their coordination with Halsey's actions in the South Pacific. The admirals ironed out a few differences concerning which specific islands would be targeted, first in the Gilberts and then in the Marshalls.

The first step in the navy's contribution to this grand strategy was the attack on the Gilbert Islands in November 1943. The units named for the assault included the 2nd Marine Division, chosen for the landing on Tarawa, and the army's 27th Infantry Division, selected for the attack on Makin. In 1943 intelligence information accurately indicated that it would be more difficult to take Tarawa than Makin, but even that prediction severely underestimated the situation. On Tarawa, the 2nd Division faced a tough and blistering Japanese defense and suffered heavy casualties. "Bloody Tarawa" entered the Marine Corps pantheon.[7]

While the island of Makin was not as heavily defended as Tarawa, the Japanese forces stationed there fought well. Nevertheless, when the 165th Regiment of the 27th Infantry Division took three days to secure Makin, Marine Corps major general Holland M. "Howlin' Mad" Smith lost his temper and lambasted the army for not moving quickly enough. Not officially in command at Tarawa, Smith was present as an observer. He was disappointed with his limited role and resentful that he was kept on board ship throughout most of the fighting. He directed much of this anger toward the army. His dissatisfaction with the army troops and with their leader, Major General Ralph C. Smith, was communicated to Vice Admiral Spruance and Rear Admiral Richmond Kelly Turner. While this incident faded without further repercussions, all of the leading officers would be involved at the Battle of Saipan when interservice rivalry and tactical disagreements emerged again. Holland Smith carried his resentment against the army from the Gilberts to the Marianas.

Figure 3. Admiral Raymond A. Spruance (*left*), commander of U.S. Fifth Fleet, and Lieutenant General Holland M. Smith (USMC), commander of V Amphibious Corps, attend flag-raising ceremonies in Charan Kanoa, Saipan, 10 July 1944; U.S. Naval Historical Center photo.

With the victories at Tarawa and Makin the war seemed to be going well for the United States, with one rapid victory after another. Beneath the surface, however, and certainly unknown to the American public, serious antagonisms were developing within the services. This situation would explode at Saipan, and Holland Smith was a central figure in this story. The Gilbert Islands offensive exposed Smith's views regarding "his" marines versus the army. Disappointed with the progress of the 165th Regiment at Makin during the Gilbert Islands attacks, Smith claimed that "any marine division" would have taken the island in one day, whereas the army took three. He complained that he was "very dissatisfied with the regiment's lack of offensive spirit," but he felt that it "probably was not the fault of the men." The marine general blamed the officers of the 165th Regiment and specifically the division commander, Ralph Smith. Howlin' Mad told Nimitz: "Had Ralph Smith been a marine I would have relieved him of his command on the spot."[8] Howlin' Mad would eventually make good on this threat during the Battle of Saipan.

Further, in his own account of the events on Makin, Holland Smith related the story of an army company that was "firing indiscriminately right and left" and disrupting other military operations. Smith got out of his jeep to reprimand the lieutenant in command, telling the young soldier that "any damn fool can see there aren't any Japs up there. . . . If I hear one more shot from your men in this area I'll take your damn weapons and all your ammunition away from you." Smith acknowledged that he was "howling mad" at this point. In contrast, when the 4th Marine Division landed on Roi-Namur and spent the night firing indiscriminately at sounds in the jungle, Smith remarked only that the marines, "like most new troops . . . had fallen prey to a trigger-happiness only exceeded by what I had seen at Makin." Despite this lapse, Smith asserted that the "division as a whole had acquitted itself well, manifesting the dash and offensive spirit which I regard as essential and characteristic in Marine Corps units."[9] Apparently, Smith did not become "howling mad" at the trigger-happy marines. In fact, he may have indulged in some trigger-happy behavior himself. While on Makin, the army and marine generals were conferring, with Howlin' Mad "nagging" Ralph Smith on the progress of army troops. An army officer ran into the command post to report that Japanese snipers had the area surrounded. In accordance with proper military procedure, Ralph Smith immediately called for rifle companies to move in that direction to deal with the threat. Colonel (later General) S. L. A. Marshall recalled that "Holland Smith picked up his carbine and stalked into the bush. He was gone for about five minutes, and then returned, rubbing his hands. 'Well, I took care of those bastards.'" Marshall called Holland Smith's action "about as ridiculous a grandstand play as I have ever seen by a general officer, which is saying a lot. The sniping continued for about twenty minutes following his boast."[10] Overall, the marines and the army forces on the Gilberts had done their jobs well under the circumstances, but Howlin' Mad's view toward the army was already apparent.

The conquest of the Gilberts took a lot of American lives. The army lost only 66 killed and 185 wounded, but marine casualties at Tarawa numbered closer to three thousand. While Tarawa was not the bloodiest battle of the Pacific war, it attained notoriety because the high casualty count occurred in only a few days. The numbers reflected not only the strong Japanese defenses on Tarawa but also the inadequate and insufficient American landing vehicles that left the marines wading ashore directly into devastating gunfire.

At the same time, the battles for Tarawa and Makin revealed a fundamental difference in marine and army tactics. The marines employed a method of direct assault, seeking to attack each target frontally and as quickly as possible. During the war the marines were often criticized for this method. Newspapers and parents back in the United States complained that marine leaders took unnecessary risks and as a result suffered too many casualties.[11] The army preferred a slower, more methodical offensive action, with artillery clearing the path for the ground troops that advanced behind the barrage. These variant tactics would again emerge on Saipan, contributing to the infamous marine-army bureaucratic battle.

Nevertheless, in the Gilberts, and especially at Tarawa, the United States learned many lessons about amphibious landings that would be applied to future targets. Americans did not possess adequate intelligence about the Gilberts; marines did not even know about the presence of the coral reef. The Americans approached the beach with an insufficient number of landing vehicles and did not have the information they needed about the tides in that area; as a result, many of the vehicles became hung up on the reef. All of these factors contributed to increased casualties. Following Tarawa, American planners realized that they needed to have recent intelligence photographs of enemy positions, better knowledge of tides and reef formations, and more landing vehicles. In addition, the admirals and their staffs were learning to appreciate the importance of airpower, and they accelerated the building of air bases on each suitable island and used these new forward positions to bomb their next target. This airpower proved to be a formidable weapon for the American offensive. Because of the eventual American victory in the war, it is easy to forget that the navy, marine, and army commanders were inventing this new type of warfare, on the beaches and in the air, as the fighting progressed. Fortunately for American forces, the lessons learned at Tarawa and Makin were applied in the assault on the Marshalls and eventually on Saipan.

While the American attack on the Gilberts was taking place in November 1943, the Joint Chiefs finally accepted King's view on the importance of the Marianas. King had long argued that the Marianas were the strategic key to the western Pacific and that American success there would cut Japanese communication lines to the rest of its empire. Not all the Joint Chiefs were convinced, but General Henry "Hap" Arnold, head of the U.S. Army Air Forces, helped tip the balance in King's favor. Arnold recognized that the Marianas would provide a perfect base for the new long-range bomber, the B-29 Superfortress, just coming off the line in American factories. When loaded with four tons of bombs the B-29 could fly up to 3,500 miles, putting the distance from the Marianas to Japan well within its target range. Saipan was closer to Japan (1,200 miles) than the closest usable Chinese airfields (1,600 miles) were. Further, Arnold and several other members of the Joint Chiefs recognized that the Chinese military was not capable of safeguarding B-29 bases in China owing to the military and political situation in that country. As King indicated and Arnold concurred, the Marianas were a better choice.

When they met at the Cairo Conference (code-named Sextant) in November 1943, Roosevelt and Churchill accepted the recommendation to include the Marianas as an objective. The final report resulting from their consultations affirmed once again the two-pronged strategy in the Pacific. MacArthur would attack through New Guinea toward the Philippines, while Nimitz would direct a naval advance across the central Pacific. Tentative dates were assigned to each target, with an attack on the Marianas scheduled for 1 October 1944. The plan recognized that the defeat of Japan on other islands might necessitate a revision and acceleration of the offensive scheme. In both the southwest Pacific and the central Pacific, the services would have to work together, with naval support provided for MacArthur while marine and army units carried out the actual landings on the targeted Pacific islands.

While the general outline of an offensive now existed, the details remained to be finalized and some interservice rivalry still had to be overcome. Fearing that an additional commitment to a drive in the central Pacific would detract from his own goals, MacArthur launched a furious lobbying campaign against the two-pronged approach, insisting on a single line of attack through New Guinea aimed at the Philippines. Early in 1944 he appealed directly to the Joint Chiefs and then to Secretary of War Henry Stimson to shift navy operations in his direction, using the example of "Bloody Tarawa" to warn of the consequences of naval and amphibious tactics. At the end of January Nimitz called a meeting of Pacific theater commanders at Pearl Harbor. Pursuing the argument along these lines, U.S. Army lieutenant general Richard Sutherland, who represented MacArthur at this meeting, asserted that an operation in the Marianas would be too costly in men and materiel. He further stated that Saipan did not possess the deep-water harbors that the navy needed as advance bases for a move toward Japan. Instead, Sutherland proposed concentrating all forces in the Pacific along the New Guinea–Philippines line. Nimitz communicated these arguments to King. At the same time, MacArthur wrote to the U.S. Army's chief of staff, General George C. Marshall, recommending that the Marianas be dropped in favor of his offensive in the southwest Pacific. King, who had already devoted considerable energy to the Marianas approach and considered the matter settled, sent Nimitz a strongly worded letter reiterating his reasons for the two-pronged approach. Calling the abandonment of the central Pacific strategy "absurd," King reminded Nimitz that the Marianas and Carolines could not be ignored, as both played a vital role in the Japanese communications network. Having already won this argument with colleagues in Washington, King pointed out that the MacArthur plan was "not in accordance with the decisions of the Joint Chiefs of Staff."[12] King remained adamant, and again his view prevailed.

With these issues seemingly resolved, the Joint Chiefs drafted Operation Flintlock, designating the Marshalls as the next target for American forces. After some discussion and compromises, naval commanders set the attack for the end of January 1944, with the newly formed 4th Marine Division and the army's 7th Infantry Division assigned the primary landing tasks. The command structure remained nearly the same as it had been in the Gilberts, with Rear Admiral Turner in charge under Vice Admiral Spruance's overall direction. Unlike the situation in the Gilberts, when he served primarily as an observer and adviser, Holland Smith was given command of the marine and army troops once they were on the beach.

American forces were able to use their new bases in the Gilberts to fly reconnaissance missions over the Marshalls and then to bomb Japanese airfields and supply ships. Combined with the air assaults launched from Task Force 58, a fast carrier force under Rear Admiral Marc A. Mitscher, the successful bombing campaigns ensured that Japanese planes would not challenge American troop landings; indeed, American ships were not seriously threatened by Japanese airpower during the entire Marshalls operation.

The important Japanese base at Kwajalein in the Marshalls was the major target. Following the uncontested capture of Majuro Island at the end of January 1944, American naval forces began heavy bombardment of Roi-Namur and Kwajalein, destroying many Japanese defenses. The 4th Marine Division landed on Roi-Namur on 1 February, while the 7th Infantry Division went ashore on Kwajalein. Both operations went well, and within a week the islands were secure.

Following the rapid success of these landings, Nimitz, in consultation with Spruance, approved an immediate attack on the major Japanese base at Eniwetok, 350 miles northwest of Kwajalein. In order to support this operation, Japanese airpower again had to be controlled, and before the landing at Eniwetok, Task Force 58 bombed the enemy base at Truk in the Caroline Islands as well as air bases in the Marianas. The attack on Truk was a complete success, destroying over two hundred Japanese planes, sinking fifteen ships, and providing crucial flanking protection for the Eniwetok operation.

This time the assault troops were the unused reserves from the Kwajalein operation: the 22nd Marine Regiment (reinforced) and two battalions of the 106th Regiment of the 27th Infantry Division.[13] These landings in mid-February also went well, and the objectives were achieved in several days. King's memoirs indicate that the admiral "was well pleased not only with Spruance's excellent planning but with the almost perfect timing of his forces in the execution of these plans."[14] As a result of this victory, Nimitz recommended that King promote Turner to vice admiral, and King approved this suggestion and added a recommendation for Spruance's promotion to full admiral (four stars). After some political maneuvering by the Marine Corps, Holland Smith was promoted to lieutenant general in March; despite this honor, Smith was annoyed that he had been promoted after Spruance and Turner. At the same time, Mitscher was promoted to vice admiral, and the force in the central Pacific was renamed the Fifth Fleet.[15] The United States was poised for a major push against the Japanese Empire.

It can be argued that American naval victories in 1943 and 1944 were comparable to the Japanese naval blitzkrieg of 1941–42. The United States moved faster than anyone anticipated, and the victories in the Gilberts and Marshalls forced decisions on the direction of future American attacks in the Pacific. With the Marshalls under control, the United States had to drive toward the west—either southwest toward the Carolines, as originally envisioned, or northwest toward the Marianas. Again, King emerged as the primary proponent for a push in the direction of the Marianas, a strategic position he had advocated for more than a year.

In anticipation of this strategy, the U.S. Navy planned a photographic reconnaissance and bombing run over Saipan. After taking control of the Marianas from Germany in 1914, the Japanese received a formal mandate to govern the islands from the League of Nations in 1920. Since 1935 these possessions had been closed to the outside world. As a result, the United States had little intelligence on the islands, with the exception of Guam, a former American colony. The immediate American goal was twofold: to acquire better intelligence and to bomb and destroy Japanese land-based airplanes. At this point Task Force 58 acquired and played a crucial—some might even say decisive—role in the progression of the war.

Marc A. "Pete" Mitscher was in command of this division of the Fifth Fleet—the fast carrier force, or Task Force 58. This innovative section of the navy revolutionized warfare from 1943 to 1945 by spearheading the American naval mobile attacks that caught the Japanese off-balance.[16] Composed of new *Essex*- and *Independence*-class aircraft carriers as well as fast battleships, cruisers, and destroyers, all of which could sail at thirty knots, this task force moved rapidly around the Pacific and used its carrier planes to weaken Japanese targets by destroying enemy land-based aircraft before the marines landed. According to the Department of the Navy:

> The preceding Yorktown class carriers formed the basis from which the Essex class was developed. Intended to carry a larger air group . . . USS Essex was over sixty feet longer, nearly ten feet beamier and more than a third heavier. A longer, wider flight deck and a deck-edge elevator facilitated more efficient aviation operations, enhancing the ships' offensive and defensive air power. Machinery arrangement and armor protection was greatly improved. These features, with the provision of more anti-aircraft guns, gave the ships much-enhanced surviv-ability. . . . The Independence class design featured a relatively short and narrow flight deck and hangar, with a small island. To compensate for this additional topside weight, the cruiser hulls were widened amidships by five feet. The typi-cal air group, originally intended to include nine each of fighters, scout-bombers and torpedo planes, was soon reoriented to number about two dozen fighters and nine torpedo planes. These were limited-capability ships, whose principal virtue was near-term availability. Their small size made for seakeeping problems and a relatively high aircraft accident rate. Protection was modest and many munitions had to be stowed at the hangar level.[17]

Mitscher sent his carrier planes to strike before the Japanese were ready and where they least expected to be attacked. Task Force 58 affirmed airpower as being at the center of naval campaigns. Naval warfare had become air battles fought over the ocean.

After carrying out a bombing strike against Truk on 17–18 February 1944, Mitscher led his carrier force on a reconnaissance mission to the Marianas. Although the fleet had to fight off several Japanese air attacks on its way to Saipan, no American vessels were damaged in these encounters. Mitscher was able to move his ships about one hundred miles off the west coast of the Marianas by February 22. The next morning American carrier planes flew over, took pictures of, and bombed Japanese installations on Saipan, Tinian, and Guam. While estimates of the number of Japanese planes destroyed varied between 135 and 168, the success of the operation was clear. At the same time, the Americans placed five submarines off the coast in case Japanese ships attempted to move away from the Marianas during the bombing runs. Again the plan worked perfectly, with at least six enemy ships sunk.

While the photos of the beaches and airfields provided important information for American planners, the quality and interpretation of the pictures proved uneven. The carrier planes involved in the attack were more concerned with the bombing mission than with the photographic objectives, and the photos obtained were often of areas with little strategic importance or difficult to decipher topographically. According to an American intelligence review, "the sorties were partially cloud covered and it was not a complete coverage. However, from these photos were made most of the maps used on this operation. This will explain why the maps were not very accurate, and proved at times to be of limited aid to the ground forces." In addition, "clouds, trees, and the angle at which the photos were taken helped hide the true nature of the terrain, so that many a cliff was interpreted on the map as a gentle slope." The lack of depth in the photos and on the maps created a serious problem: "For some reason neither [photos or maps] showed accurately the extreme ruggedness of the Saipan terrain." This appraisal was acknowledged in the intelligence assessment which admitted that the most useful map was Japanese: "This map proved to be of great value to infantry units as well as the artillery as it gave ground forms and elevations much more accurately and in greater detail than the Special Air and Gunnery Target Area Map, which was made from vertical and oblique photographs." Fortunately, the submarine *Greenling* sailed around the Marianas in April and snapped good-quality pictures of the landing beaches and approach routes.[18]

Admiral Spruance was aware of the mediocre quality of the photos but decided not to risk another major reconnaissance mission so soon after the February excursion; he did not want the Japanese to realize that Saipan was his next target. By not paying too much attention to the Marianas in pre-invasion bombings or photographic missions, the Americans were able to keep the Japanese guessing about their objectives. Of course, the primary factor in maintaining this element of surprise was the speed of the overall American advance in the Pacific. By the time the Japanese recognized the American threat, it was too late to rush supplies to the Marianas. The United States controlled both the air and sea lanes by early 1944, and Japanese merchant and supply shipping was seriously damaged and diminished by American bombing and submarine patrols.

The United States conducted additional photo flights over the Marianas on 18 April and 29 May, and the new photos revealed some of the defensive measures and weapons on Saipan. Reports noted "feverish defensive preparations" in the Tanapag Harbor area, and "it was believed possible that troop reinforcement of Saipan was being attempted." Nevertheless, American intelligence underestimated both the quantity of weapons and the number of enemy soldiers. The final American intelligence estimates of 13 June, only two days before D-Day, indicated that the Japanese had between 15,000 and 17,600 soldiers on Saipan. The American military believed that only 9,000 to 11,000 of those were combat troops and that the rest were primarily construction and maintenance workers. In actuality, the Japanese had close to 30,000 defenders on Saipan. As a result of this inaccurate intelligence, American forces encountered greater resistance than anticipated in the conquest of Saipan.

The Americans were not the only forces operating with faulty intelligence, as the Japanese also missed the significance of the impending battle. Captured Japanese documents indicated that as late as 14 June, the day before the American landing, the Japanese anticipated an invasion only in late June or in August: "It is a certainty that he [the U.S. forces] will land in the Marianas Group either this month or next." Fortunately for the Americans, the photo missions had not changed the Japanese conviction that the Palaus would be the American objective after the Gilberts and Marshalls.[19]

The rapid success of the Marshalls operations allowed the Joint Chiefs to accelerate the timetable for the rest of 1944. The Joint Chiefs held a crucial planning meeting in Washington on 11–12 March 1944, with both Admiral Nimitz and Lieutenant General Sutherland, who again represented MacArthur, in attendance. MacArthur's attempt to slow the offensive in the central Pacific and to focus all attention on his own theater of operations once more proved unsuccessful. Realizing that he could not stop the navy's advance, MacArthur wanted to accelerate his own offensive so that the navy did not get too far ahead of him. The Joint Chiefs gave MacArthur permission to jump four hundred miles across New Guinea and occupy Hollandia. At the same time, King won his argument when on 12 March the Joint Chiefs ordered the newly designated Fifth Fleet to bypass the Carolines and instead aim at the Marianas. The new target date was 15 June.

As King had advocated, the goal was to disrupt Japanese communications and establish American air bases in this strategic location. For the first time as part of a major naval operation, creating air bases took precedence over finding deep-water harbors. This new objective accurately reflected the growing strategic importance of long-range bombing. In addition, King and the Joint Chiefs had one other goal in mind for the Marianas operation: they hoped that the threat to Japan would be so immediate that the Imperial Navy would be forced to defend the Marianas by attacking the American fleet.

Unlike 1942, when the Japanese were the aggressors in the Pacific, it was now the Americans who hoped for a decisive battle like Midway. The Marianas operation would be the first U.S. assault on Japan's inner defense line, and the Japanese would have to protect this territory. A Japanese document dated 20 May 1944 called the Marianas "the final defensive positions of the homeland," a sentiment repeated in a Japanese order on 14 June: "The Marianas are the first line of defense of the homeland."[20] As a result, American expectations were fulfilled both on land and sea, as the Japanese defended the Marianas almost to the last man while the Japanese navy also emerged for a major fight.

With so much at stake in the invasion of the Marianas, Nimitz realized that a meeting with MacArthur was necessary in order to ensure close cooperation and coordination. To demonstrate his importance and power, MacArthur preferred to stay in Australia and force others to come to him. At the end of March 1944 Nimitz flew to Brisbane. At first the discussions seemed to go well, but when the two began to discuss areas of jurisdiction, MacArthur became angry. He exploded when Nimitz hinted that a collapse of Japanese power could result in an American jump directly to Taiwan and China, sidestepping the Philippines, for a final assault on Japan. According to Nimitz, MacArthur "blew up and made an oration of some length on the impossibility of bypassing the Philippines, his sacred obligations there—redemption of the 17 million people—blood on his soul—deserted by American people." While in the end the navy agreed to help cover MacArthur's invasion of Hollandia, Nimitz developed a clear understanding of the general's persona: the admiral reported that MacArthur was "highly intelligent, with a magnetic personality, but also with an unfortunate tendency to strike poses and to pontificate."[21]

MacArthur proceeded with his advance on New Guinea, using a brilliant plan that allowed his troops to capture Hollandia in April 1944. Following that victory he continued his thrust across New Guinea, outflanking and outsmarting the Japanese defenders. MacArthur's motives were not totally selfless, as he wanted to accelerate his timetable to prevent Nimitz and the navy from claiming all the glory in the defeat of Japan.

The Japanese slowed MacArthur's advance at Biak Island, preventing the general from offering "Biak's airstrip to Nimitz for the Saipan operation."[22] These two aspects of MacArthur's identity—his military brilliance and his egotistical competitiveness—always coexisted next to the "blood on his soul" from his defeat in the Philippines in late 1941 and early 1942.

As mandated by the Joint Chiefs, the navy provided logistical support for MacArthur. Task Force 58 attacked the major Japanese base at Truk in the western Carolines as well as the headquarters of the Imperial Fleet in the Palaus. The Americans wanted to establish air supremacy in order to prevent Japanese land-based planes from reaching either MacArthur's forces in New Guinea or the marines once they landed on Saipan. At the end of March the attack on the Palaus destroyed 150 Japanese planes and more than 100,000 tons of shipping, while the Americans lost only 25 aircraft. One month later the Americans hit Truk again and destroyed 93 planes while losing 27.[23]

Mitscher's Task Force 58 deserved tremendous credit for its actions in the first half of 1944. The raids on Truk in February, March, and April, on the Marianas in February, on the Palaus in March, and back to the Marianas in June kept the Japanese guessing and constantly shifting their naval and air resources to avoid the American carriers. Of course they could not escape, as the carriers could hit targets from hundreds of miles away. The Japanese plan for a massive naval battle with the United States counted on land-based planes on Saipan, Guam, and elsewhere being able to strike American ships, but by the time the battle started those planes no longer existed.

After Mitscher's carrier planes bombed the Marianas, including Saipan, on 22–23 February 1944, Task Force 58 left to hit other targets in the Pacific before returning in June in advance of the main American Expeditionary Force. Before the American fleet under Spruance and Turner reached Saipan on 14 June, Task Force 58 sailed toward the Marianas to destroy Japanese airpower and clear the way for the amphibious landing. The Japanese had unwittingly assisted this process by transferring half of their planes in the direction of New Guinea to help defend Biak against the continued advance of MacArthur's troops. MacArthur was pushing across New Guinea toward the Philippines while the navy was crossing the central Pacific, taking one island group after another from the Japanese. This two-pronged American advance across the Pacific proved successful in weakening Japanese defenses. Although this strategy divided American forces, in practice it stretched Japanese resources beyond their capabilities.

With MacArthur's bold move through New Guinea, followed by his strike against Biak, Japanese military planners guessed that the next major American objective was the Palaus rather than the Marianas. The Japanese military began to concentrate their forces in the Palaus. Moving planes toward Biak and the Palaus appeared logical to the Japanese given the speed of MacArthur's thrust. The American strategy devised by Admiral King in Washington and by Admiral Nimitz at Pearl Harbor envisioned the invasion of the Marianas first and the attack on the Palaus subsequently. The Japanese, already on the defensive throughout the Pacific, made the wrong decision, and it cost them dearly. They were unable to mass their air and naval forces to stop the American advance in the Marianas.

Mitscher's Task Force 58 raided the Palaus in March 1944. To escape American carrier planes, the Japanese navy sailed for Tawitawi Island in the Sulu Archipelago in the southwestern Philippines. As part of this same redeployment, the Japanese moved their land-based planes out of the Marianas and flew them southwest. When Task Force 58 bombed Saipan in June, the Japanese were still not sure whether this attack was simply another quick strike by Mitscher or the beginning of a major invasion. Throughout these events, Japan continued to plan for and anticipate a confrontation with the American fleet wherever the next large-scale attack would take place; unfortunately for the Japanese, their transfer of ships to Tawitawi Island left their fleet sixteen hundred miles away from the U.S. Navy at the time of the Marianas invasion.[24]

In all of these operations the outcome was positive for the Americans, not only because the numbers favored the United States but also because the United States was producing far more planes than Japan. The Japanese could ill afford the loss of either aircraft or pilots. Having achieved his objective of neutralizing Japanese airpower in the western Carolines and Palaus, Spruance was ready to move on to the Marianas.

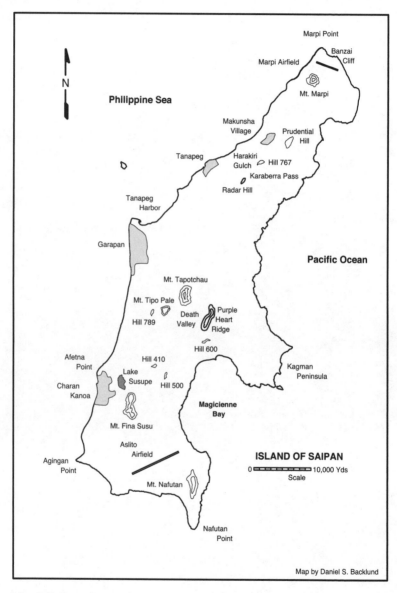

Map 2. Saipan

CHAPTER TWO

THE TARGET

In the course of his attempt to circumnavigate the earth in the service of Spain, the Portuguese explorer Ferdinand Magellan landed on Guam in 1521 to procure supplies. According to most books on this subject, Magellan's sailors called the discovery Las Islas de los Ladrones, or the Islands of Thieves, because the natives attempted to steal from their ships. It is just as likely that the European sailors stole from the natives. Undoubtedly, serious communication problems prevented the native population from understanding the European concept of trade. More than one hundred years later, in the 1660s, the Spanish began serious missionary work on the islands and gave them their modern name, Las Marianas, in honor of Queen Maria Anna (Mariana), the second wife of King Philip IV. The Marianas remained under Spanish control until 1898, when the United States took possession of Guam in the Spanish-American War. The following year Spain sold the other islands, along with the Caroline Islands, to Germany for about four million dollars. At the end of 1914 Japan occupied the islands, and following the war the Treaty of Versailles awarded the German Marianas and Carolines to Japan: "German Islands North of the Equator. The mandate shall be held by Japan." While technically the islands were part of the League of Nations mandate system, in practice they became Japanese possessions. The United States retained Guam until the Japanese occupied it two days after the attack on Pearl Harbor.

The Marianas comprise fifteen islands, but only the four southern islands—Saipan, Tinian, Rota, and Guam—are sufficiently large to be of economic or military value. The biggest is Guam (206 square miles), located about one hundred miles southwest of Saipan. Despite Guam's strategic location, the U.S. government largely ignored it between the wars. In contrast, the Japanese government worked hard to develop Saipan, Tinian, and Rota, bringing large numbers of workers from Japan, Korea, and Okinawa to develop sugarcane fields, sugar refineries, and distilleries, with the finished products mostly exported back to the Japanese home islands. During World War II, Japan built airstrips on all three islands.

Saipan is more than 3,200 miles from Hawaii, almost 1,350 miles from Kwajalein, 1,500 miles from the Philippines, and approximately 1,260 miles from Tokyo. While Tinian produced large amounts of sugar, and Rota possessed phosphate mines, Saipan remained the most important island economically and militarily to the Japanese. With a width that varies between 2.5 and 5.5 miles and a length of 12.5 miles, Saipan covers approximately seventy-five square miles. Owing to the island's location fifteen degrees north of the equator, the weather is warm in the summer, with tropical breezes, overcast skies, and frequent afternoon thunderstorms. Enjoying plentiful rain and good soil, Saipan supported the cultivation of corn, citrus, coffee, tapioca, pineapple, and sugarcane, the last of which was processed either in the capital city of Garapan or in the smaller town of Charan Kanoa. Mt. Tapotchau, 1,554 feet high, dominates the center of the island, and to its west is Mt. Tipo Pale at 1,133 feet. Those mountains and the surrounding area are covered with thick brush and forest growth and are home to numerous caves, ravines, and valleys. From Mt. Tapotchau the mountainous terrain continues for about seven miles to the northern end of the island, where Mt. Marpi rises to 833 feet. Elevation tapers off south of Mt. Tapotchau, dropping to Mt. Fina Susu at less than three hundred feet. The southern tip of the island, while still hilly, includes some flatter terrain, sugarcane fields, and areas of jagged coral outcroppings. Overall the island's topography is varied, with beaches, jungles, swamps, mountains, hills, valleys, caves, and dense sugarcane fields. Regardless of the specific land feature, Saipan is well suited to defense, with every hill and cave perfect for defenders and treacherous for invaders.

Before World War II, Japan had invested in air bases in the Marianas. Aslito Airfield, located on the southern end of Saipan, was the primary base. Started in 1934, Aslito had a landing strip of 3,600 feet. From 1941 until the American threat materialized in 1944, Aslito was considered safely behind the lines of combat and was used as a maintenance and repair center for planes on their way to and from battles in other parts of the Pacific. In addition the Japanese built a seaplane base near Tanapag Harbor and a landing strip of 3,280 feet near the town of Charan Kanoa. Morison pointed out that the Charan Kanoa runway ran north-south, "crosswise to the prevailing wind, making so short a strip practically useless for anything bigger than a Piper Cub." In practice it could serve only as an emergency landing strip. Like the base at Aslito, the naval base at Tanapag served primarily as a transit point for ships and soldiers bound for other islands. Shortly before the American invasion the Japanese had begun to construct a 4,300-foot runway at Marpi Point on the northern end of the island.[1] Prior to D-Day the Japanese had approximately 152 planes on Saipan, but most of those were destroyed or rendered inoperable after strikes from Task Force 58 just before the landing. The Japanese also had airfields on nearby Tinian, Rota, Pagan, and Guam. All of these bases would become primary targets for the American forces.

In addition to building air bases, the Japanese military attempted to fortify the Marianas in other ways. This effort intensified after February 1944. Previously the Japanese government had neglected its defenses in the Marianas. As Japan had advanced south in the early years of the war, Saipan had not been strongly fortified, since it was too far behind the empire's expanding perimeter to function as more than a transfer point for soldiers being shipped elsewhere. From Tokyo's perspective, it did not make sense to strengthen the Marianas when they appeared safe for the foreseeable future. However, as a result of the rapid American advance in the Gilberts and Marshalls in 1943 and early 1944—almost as shocking to the United States as it was to the Imperial Japanese forces—the battle lines suddenly moved toward the Marianas. In February 1944 Mitscher's fast carriers launched attacks against Truk and the Marianas, and the Japanese military began to rush men and supplies toward the Marianas, with special attention paid to Saipan and Guam.

In May 1943 the Japanese had fewer than a thousand military person-nel on Saipan, and in February 1944, just before the massive increase, just under fifteen hundred. Their attempt to reinforce Saipan in the spring of 1944 did not leave enough time to turn the island into a defensive fortress before the American assault. U.S. submarines attacked and sank large numbers of ships carrying men and equipment to Saipan. On 29 Febru-ary 1944 the *Trout* sank the troop transport *Sakito Maru*. Japanese ships retaliated and destroyed the *Trout* with depth charges. Nevertheless, only seventeen hundred of the forty-one hundred Japanese soldiers on board

Sakito Maru made it to the island; most of the seventeen hundred survivors were soon moved to Guam in order to reinforce that possession. Reinforcements continued to be rushed to Saipan, with the final Japanese attempt to fortify the Marianas occurring less than ten days before D-Day. By that time the United States controlled the waters around the Marianas, and U.S. submarines sank five of the seven Japanese ships carrying the 118th Regiment. Japanese ships rescued many of the soldiers, with twenty-five hundred men surviving the submarine attacks, but often they arrived on the island without weapons or ammunition.[2] Between February and June 1944, Japan sent more than forty-five thousand troops to the Marianas, but not all of them were destined for Saipan. Arriving without their equipment and generally short of officers, several thousand troops had to be quickly integrated into an improvised battle plan. As Denfeld indicated in his work on Japanese fortifications:

> With an enemy invasion imminent, the Japanese rushed reinforcements to the Marianas. These included two Japanese army divisions, the 29th and the 43rd. Other smaller units joined them to bolster the defense of key islands in the Marianas. Reinforcement efforts were seriously challenged by American submarines which cruised off the Marianas in substantial numbers. Submarines were responsible for sinking many transport ships containing critically needed troops, weapons, equipment and building materials. Approximately nine transports were sunk en route to the Marianas with losses totaling over 3,600 men and considerable amounts of supplies and equipment. In spite of the effectiveness of the submarines, 40,000 Japanese reinforcements did reach the Marianas where they were immediately put to work constructing defenses.[3]

The highest-ranking Japanese officer in the area was Lieutenant General Obata Hideyoshi, who commanded the 31st Army and was in charge of defending several island groups—the Marianas, the Palaus (Peleliu), and the Bonins (Chichi Jima). In March 1944 Vice Admiral Nagumo Chuichi, who had commanded the Japanese attack on Pearl Harbor in 1941, took charge of the newly formed Central Pacific Area Fleet, but according to a Japanese naval commander quoted by Crowl, this administrative change had "no tactical significance." Morison indicated that Nagumo, once one of the most important admirals in the Japanese navy, now commanded "a small area fleet consisting of patrol craft, barges and ground troops."[4] Paradoxically, he was one of Japan's most experienced yet worst naval officers. When he led the carrier task force that attacked Pearl Harbor in December 1941, his errors there saved the United States from an even more devas-

Figure 4. Admiral Nagumo Chuichi, commander of Japanese task force that attacked Pearl Harbor and commander of naval forces on Saipan; photo from 1941 or 1942; U.S. Naval Historical Center photo.

tating defeat. He performed poorly at Midway, then was sent to Saipan because it seemed to be safely behind Japanese lines. His ultimate fate on Saipan certainly added to the satisfaction of the American victory.

Japanese command structures were complicated, at least to the Americans, and in addition the services often did not cooperate with each other. Throughout the war the Japanese suffered from a lack of coordination between the services, as army and navy leaders in Tokyo attempted to ensure their own superiority in the command structure and to take credit for victory. To avoid the consequences of these disputes, Obata and Nagumo had agreed to split their command in this part of the ocean, each taking responsibility for his own branch. Prior to the American landing, Obata left the island to inspect defenses in the Palaus, and on his way back he found himself stranded on Guam as the battle raged and prevented his return to Saipan. In his absence, Lieutenant General Saito Yoshitsugu, commander of the Northern Marianas Defense Force and the ranking officer on Saipan, ran the show. It would not matter. Obata experienced defeat on Guam, while Saito and Nagumo died on Saipan.

Following Obata's departure from Saipan for his inspection tour of the Palaus, the main Japanese units remaining on the island were Saito's 43rd Infantry Division (reinforced) and Colonel Oka Yoshiro's 47th Independent Mixed Brigade. Each was divided into three units, similar to the American system. Saito's infantry of nearly thirteen thousand men included three regiments: the 118th under Colonel Ito Takeshi (twenty-six hundred men), the 135th under Colonel Suzuki Eisuke (three thousand), and the 136th under Colonel Ogawa Yukimatsu (thirty-six hundred). Oka's twenty-six-hundred-man brigade was divided into three battalions of 618 men each: the 316th under Captain Edo Susumu, the 317th under Captain Sasaki, and the 318th under Major Nagashima. In addition to these infantry forces, the Japanese had an antiaircraft company, engineering regiments, a large supply of mortars and artillery, and approximately forty-eight tanks. More than six thousand naval personnel under Nagumo's command were stationed on the island. According to Crowl, "The largest single element of the naval forces was the 55th Naval Guard Force, which was chiefly responsible for manning coast defense guns." This force, commanded by Captain Takashima Sanji, included two thousand men. The next-largest naval unit was the eight-hundred-man Yokosuka 1st Special Naval Landing Force under Lieutenant Commander Karashima Tatsue. Other naval forces included a construction department, a communications unit, a transportation department, a supply department, and scattered elements rescued from the ill-fated resupply efforts earlier in the year. From the beginning of the year Japanese military strength had grown significantly and totaled 25,469 army troops and 6,160 naval forces. Despite this apparent strength, the Japanese started the battle with serious flaws in their defenses.[5]

Many of the Japanese on Saipan were there accidentally, some detached from their regular units and some without adequate weapons. Soldiers came from a variety of random regiments, remnants and survivors from the convoys that had been victims of American attacks. In addition, because some of them arrived so late or by accident, the defenders were not well integrated into an overall battle plan. The total of approximately thirty thousand defenders was more than double what the Americans expected, but fortunately for the American forces, even those Japanese soldiers who had weapons were at a disadvantage, as Japanese bolt-action rifles were of lesser quality than the American semiautomatic M1 Garand. The major Japanese rifle manufactured during the war was the Arisaka Type 99. The Japanese continued to use a bolt-action rifle (Type 38 or Type 99) even after the Americans had switched to the M1.

In addition to being supplied with inferior-quality weapons, Saito's troops had only partially completed their defensive plans by 15 June. Until they saw the American fleet offshore in June, the Japanese believed they had until November to assemble their defenses. As a result, building materials were unused and many weapons were only partially ready on D-Day.

During the battle, marines occasionally discovered Japanese weapons that had not been deployed in time for the invasion. According to Private First Class Robert Kane, who served in the 2nd Marine Division: "I had occasion to be in a section of the mountain that I hadn't seen—we found two emplaced big guns. I believe they were either 16-inch or 18-inch guns, which were supposed to be on a battleship, but since we sunk their navy, they sent them to Saipan. They never got them in operation because they were pointed in the wrong direction."[6] In addition, many other weapons that could have aided the Japanese effort were never unpacked. "It also accounts for the fact that whole trainloads of new and crated guns were found in the Garapan and Charan Kanoa yards. On Nafutan Point several large-caliber guns were captured that had been hauled up and put in place, but could not be used because their installation was not complete. Bunkers, dugouts, and blockhouses were still building."[7]

As Denfield indicated, "An American engineer survey [in July 1944] noted several examples of uncompleted defensive works, which included three 140mm guns loaded on rail cars waiting to be installed. At one battery, three 120mm DP Type 10 guns were laying on the ground near their emplacements. Engineers also discovered the following weapons in the Garapan Naval Depot: three 120mm coastal defense guns, one 140mm coastal defense gun, thirty-two 120mm Type 10 (1921) guns and six Type 3 200mm anti-boat guns."[8] As noted in Love's work on the 27th Division, "One [Japanese] prisoner of war later said that, had the American assault come three months later, the island would have been impregnable."[9] While that assessment clearly exaggerated the situation, the Japanese would have been better prepared if the original American timetable of early November and Japanese expectations of a fall invasion had been realized.

Despite their shortcomings, the Japanese had a lot of firepower on the island, especially on hills and ridges that could target the beaches. For example, approximately a thousand yards to the southeast of Green Beach, "the 9th Field Heavy Artillery Regiment had twelve Type 4 (1915) 150mm howitzers supported by 30 Type 94 (1934) 75mm mountain guns." To the east of Green Beach were four 150-millimeter howitzers, which "laid down some of the most deadly fire encountered by the landing forces." In addition the Japanese had "a battery of two six-inch British Whitworth Armstrong (Model 1900) guns" at Agingan Point, although these were damaged by the pre-invasion naval bombardment. In total "the Japanese had about 34 guns emplaced and operational at the time of the American invasion of Saipan. Another twelve guns were at batteries but were not operational and three were found loaded on railcars for shipment to battery positions. Forty-two guns were in storage at the Garapan Naval Depot at Tanapag."[10] The Japanese had also constructed a series of concrete pillboxes, blockhouses, and other fortifications, and of course they planned to use natural defensive structures, including caves and other rock formations, to their advantage. The many caves and coral outcroppings provided natural defensive positions for the Japanese soldiers. Many of the caves were deep enough to provide the defenders with total protection from American gunfire, artillery, or naval shelling.

The Japanese "Outline of Defensive Plan of Northern Marianas Force" of May 1944 indicated that they were optimistic about the coming battle and expected to stop the Americans on the beaches. Their orders were clear in this regard: "Various units will so prepare their defensive strength, beginning with the immediate construction of defensive positions, that when they are fully developed they can destroy the enemy landing force on the beach. We will transform these islands into a fortress so that we can expect absolutely to hold our airfields." The Japanese planned to counterattack "from strategic points supported by artillery and tanks."[11]

Lieutenant General Saito had divided the island into four defensive sectors—Central, Navy, Southern, and Northern. The Central Sector was defended by the 136th under Colonel Ogawa Yukimatsu. Just to his north was the Navy Sector, which included the capital city of Garapan and was defended by the 5th Base Force (55th Keibitai, 1st Special Naval Landing Forces). The Southern Sector included the other major city, Charan Kanoa, and was under the command of Colonel Oka's 47th Independent Mixed Brigade. The Northern Sector was patrolled by the 135th under Colonel Suzuki. The 3rd Independent Mountain Artillery Regiment and the 3rd Battalion, 10th Field Artillery Regiment, were ordered "to defend the front on the west coast south of Garapan and to deploy part of their force in defense of the airfield area." In all cases the Japanese placed their batteries in order to create "interlocking sectors of fire."[12] Guns were situated so that they could fire toward the water but at the same time across the beach, thereby establishing a crossfire pattern as the enemy came ashore.

Despite the natural advantages provided by the island's topography,

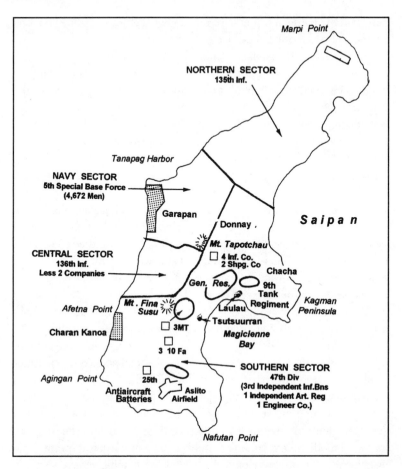

Map 3. Japanese defense sectors on Saipan

Japanese commanders were committed to an offensive approach that dissipated their intrinsic strength. According to a Japanese battle plan quoted by Crowl, "It is expected that the enemy will be destroyed on the beaches through a policy of tactical command based on aggressiveness, determination, and initiative."[13] While this aggressiveness had worked well for the Japanese earlier in the war, when they were on the offensive, the Japanese military was slow to adjust to the new reality of 1944. Rather than attacking the American lines, which almost always proved disastrous for the Japanese, they should have fortified their defensive positions and waited for the marines to move forward. While a more defensive orientation might not have won the battle, it would have inflicted greater losses on the attackers and possibly slowed their advance.

As the battle for Saipan neared, the American troops enjoyed several advantages—more troops, better weapons, superior firepower, and air dominance. At the same time, some issues remained unresolved in the American plan. Of course the Marianas invasion was primarily a navy operation, simply because the central Pacific was assigned to the navy. Further, Saipan was an island, so the only way to get there was by ship. But difficulties related to this specific island were not resolved in advance. It made sense to use the navy's shock troops, the marines, for amphibious landings on beaches such as Tarawa and Roi-Namur. Those atolls were small and perfectly suited to marine offensive tactics. For example, Tarawa (or Betio Island, which had been the specific target of the marines within Tarawa atoll) was two and a half miles long and eight hundred yards wide; Roi was approximately twelve hundred yards wide, Namur only eight or nine hundred yards wide. In each case, the taking of the beach assured victory on the rest of the relatively small island.

Saipan was totally different. Its seventy-five-square-mile area established it as a large landmass compared to previous marine objectives (with the exception of Guadalcanal), and a beach landing, for which the marines were so well trained, was only one aspect of the total goal. While marines would fight across any terrain they encountered, their original amphibious mission conflicted with the larger picture on Saipan. In terms of military conceptualization, it was the army, not the marines, that was trained to drive over long distances with artillery and tanks. In the Marianas the marines had the job of landing and inflicting a quick defeat on the Japanese forces; the army was only considered the floating reserve. No one contemplated what might have happened if the Japanese refused to stop fighting after the beach had been taken and instead retreated into the interior of the island and put on a furious defense. What tactics would then be most useful in defeating the enemy? Would marine assault tactics continue beyond the beach? Would the army, with its more methodical approach, take over beyond the beaches, or would it continue in a support role? Would marine and army tactics be coordinated to create a seamless unit operating with a shared understanding of how to proceed?

CHAPTER THREE

OPERATION FORAGER

Admiral King was correct about the crucial nature of the battle for Saipan, and others also recognized the significance of the impending fight. Holland Smith called Saipan "the decisive battle of the Pacific offensive," and according to the U.S. Strategic Bombing Survey, the Japanese understood the same reality: "Almost unanimously, informed Japanese considered Saipan as the decisive battle of the war and its loss as ending all hope for a Japanese victory."[1]

For the assault on the Marianas, code-named Operation Forager, Admiral Nimitz chose to stay with the team that had worked so well for the U.S. offensive in the Pacific thus far. Admiral Spruance remained in command of the entire naval force known as the Fifth Fleet. Spruance was one of the best American leaders of the war, although most Americans today do not recognize his name. Unlike General MacArthur or General George Patton or Admiral "Bull" Halsey, Spruance was "inherently a quiet man" and decidedly not flamboyant. While some of his colleagues called him "old frozen face," he was extremely competent and an excellent naval officer.[2] Yet he remains one of the most underrated American military leaders of the war.

Vice Admiral Turner continued as commander of the amphibious fleet as well as head of the Northern Attack Force that would move against Saipan and Tinian. One of the most aggressive American commanders of the war, he had already seen action in some of the major battles in the

Pacific, including New Georgia, the Gilberts, and the Marshalls. His comrades agreed that Turner was a hard worker who drove himself and those
around him to their limits. One officer called him "the meanest man I
ever saw, and the most competent naval officer I ever served with." Rear
Admiral Frank Jack Fletcher observed: "Any Captain who relieved Kelly
Turner was in luck. All he would have to do is back off the thumb screws
a bit to have the perfect ship." Others remarked on the "relentless tenacity with which he cracked his whip over those who formed his team. He
drove them ruthlessly but none more so than himself." Possibly the pursuit
of perfection in himself and those around him led to his alleged abuse of
alcohol. Although his drinking never interfered with his performance as a
naval officer, it increased as the war went on. Turner drank heavily every
night, but his battle performance continued to be first-rate. Spruance had
great respect for Turner as a commander and protected him from Nimitz
and others who occasionally lost patience with his drinking and his temper.
According to Holland Smith, who worked closely with Turner in several
campaigns, "Kelly Turner is aggressive, a mass of energy and a relentless
task master. The punctilious exterior hides a terrific determination. He
can be plain ornery. He wasn't called 'Terrible Turner' without reason."[3]
Despite his nickname, Turner was a commander that a sailor or marine
wanted on his side during battle.

Turner designated Holland Smith as commander of the Northern
Troops and Landing Forces headed for Saipan and Tinian as well as commanding general of all marine and army troops once they had been committed to combat. To all appearances Smith was the perfect choice to lead
the amphibious landing at Saipan. Between the wars he had pressed the
military hierarchy to devote greater resources to landing vehicles and the
kind of training necessary to prepare for sea-to-land assaults. To facilitate
this style of offensive he insisted that the navy adopt the innovative Higgins
boat as a landing vehicle. Higgins assault boats (LCVPs, or landing craft
vehicles, personnel) were specifically designed to land troops and materiel
on an invasion beachhead. More than thirty-six feet in length, the boats
carried thirty-six men or eight thousand pounds of supplies, could travel at
nine knots, and were defended by two .30-caliber machine guns. Smith's
persistence in this area finally paid off, and the navy began to use these
vehicles.[4] In 1940 and 1941 Smith instructed new marine units on the
techniques of amphibious warfare, pushing his troops as hard as possible
to prepare them for real combat, always believing that the Marine Corps
would inevitably play the crucial role in the coming war.

Ironically, Smith's devotion to marine tactics also made him an unfortunate choice to lead the attack on Saipan. He did not respect the contributions of the other branches of the military and saw the army and navy as impediments to his vision of a Marine Corps victory. When problems developed on Saipan, Smith looked for someone to blame, never questioning his own battle plan, his own tactics, or his communication with officers in the field. He assumed that all officers, even those in the army, would fight the battle using Marine Corps tactics. His disagreement with and dislike—even disdain—for the army was clear. If the battle for Saipan had been won in three days of marine glory, as Smith anticipated, none of the subsequent issues would have emerged. Of course the marines themselves knew better, and as Harlan Rosvold of the 2nd Armored Amphibian Battalion observed: "The folks who never had to go ashore and participate in the actual fighting always had optimistic and usually unrealistic estimates of how fast the Marines could accomplish the job at hand."[5] Battles rarely proceed as imagined, and the best officers know that flexibility and adaptability are necessary as the fighting progresses.

In fact, Smith considered both the army and the navy resistant to modern ideas. In his memoir, *Coral and Brass*, Smith referred to the "Navy's mental arteriosclerosis" and disparaged its desire "to continue running the show" after marines had been dropped on the beach in amphibious operations. He railed against the defensive training emphasized in American military schools between the wars (he favored the offensive approach of his military hero, Napoleon). He was contemptuous of the army and its tactics, remarking that "MacArthur was in supreme command in his own theater and could pick his own targets. He picked the easiest." Smith's animosity toward the other services, but especially the army, erupted during the Battle of Saipan in one of the most notorious interservice controversies of World War II. Smith's temper, evident throughout his career and in his memoir, earned him the nickname "Howlin' Mad." Smith feigned ignorance about his nickname: "How I got the name 'Howlin' Mad' I don't know but it was pinned on me while I was stationed on Luzon."[6] Not surprisingly, Smith acquired some enemies. Army historian S. L. A. Marshall described Smith as "a bully, something of a sadist and . . . tactically a chowderhead."[7]

Under Smith, Major General Thomas E. Watson led the 2nd Marine Division, veterans of "Bloody Tarawa," while Major General Harry Schmidt commanded the 4th Marine Division, veterans of Roi-Namur. The floating reserve, which could be committed to battle wherever needed, consisted of the 27th Infantry Division under the leadership of Major General Ralph

Smith. Ralph Smith was a highly regarded officer who spoke French and had been trained in military intelligence and tactics. Between the wars "he had spent most of his time attending advanced military schools, teaching at West Point, Ft. Leavenworth, and Ft. Benning, and had spent four demanding years as a member of the General Staff. . . . At that time the War Department General Staff was a very select group of only eighty-eight officers. Each was a graduate of the War College," as noted by historian Harry Gailey. The General Staff, which served under Chief of Staff George C. Marshall, also included Generals Dwight Eisenhower, Albert Wedemeyer, Omar Bradley, and Walter Bedell Smith. Ralph Smith worked on military intelligence, and his area of expertise was Europe—more specifically, the French army. Nevertheless, the demands of war led him to command a division that served in the Pacific. He was intelligent, with a calm and mild personality, in some ways the very opposite of Howlin' Mad. S. L. A. Marshall remarked on his "extreme consideration for all other mortals."[8]

Another army division, the 77th Infantry, was to remain in Hawaii as a backup reserve unit. Due to the commitment of shipping in the invasion of Europe, the United States did not have enough available transports to bring the 77th along with the rest of the invasion force. The plan called for sending ships back from the Marianas to Hawaii, more than three thousand miles, to pick up the 77th Division only if necessary. Eventually the 77th would join the 3rd Marine Division on Guam.

With the leadership structure in place, preparation and training for the invasion began. Early in 1944 the 2nd and 4th Marine Divisions and the 27th Infantry Division assembled in Hawaii, each on its own island, to practice for the attack. Unfortunately, many of these troops were still recovering from dysentery, dengue fever, and other maladies previously picked up in the Pacific.

The 2nd Marine Division was sent back to Hawaii after the Battle of Tarawa to rest and break in replacements for the men who had been killed. The official history of the division noted that marines recalled the difficulty of the ride home from Tarawa among the large number of wounded: "The 2,000-mile voyage from Tarawa was in itself a postscript to horror. The transports reeked of the awful smell of the island, of disinfectant, and of blood. There were no fresh clothes for unwounded Marines, and almost everyone had lost his gear in the shuffle of battle. Every day there were funerals aboard the transports, and flag-covered bodies slipping into the silent seas."[9]

The 2nd Division was based in the middle of the big island of Hawaii, in an area about six thousand feet above sea level in the shadow of Mauna Kea and Mauna Loa volcanoes, both well over thirteen thousand feet high. In memory of their bloody introduction to amphibious warfare as well as to honor their victory, the marines called their base Camp Tarawa. The area was extremely cold in the winter, which was when most of the marines arrived. In addition, the camp was not completed when they arrived, and they had to assemble their shelters in the cold, mist, and fog. The goal was to allow sick marines to heal and new marines to be trained and acculturated by the veterans. By springtime the division was preparing for its next assignment. While their next target remained a secret, the marines began to practice crossing sugarcane fields.[10] Despite all of these exercises, Captain Harry Phillips, who served with the 8th Marines, 2nd Marine Division, later recalled that "there is no training that can get you ready for war."[11]

At Camp Maui, the 4th Division was thirteen hundred feet above sea level on the slopes of the ten-thousand-foot-high Haleakala volcano, living in "tents that had wooden decks and a bare electric bulb," recalled Private First Class John Lane. "Cold water sufficed for showering, shaving, and doing one's laundry."[12] Toilet facilities were rustic, a real problem for marines still recovering from dysentery. Private First Class Carl Matthews recalled that "a ten or twelve foot urinal had been fashioned from sheet metal and hung on one wall. Another cubicle had lavatories on one wall . . . beyond that the shower, with ten or twelve spigots that emitted the coldest water this side of the North Pole. There was no roof."[13] This created a problem because of the heavy rains. His first night at camp, Private Alva Perry put his shoes under his bed, and "the next morning all our shoes were found at the bottom of the company street. They had floated down during a downpour."[14]

In their spare time, marines would play sports or cards, write letters, drink beer (rationed at two per day), or for a special diversion watch Esther Williams movies. There was a PX in the area, but it was small and sold only soap, razor blades, cigarettes, and Aqua Velva (which a few marines drank for its alcohol content). When ordered to load the truck carrying supplies to the PX, some marines managed to find an extra case of beer, with the "surplus" case hidden in the deep brush near the camp. "Later, when darkness fell, we would retrieve the cases and bring them to our tents for a well earned party," recalled Corporal Robert Graf of upstate New York.[15] The pineapple farm next to Camp Maui provided another treat.

The marines were warned that the private farm was off-limits, but by the end of the first night Matthews and many other marines had enjoyed the taste of fresh pineapple.[16]

Mostly the marines prepared for their next assignment. They practiced amphibious maneuvers on the beach of Maalaea Bay on Maui's west coast and used the slope and crater of Haleakala volcano as a challenging obstacle course. In the process they learned a few basic rules that could save a marine's life in battle. Tibor Torok, a member of the 4th Division, remembered several: "Do not wear any objects that might reflect the sun, keep off the skyline, where you are easily seen, when crawling on your belly, keep your butt down." Along these lines marines wrapped their dog tags with tape so they would not reflect the sun or rattle.[17] In May the 2nd and 4th Divisions held joint maneuvers. Lieutenant John C. Chapin described the constant practice:

> To us in the lower echelons it was just the same old stuff that we'd been doing for a solid year: filing up from compartments below decks to your assigned boat station, going over the side, hurrying down the net to beat the stopwatch, into the heaving LCVP (Landing Craft Vehicle, Personnel), and away. Then the interminable hours of circling, meanwhile getting wet, hungry and bored. The K rations (in a waxed box) tasted like sawdust; the weather got rougher and rougher. Some of the men got seasick, and all of us were soaking wet and cold. . . . The next day it was the same thing all over again.[18]

While the marines prepared at Camp Tarawa and Camp Maui, the army encamped at Schofield Barracks on Oahu, about twenty miles from Pearl Harbor. Unlike the makeshift facilities used by the marines, Schofield Barracks was relatively comfortable. Nevertheless, the soldiers trained hard and endured forced marches in the hot sun, practiced bombing raids (with sacks of flour dropped on them), and engaged in target practice. Like the marines, they ran through an obstacle course, studied the difficulties of moving through sugarcane fields, and worked on amphibious landings. In all, forty-seven training areas were available to the marines or shared with the army. In preparation for Saipan all the troops trained on rifle ranges, with grenades, bazookas, mortars, and artillery, and in formations in coordination with tanks and other armored vehicles. At the same time, both the marines and soldiers practiced across different topography and terrain, including beaches, jungle, caves, and concealed emplacements.[19] Nevertheless, the tactics experienced by each service reflected its own strengths and traditions, with the marines emphasizing amphibious landings and the army practicing close infantry-tank and signal corps coordination. The two groups never trained together, however, and made no attempt to reconcile their different tactics.

For organizational purposes and in order to create manageable attack units, each marine division was subdivided into three regiments, and each regiment was further broken down into three battalions. The 2nd Division consisted of the 2nd, 6th, and 8th Regiments, while the 4th Division included the 23rd, 24th, and 25th Regiments.[20] These six regiments were the division's rifle or infantry units—the frontline combat troops. Each division included other units as well, including an artillery and howitzer regiment, an engineer regiment, a tank battalion, an amphibious tractor battalion, a joint assault signal company, and a medical battalion. Battalions, which consisted of approximately nine hundred officers and men, were further divided into companies (about 250 men), and companies were divided into platoons (60 men). The actual strength of the 2nd and 4th Divisions was roughly 19,500.

The 27th Infantry Division was similarly divided into three regiments: the 105th, which had little battle experience; the 165th, which had fought on Makin and was practicing for the invasion on Saipan; and the 106th, which had fought on Eniwetok and would serve as the reserve regiment within the division.[21] By the end of May 1944 all of these forces seemed well prepared for the operation, the largest amphibious landing thus far in the Pacific war. Simultaneously training troops for the invasions of France and the Marianas, the United States was assembling and preparing to project the largest sea-to-land military force in world history.

With all three combat divisions training in Hawaii, the U.S. military had the opportunity to encourage close cooperation between the services. Unfortunately, this would not be the case, as relations between marines and army soldiers were not always cordial. There were resentments on both sides, with soldiers seeing marines as glory seekers and marines viewing the army as soft and pampered. According to Private Lane of the 4th Marine Division, "dealings with the Army were not so friendly. Always better equipped and fed than the Marine Corps in those days, the Army was both a focus of resentment and a target of opportunity for Marines everywhere." Sometimes marines would steal food or movies from nearby army bases.[22] Most importantly, the marines and the army did not engage in joint maneuvers in Hawaii in preparation for their next operation. Not coordinating tactics and not practicing together were serious mistakes.

The marine-army rivalry had been festering even before the battle for

Saipan started. Lieutenant General Robert Richardson, based in Hawaii, was in administrative command of army troops in the central Pacific area, and he was not comfortable with his soldiers serving under Marine Corps officers. Richardson, like other army officers, did not believe that Marine Corps officers were capable of leading a large number of troops into battle. Many army officers held that marine leadership was best exercised over small units with specific and limited objectives. At the end of 1943, Richardson wrote to Admiral Nimitz and expressed concerns about Holland Smith's leadership abilities. Richardson opposed having army soldiers serve under the tactical command of Marine Corps officers. In February 1944, as the command structure for Saipan was being organized, Richardson reiterated to Nimitz his opposition to Marine Corps control of army soldiers. When Nimitz dismissed his objections, Richardson warned Nimitz that he intended to pursue the issue in person in Washington. He planned to tell General George C. Marshall of his position and specifically of his objection to Holland Smith in this leadership capacity. Nimitz alerted Admiral King regarding Richardson's intentions and reported further on the conversation: "Richardson then proceeded to indict in a courteous manner, but in extremely positive terms, the competence of Holland Smith in particular, and of senior marine officers in general, to command large bodies of troops."[23]

Richardson was not the only army officer concerned about Howlin' Mad's leadership abilities. After returning from Makin, S. L. A. Marshall, who had witnessed Smith's grandiose stand against Japanese snipers, told Major General Charles H. Corlett of the army's 7th Infantry Division that "Smith was determined to make trouble for any army general who came under him." When Corlett and Howlin' Mad conferred on operations, Smith "quickly began ridiculing Ralph Smith." Corlett told Holland Smith that his comments were inappropriate, and Smith "stomped out." The situation did not improve after Corlett's 7th Division invaded and captured Kwajalein. When the battle ended, Howlin' Mad called a press conference and told reporters that the army "had done a poor job on Kwajalein compared to the fight of the marines at Roi-Namur. That was too much for Corlett," Marshall recalled. Corlett "broke in to inform the correspondents that the Corps commander didn't know anything about either battle since he had been kept aboard ship the whole time." Aware of all of these events on both Makin and Kwajalein, Marshall "made out a full report on my observations of Holland Smith that was handed to the War Department several months prior to the Smith vs. Smith blowup at Saipan."[24]

Despite the opposition of both Richardson and S. L. A. Marshall, Holland Smith received the command assignment over the Amphibious Corps for the invasion of Saipan. While army-marine relations remained problematic, the mission proceeded as if all of these issues had been resolved. Unfortunately, a smooth operation was made unlikely by Smith's negative attitude toward the army as well as the army's doubt that a marine officer had the ability to lead a large operation.

Interservice rivalry was not the only difficulty confronted by U.S. forces targeting the Marianas. Military operations in the Pacific involved logistical and supply problems that dwarfed those encountered on the western front in Europe. Unlike the invasion of northern France, which carried soldiers nearly one hundred miles across the English Channel, the invasion of the Marianas involved moving the attack fleet three thousand miles from Hawaii. Of course, the ships had to transport all supplies—food, medicine, ammunition, guns, and tanks—for the duration of the battle, as there was no nearby American supply base to replenish these items as they were depleted. The base at Eniwetok in the Marshalls was stocked with supplies, but it was still more than a thousand miles from Saipan.

The success of the campaign also depended on the ability of the U.S. forces to establish control of the sea and air lanes. Just as the invasion of France was not practical until the Battle of the Atlantic had been won, so too the United States could not move against the Marianas until Japanese submarine and airpower had been eliminated. The American attacks on Truk and the Palaus as well as the steady diminution of the Japanese sub forces had accomplished this objective and opened the way for the American advance. By mid-May 1944 all the factors necessary to launch the next invasion seemed to be in place. Suddenly, however, a new problem arose before the attack force ever left Hawaii.

Rear Admiral Harry Hill had recommended an experiment to reinforce landing vehicles with mortars. "On the suggestion of Rear Admiral Harry W. Hill," Dyer indicated, "each of the three LCTs was equipped as a gunboat with six 4.2-inch Coast Guard mortars and 2,500 rounds of projectiles. These were desired primarily to protect the left flank of our Landing Force against Japanese reserves moving down the coastal road from Garapan. By having the LCTs steam parallel to the beaches, they would also be able to cover the landing beaches with a blanket of heavy mortar fire while the assault waves were being formed." Specially equipped LCTs were tied down on the decks of the larger LSTs. Dyer continued: "During heavy weather en route to the rehearsal area the night of 14–15 May, two of the three specially equipped LCTs carried away their securing gear from the LSTs on which they were mounted and riding and slid into Davy Jones Locker with considerable loss of life." Often marines or sailors would sit under the LCTs for shade, to play cards, or write letters. When the LCTs disappeared into the ocean, they took nineteen men with them. While Hill was not at fault for this accident, he felt responsible and canceled the plan to add mortars to the landing vehicles.[25]

Despite this setback, rehearsal landings proceeded as scheduled. On 16 and 17 May marines practiced amphibious landings at Maalaea Bay on Maui, and on 19 May they hit the beach again on Kahoolawe Island, a deserted area off Hawaii used for military practice, and "this time troops approached the shore under actual cover of naval and aerial fire."[26] All aspects of the landing went well, but Vice Admiral Turner reacted to the LCT accident by ordering the LSTs with the remaining mortars to be unloaded when they arrived at Pearl Harbor. This led to a greater calamity—an incident that reminded many witnesses of the attack of December 1941.

This devastating accident occurred on 21 May at West Loch at Pearl Harbor. Many of the forty-seven LSTs designated for the Marianas campaign were loaded with antiaircraft shells and powder, rockets, machine-gun ammunition, and gasoline in drums next to the ammunition. The area was crowded with LSTs and other vessels and "lashed together in groups of two to eight," according to Carl Matthews. As troops were removing mortars from one of the LSTs, an explosion set off a conflagration, the fire spreading rapidly due to the concentration of ammunition and gasoline on the nearby landing craft. Lane remembered: "Exploding gasoline drums, jeep engines and whole jeeps, parts of ships, guns, equipment shrapnel, fragments of metal, all rained down on the waters of the West Loch as ship after ship was touched off in a kind of chain reaction." Matthews recalled bodies and parts of bodies flying through the air, and "many bodies were found in the sugar cane fields, blown there by the explosions. . . . The sky above Pearl Harbor was blackened and heavy smoke billowed from the LST moorings. Flames were shooting hundreds of feet into the air. When the smoke cleared there was no doubt that we had suffered a serious disaster." Corporal Graf recalled: "Unexpectedly a tremendous explosion filled the air. . . . I saw the tarp overhead covered with flame. . . . Fragments of shrapnel were falling everywhere. . . . Fire was falling upon us. . . . Burning oil covered the water . . . the gas drums on our LST started exploding."[27]

The cause of this disaster was never determined, but sparks from a welding torch, smoking, or carelessness with ammunition have all been suspected. The situation in the water became chaotic, with fires and explosions and boats trying to flee and crashing into each other. Winton Carter, who served with the 2nd Armored Amphibian Battalion, recalled: "Several LST's in attempting to leave the area ran into other vessels. Some sailors leaped overboard and were ground up in the churning propellers." Despite the continuing danger, several marines distinguished themselves by risking their lives in order to rescue other men. Arthur J. Auxer Jr., Merle B. Carpenter, and Louis Sangouard of the 2nd Armored Amphibian Battalion all received the Navy and Marine Corps Medal for helping men who were injured and disabled. Specifically, Auxer and Carpenter were praised for encountering and rescuing "injured men from the water who had become physically disabled by the explosions. As he [both Auxer and Carpenter] was moving away from the enveloping blaze and explosions, his vehicle caught fire which was immediately put out by his prompt actions, saving the casualties and the armored amphibian. Later, he returned again, heedless of his own personal safety, and assisted in driving four other armored amphibians away from the burning ship." Sangouard was acknowledged because "he rescued a drowning man from flaming oil-covered waters."[28] Although they did not receive individual medals for their actions, navy corpsmen also went into action immediately, "tending the wounded seemingly unaware of the danger to themselves."

According to Dyer, Vice Admiral Turner himself played a role in putting out the fires and even threatened one fleeing sailor with death if he did not return to the scene to help fight the blaze. The accident resulted in at least 163 killed and almost 400 wounded. The loss of six LSTs and three LCTs so close to the planned departure for the Marianas also strained American resources, but replacement landing craft and vehicles, as well as replacement marines, were found and the invasion schedule was not seriously disrupted.[29]

Assembling and organizing all of the components of the operation took considerable time, planning, and coordination. The marines of the Northern Attack Force sailed from Hawaii at the end of May and then regrouped and refueled at Eniwetok, just over a thousand miles from Saipan. The 27th Infantry Division left Hawaii at the same time and sailed to Kwajalein before heading for Saipan. Almost simultaneously the United States launched another reconnaissance mission over the Marianas, with photographically equipped navy Liberators (B-24s) flying from Guadalcanal to Eniwetok to Saipan. Morison praised their efficiency: "Prints of Saipan from negatives taken 1 June were finished in time for gunnery officers of the Northern Attack Force to study en route to the target."[30] While the photographs revealed that the Japanese had increased their antiaircraft gun emplacements as well as other weapons, the Americans remained misinformed about the number of Japanese defenders on Saipan.

The fleet that left Eniwetok for the Marianas was an impressive sight. It included over 535 ships of various types: 11 aircraft carriers, 7 battleships, 86 destroyers, 11 cruisers, 44 minesweepers, 91 LSTs, fifty LCIs (158-foot landing craft, infantry, which could transport two hundred men to the beach), and 36 LCTs. Task Force 58 added 93 ships. On board were more than 166,000 marine and army troops; of those 127,000 were assault troops, with 71,000 designated for Saipan.[31] As the armada moved across the Pacific, security issues remained crucial, as Japanese submarines could have been lurking in the waters at any point. One safety measure ensured that there would be no lights on deck. Guy Gabaldon, a scout in the 2nd Marine Division, recalled one of the security measures: "The hatches leading down below have thick, double, black curtains, a few feet apart, so that when one passes through, no light is seen from the outside."[32] For the most part the journey was uneventful and even boring, despite the anxious anticipation by the troops preparing themselves mentally as well as physically for the coming battle.

Sergeant Jim Evans of Chicago, who had joined the Corps at the age of sixteen, remembered the voyage from Hawaii to Saipan as rather miserable. The troops endured smelly accommodations, ate a lot of C-Rations, and sailed through a couple of storms at sea. To pass the time they played cards, tried to find a shady or cool spot for a nap, and listened to music played by Tokyo Rose. Between recordings of American music she warned that Japanese troops were waiting to destroy the Americans, wherever they might land.[33] Corporal Graf remembered playing checkers or chess and reading Perry Mason and Charlie Chan mysteries on board ship.[34] As they had in Hawaii, the marines sought out alcoholic beverages to help pass the time. They had to brew their own, often "borrowing" ingredients such as potatoes, yeast, and sugar from the mess. By replacing the water in the kegs on the life rafts with their fermenting mixture, they were rewarded with "potent booze." Others passed the time "sharpening our K-bars and bayonets, oiling our rifles," and trying to guess which island they were going to invade.[35] Captain Harry Phillips summarized the situation: "We knew we were going to a party but we didn't know where."[36]

The troops did receive one piece of good news along the way. While sailing for Saipan they learned of the other amphibious assault, which started on 6 June on the western front. Operation Overlord, the landing in Normandy, successfully placed more than 150,000 Allied troops in northern France by the end of the first day. Marines and soldiers on the way to Saipan heard the terse announcement over the ship's loudspeaker: "Now hear this! The invasion of France has started. Supreme Headquarters announced that the landings to date have been successful. That is all." The news of the initial success of this massive campaign boosted the morale of the troops and drew loud cheers. It also demonstrated the enormous productive capacity of the United States, which was launching two vast and impressive naval-supported amphibious invasions almost simultaneously, one across the English Channel and the other in the central Pacific.[37]

Finally, once the marines left Eniwetok and the army departed from Kwajalein, the troops were informed about their destination. They were briefed on the topography of the islands, the Japanese defenses, and the offensive plan. The 2nd Marine Division prepared a pamphlet that alerted the men to some of the conditions on Saipan. "Because of the widespread use of human feces (night soil) as fertilizer, uncooked, locally grown vegetables or fruits should not be used." Marines were warned that an "enormous number of flies" on the island "will carry the organisms of dysentery and typhoid from the feces of the Japs to the food of our troops." In addition there were mosquito-borne diseases such as dengue (breakbone) fever. Flies and mosquitoes were not the only dangers. The marines were also cautioned about gonorrhea and syphilis: "It should be assumed that many women on the island are infected with one or both diseases, and contact with them must be avoided." Besides Japanese soldiers, booby traps, and mines, the marines had to stay away from fruit, vegetables, flies, mosquitoes, and women with venereal diseases.[38]

As they approached their destination, one medical officer warned a battalion of the 14th Marines: "In the surf beware of sharks, barracuda, sea snakes, anemones, razor sharp coral, polluted waters, poison fish, and giant clams that shut on a man like a bear trap. Ashore, there is leprosy, typhus, filariasis, yaws, typhoid, dengue fever, dysentery, saber grass, insects, snakes, and giant lizards. Eat nothing growing on the island, don't drink its waters, and don't approach the inhabitants."[39] In reality the marines did not confront giant clams, but they did face a formidable foe, dug in and determined to contest every foot of Saipan.

CHAPTER FOUR

"A CONDEMNED MAN'S BREAKFAST"

In June 1944 one of the largest American armadas ever assembled converged on the Mariana Islands. Hundreds of ships and tens of thousands of troops prepared for the crucial battle for control of Japan's essential outpost on Saipan. This concentration of American power ranks among the most impressive in the entire war. Two-thirds of the troops were marines, and many of them were battle veterans. The 2nd Marine Division had prevailed at the bloody battle for Tarawa in 1943, and the 4th Marine Division had invaded Roi-Namur in February 1944. In both of those battles, the first in the Gilbert Islands and the second in the Marshall Islands, regiments of the army's 27th Infantry Division participated and took important objectives. All of these divisions were among the best available in the Pacific. They had to be: Saipan was a crucial battle in the effort to defeat Japan.

The battle plan called for the 2nd and 4th Marine Divisions to carry out the invasion of Saipan on D-Day, 15 June. The 3rd Marine Division was scheduled to invade Guam three days later, once Saipan was secure. The 27th Infantry Division, designated the floating reserve, was prepared to assist on either island. In addition to the three combat divisions destined to hit Saipan, U.S. forces included several artillery battalions. The largest of the attached units participating in the invasion was the army's XXIV Corps Artillery, under Brigadier General Arthur M. Harper. The 2,682 troops in the XXIV Corps Artillery fielded two battalions of 155-millimeter guns and two battalions of 155-millimeter howitzers and would provide crucial support for the ground troops as the battle progressed. In addition there were artillery regiments attached to each marine division. The artillery of the 14th Marines had the specific task of covering the 4th Marine Division, while that of the 10th Marines would land in support of the 2nd Marine Division. While each artillery unit was attached to a specific division, each was expected to assist wherever necessary along the combat line.[1] Private First Class Rod Sandburg, who served with the 3rd Battalion, H Battery, 10th Marines, explained the organizational structure of his unit:

> For example the Second Division had one battalion of 105-millimeter howitzers or guns, which were twelve in number, and they were called Corps Artillery. The Marine Corps had only howitzers and most called them guns. There are four Batteries to a Battalion with Guns and one Battery called H&S (Headquarters and Service), which had only small arms as they were usually behind the Batteries in a Battalion. Their job was to run the FDC (Fire Direction Center) where the forward observers gave them Targets to fire on and they in turn called them down to the Guns. Each division has one regiment of artillery. The Second Division had the Tenth Marine Regiment that I was in: 3-H-10.[2]

The command structure for the Marianas campaign was complicated. The U.S. Navy was in overall charge, with Admiral Spruance commanding the Fifth Fleet and coordinating the invasions of Guam and Tinian with that of Saipan. Spruance also had to prepare for a possible Japanese naval response to the American offensive and anticipate how he might achieve all of these objectives concurrently. The Fifth Fleet was divided into two major sections: the Joint Expeditionary Force and Task Force 58. The Joint Expeditionary Force was further divided into the Northern Attack Force, which would invade Saipan and Tinian, and the Southern Attack Force, which targeted Guam. Admiral Turner commanded the entire Joint Expeditionary Force, and he would also lead the Northern Attack Force (Task Force 52) in the invasion of Saipan.[3] General Holland Smith was in charge of the troops, both marine and army, once they landed on Saipan and Tinian.

In June 1944 Vice Admiral Mitscher wanted to hit Saipan before the Japanese could fly in reinforcements from other islands, and Spruance gave permission for that action to begin on 11 June rather than 12 June as originally scheduled. The plan was successful, as 225 aircraft launched from more than two hundred miles away surprised the Japanese defenders and destroyed or damaged 147 enemy planes. The United States lost only a few pilots and eleven planes, ensuring American control of the air and the unimpeded bombing of the islands for the next couple of days. Against heavy but mostly ineffective antiaircraft fire, planes from Mitscher's fifteen carriers continued to bomb Saipan and the other islands in the Marianas until the invasion began. The U.S. Strategic Bombing Survey noted: "During daylight hours of 12–14 June all targets were kept under maximum air attack, with the objectives of destroying aircraft, rendering airfields temporarily unusable, destroying coastal defense and AA [antiaircraft] positions, and burning the cane fields."[4] When Japanese ships tried to escape the island, Mitscher's planes decimated the fleeing vessels.

On 13 June Mitscher's battleships commenced the sustained shelling of Saipan in order to destroy Japanese defenses, but the shelling did not target specific emplacements and did little damage to Japanese fortifications. There was a practical reason for this random barrage. The waters near the island had not yet been checked for mines, so the American fleet remained between ten thousand and sixteen thousand yards offshore, from which precise targeting was impossible. After ten minesweepers, deployed in a range from two to six miles off Saipan, found no mines in the area, the big ships moved closer to the island and resumed the shelling. At the same time, patrol planes and destroyers watched for Japanese submarine activity. On 14 June, the day before the scheduled landing, the seven battleships, eleven cruisers, and twenty-six destroyers of Turner's Joint Expeditionary Force joined those of Task Force 58 in pounding defenses on the island.[5] Several of the battleships targeted the western beaches where the marines would land the next day. The battleship *Tennessee* moved three thousand yards off Agingan Point and fired at the beach. At noon it sailed a short distance to the north in order to hit Afetna Point, a strategic target in the center of the landing area on D-Day. At the same time, the battleship *California* blasted Tanapag Harbor from its position near the northern end of the landing beaches.[6] Spruance watched the action from his flagship, the cruiser *Indianapolis*.

Despite the overwhelming firepower that emanated from the ships, Japanese emplacements remained mostly intact. Saipan was too large for a shelling of this duration to have a major impact. The Japanese defenses were well camouflaged, hidden in caves, movable, or simply too numerous for the navy ships to destroy. Many Japanese guns were hidden on the reverse slopes of hills or behind the crest, and they survived the naval bombardment that either hit the front of hills or went over the heads of the defenders. The Japanese military reported heavy damage to the towns of Charan Kanoa and Garapan but few personnel losses. Nevertheless, the sound and intensity of the barrage had a psychological impact on the defenders. According to one Japanese soldier, it was "too terrible for words."[7]

Once the entire Joint Expeditionary Force was in place, preparations for the landing intensified. At Tarawa in 1943 the marines lacked accurate information on the reefs or the tides, and they suffered heavy casualties for that mistake. To avoid the same error at Saipan, the navy scouted the waters with underwater demolition teams (UDTs). Approximately two hundred divers, half under Lieutenant Richard F. Burke and the other half led by Commander Draper L. Kauffman, carried out their reconnaissance mission near the primary landing area. A third team, of approximately eighty divers, searched the area to the north near Tanapag Harbor. Dropped near the reef, the divers swam toward the shore to check the depth of the water, search for underwater obstacles, measure the height of the barrier reef off the landing beaches, and plant radar beacons to help guide the landing vehicles on D-Day. The UDTs also charted the distance from the reef to the beach (it varied from five hundred to one thousand yards) as well as the best paths over or through the reef to the landing zone. Despite performing this action during daylight hours on 14 June, the teams suffered only light casualties. In all areas reports were favorable for the attackers. The Japanese had mined and fortified some of the beaches around Saipan, especially those on the southern end of the island near Aslito Airfield, but not the approach chosen by the American forces on the western side. Further, the UDTs reported that the coral reef was generally flat on top and not especially tall, leaving room for the amphibious tanks and tractors to cross and move toward the beach.[8]

Of course, the divers could not report what they did not see: after they left, Japanese swimmers planted flags in the water and on the reef at regular intervals to assist their gunners in targeting the incoming landing vehicles. The Japanese now knew where the American landing would occur. While some observers felt that the flag placements helped the Japanese gunners with their targeting of the approach to the island, others indicated that with or without the flags, Japanese artillery had the beaches well sighted and the marines were in for a tough landing. Lieutenant Colonel Wendell Best asserted that "the fire would have been equally devastating without the flags."[9]

At first everything proceeded according to plan for the Americans. They had quickly established air supremacy to prevent Japanese attacks on American ships and landing vehicles. The navy had shelled the island for three days to cripple Japanese defenses, and on the morning of 15 June the marines left their ships on schedule. Debarking on time was the last perfect moment in the long and bloody battle for Saipan.

While accounts vary on the time of reveille, in general marines were awakened at 0200 (2:00 AM) to prepare for the invasion.[10] Actually "not many of us slept much that final night before our first battle," recalled Robert Wollin of the 2nd Armored Amphibian Battalion.[11] Some showered for the last time for several weeks, some for the last time ever. They headed for the mess for breakfast, although many could not eat before the big battle. Private First Class William Jeffries acknowledged that, "It is hard to eat about 3 or 4 in the morning when you know what lies ahead of you when you are going in for a combat landing."[12] While some marines remembered a wonderful breakfast of steak and eggs, others talked about pancakes, red beans, crackers, apples, an orange, toast and jam, and coffee. For Private First Class Marshall E. Harris of the 2nd Armored Amphibian Battalion, it was one of the best meals ever: "Lo and behold, here was a great morning meal—sizzling steaks cooked to your liking, fried potatoes, eggs, bacon, ham and fresh milk, toast, butter, and juice of all kinds."[13] Marines called it their "last meal" or "condemned man's breakfast," according to Private Alva Perry.[14] Different ships served different food. Still many marines were too nervous to eat much—"Some of us eat like it's another day on the farm. Some of us are a bit edgy and don't feel hungry," observed Winton Carter of the 2nd Armored Amphibian Battalion.[15] Others recalled warnings from previous battles—they did not want to have a full stomach in case they took a bullet in the gut. In any case, some ate it all and then lost their breakfast while on the landing vehicles on their way in to the island. "Nervous stomachs, rough seas, digesting of steaks, excitement of the very first battle for most of us, etc. resulted in the use of many of the empty cardboard tubes we had aboard our tanks," noted Harlan Rosvold, another member of the 2nd Armored Amphibian Battalion.[16] The tubes were actually containers for 75-millimeter shells; on the beach they were used for nighttime bathroom emergencies.

On board the amphibious assault command ship *Rocky Mount*, which served as Turner's flagship, Turner and Holland Smith conferred on the attack. All factors, including the partly cloudy weather, indicated that the offensive should proceed, and at 0542 Turner issued the command to "Land the Landing Force."

By 0700 landing ships were lined up and ready to bring the marines onto the beaches. The naval barrage was halted to allow for half an hour's aerial bombing from 160 carrier planes.[17] In addition to hitting Japanese defenses, the air attacks were designed to make sure that no Japanese planes would be able to harass the marines as they moved ashore. At 0730, with one hour to go until the landing, the airplanes returned to their carriers and the battleships resumed their shelling. Both the aerial and naval bombardment displayed impressive coordination and firepower. Everything seemed to be in place.

After breakfast, Private First Class Orvel Johnson prepared for the landing. The narrow aisles between bunks on the assault transport *Calloway* were not wide enough for all marines to stand up and dress at the same time, so marines took turns getting up to inspect their gear. Johnson checked his weapon (Browning automatic rifle, or BAR), ammunition, combat knife, canteens, and food rations, but he remembered "not to take ashore any maps that had been used during our preparatory training for the invasion—in case they might fall into the hands of the enemy."[18] Private Carl Matthews went through a similar process: "I re-cleaned my rifle, secured the semaphore flags to my pack, checked the small radio I was to carry, filled my extra canteen, and thought a lot about home—Hubbard, Texas, Mother, Dad, and my two little sisters—so far away at that moment."[19] Private Rod Sandburg indicated that everyone also carried a first-aid package with some sulfa powder and two vials of morphine that they hoped they would never need.[20] Others, like Winton Carter, added other necessities to their checklist: "Plenty of clean socks. 2 cartons of smokes. Dog tags. Lord don't leave me now."[21] Sergeant Gene Brenner noted the deep emotions many marines experienced: "The air was electrified yet there was calm and a Blessing came over the loudspeaker to all the ships, a general absolution as I recall. Most everyone felt that there was a good possibility that they might meet their maker very shortly."[22] The chaplain included appropriate words for each denomination: "With the help of God we will succeed . . . most of you will return, but some of you will meet the God who made you. . . . Repent your sins . . . those of the Jewish faith repeat after me . . . now Christian men, Protestants and Catholics, repeat after me."[23]

Each marine climbed the ladder out of the hold and moved toward his boat station. Private Johnson "went over the side of the ship and down the landing nets to our awaiting landing craft." He had enjoyed his breakfast, "one of the best meals we had while at sea," but now he moved toward his assigned amtrac, an amphibious tractor designed specifically for climbing over reefs and carrying troops to beachhead landings. "Each LST carried seventeen LVT's [landing vehicles, tracked], loaded in two rows of eight with the odd one secured on the ramp."[24] Each LST also transported three hundred marines. Rows of amtracs were parked next to each other on the huge deck, and while drivers and crew members untied their vehicles, marines in full gear scrambled across the hoods of the amtracs until they found their number. Although they had all practiced this maneuver many times, platoon leaders came by to make sure that each man had his equipment in order. With all of the amtracs starting their diesel engines at about the same time, fumes filled the air and nearly asphyxiated the marines. With his amtrac finally in the water, Johnson watched the smoke rising from Saipan as his driver circled, waiting until all the other amtracs in his "wave" had been assembled.

Private Matthews was also admiring the naval bombardment as his amtrac prepared to debark: "The big Navy guns were now firing over our heads . . . round after round they fired and sometimes, we could see the explosions on the hillsides where the shells landed. Navy planes were bombing and strafing the beaches." Lieutenant James Stanley Leary Jr., leader of Matthews's 2nd Platoon of Company G, "watched with the most serious expression I [Matthews] had ever noticed and I wondered what his thoughts were. He was, probably, thinking about home, just like the rest of us. He was also aware that some of us—men in his command—could be dead in a matter of hours."[25]

Before the marines started forward, the navy carried out a demonstration (fake attack) north of the intended landing beaches. On D-Day in Europe nine days earlier, elaborate feints had been carried out to convince the German defenders that the attack would be focused at Calais rather than at the Normandy beaches. The Allies constructed a decoy army under General Patton's command across from Calais and continued bombing runs on those German positions until the last minute. At Saipan the feint was not as intricate, but the 24th Marines of the 4th Marine Division and the 1st Battalion, 29th Marines (attached to the 2nd Marine Division), did make one demonstration run on D-Day morning toward Tanapag Harbor, approximately six thousand yards north of the actual target beaches. Supported by naval gunfire, landing vehicles moved to within five thousand yards of the shore and then returned toward their ships. Later, Major Yoshida Kiyoshi, a captured Japanese intelligence officer, told American investigators that "though our diversionary maneuver in the Tanapag area had not led the Saipan defenders to believe that we would land there they nevertheless kept the 135th Infantry Regiment in that northern area and did not commit it south of Garapan until our main landings were clearly established."[26]

At 0813 the amtracs began to move forward for the real attack. Initially beyond the range of Japanese artillery, the landing vehicles soon closed the distance, and as they "moved closer to the beach shells begin hitting and exploding in the water" all around the marines. Carl Matthews was watching the action when "one of the tractors on our left received a direct hit and it disintegrated. Other shells were coming much too close to our own tractor. It was in that moment that I made the decision to do less looking and begin some serious praying. I glanced behind me and there were several mean and ugly Marines already on their knees."[27] At the same time, Orvel Johnson's amtrac raced for shore, changing direction to avoid the Japanese artillery shells. "We heard the screaming shells, the horrendous explosions, saw the geysers of water and aerial bursts, the spray of flame, smoke, and shrapnel."[28] As the amtracs took evasive maneuvers to steer clear of the Japanese gunners, the neat "wave" lines were broken, and companies that were supposed to land together were scattered. This amphibious landing was going to be difficult and deadly. The marines hit the beaches at 0843.

As landing vehicles moved ever closer to the island, navy guns continued to bombard the defenders. Of course the battleships had to target high enough to miss their own men now in the water between them and Saipan. The crews of two battleships—*California* near the north end of the landing beaches, *Tennessee* at the southern end—must have undertaken their assignments with particular satisfaction. Both ships had been on "battleship row" and sustained damage during the attack on Pearl Harbor in 1941. Resurrected from that disaster, they were part of the armada sent to pulverize the Marianas. The exhilaration would have been further enhanced if the sailors had known that Vice Admiral Nagumo, the commander of the Pearl Harbor attack, was on Saipan. In any case, all the battleships involved in this bombardment aimed at the Japanese positions overlooking the beaches. While observers noted the noise and power of the 14- and 16-inch shells, the defenders remained dug in and well protected and did not suffer extensive losses. Their military strategy was to attack and stop the Americans on the beach.

As Privates Johnson and Matthews and other marines raced toward the beach that morning, the Japanese gunners checked their sights, hoping to blast the marines off the landing beaches. Both sides expected a quick victory: the Americans anticipated a three-day battle, while the Japanese looked forward to driving the invaders back into the ocean.

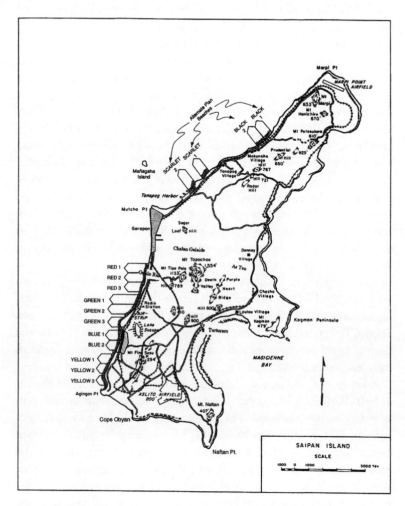

Map 4. D-Day, 15 June

CHAPTER FIVE

THE 2ND MARINE
DIVISION LANDS

The crews of the amphibious tanks had heard many rumors and warnings while on their way from Hawaii to Saipan. Of course, Tokyo Rose always tried to spread alarm and fear among the troops. "If the Marines in Pearl Harbor knew the reception that is prepared for them," she said, "they would jump overboard rather than go."[1] While the men scoffed at such admonitions, other warnings were more ominous. Private First Class G. Milton Shirley, in Company D of the 2nd Armored Amphibian Battalion, overheard an officer telling his troops: "Now this operation is going to be spearheaded by the second armored amphibian battalion. God help them poor devils." On 14 June, as Private Al Scarpo (also of Company D) recalled, a major in the 2nd Marine Division remarked, "Tomorrow morning we're going to hit the beach. There will be boats (LVT's) to take us in but there will be none to bring us back. Only two kinds of men will stay there . . . the dead and the ones who are going to die."[2]

Marines were not supposed to overhear such discouraging comments; officially, marine officers tried to boost the morale of the attacking troops. One week before D-Day, Lieutenant Colonel John C. Miller Jr. of the 3rd Battalion, 8th Marines, had written to his men: "We marines are known as the best of fighting men throughout the world. Who is there to doubt it? Perhaps the Japs will for awhile—for his Little Yellow Relatives on Guadalcanal, Tarawa, Makin, Kwajalein and Eniwetok never got back to Saipan with the word. We must prove it to him the hard way. . . . I will see you on

Figure 5. K Company, 3rd Battalion, 6th Marines, 2nd Marine Division, on Saipan; courtesy of Private Ray "Chick" Hill (USMC).

the beach. Keep a cool head, a true aim, God Bless you, and get in there and FIGHT. THE HELL WITH THE RISING SUN."[3]

On 14 June, the eve of D-Day, Major General Thomas E. Watson, commanding general of the 2nd Division, had encouraged his troops: "The task now before us is another 'must.' We are proud to help do the job. Just as in previous operations we breached the wall of the Japanese outer ring of defenses, we shall now crash through the inner defense line by the destruction of the enemy forces on Saipan. . . . You will be fighting side-by-side with another battle-tried Marine Division; units of the United States Army are fighting with us; and, the finest and greatest naval force in history supports us."[4]

The plan was straightforward. The western coast of Saipan was divided into landing beaches stretching for six thousand yards. Each beach was code-named: Red Beach 1, Red Beach 2, Red Beach 3, and so on for the remaining eight areas designated by Green, Blue, and Yellow. The 2nd Marine Division was to land on the northern beaches, Red and Green, while the 4th Marine Division hit the southern beaches, Blue and Yellow. A landing dock on the northern end of the town of Charan Kanoa served as the dividing line between the two divisions. Potential landing sites on the other sides of the island had been considered but ruled out due to a variety of problems or obstacles. Only the west coast would allow the two divisions to land side by side. The marines used their standard triangular assault formation; that is, each division landed with two regiments abreast and one in reserve. Similarly, each regiment landed with two battalions abreast and one in reserve. From north to south, the order of regiments in the assault was 6th Marines, 8th Marines, 23rd Marines, and 25th Marines. Breaking the landing down further, the 2nd and 3rd Battalions of the 6th Marines would land on Red Beaches 2 and 3, and the 3rd and 2nd Battalions of the 8th Marines would hit Green Beaches 1 and 2. At the same time, the 3rd Battalion, 23rd Marines, would land on Blue Beach 1; the 2nd Battalion, 23rd Marines, would hit Blue Beach 2; the 2nd Battalion, 25th Marines, would land on Yellow Beach 1; and the 1st Battalion, 25th Marines, would come in on Yellow Beach 2.[5]

The attack plan envisioned the 2nd Marine Division anchoring itself on the coast and turning left or northward, while the 4th Marine Division used the 2nd Division as a kind of gate hinge. The 4th Division would proceed eastward and then swing north. Both divisions would sweep to the northern end of the island, destroying the Japanese defenders in their path. The entire process was scheduled to last three days.

Shortly before 0800, Admiral Turner postponed the landing time ten minutes to 0840 to allow the ships more time to move into formation. He knew that an amphibious landing is one of the most difficult military actions conceivable, and it was crucial to make sure that the invasion started properly. Hundreds of ships and thousands of men have to be perfectly coordinated in a relatively small space. First the LSTs had to stop, lower their bow ramps, and launch their LVTs into the water; the amtracs would then carry the marines over the reef to the beach.[6] Saipan was four thousand yards away, or approximately twenty-seven minutes.

In most cases the launching procedure took place without incident, although timing the waves was not a simple task. Corporal Roy William Roush described the scene: "When we were about four miles offshore, the huge front doors of all the LST's opened and the ramps extended in order to launch the amtracs. . . . The sea was a bit rough which made it difficult and tricky to launch the amtracs off of the front ramp into the open sea. As each amtrac moved to the outer end of the ramp, it would wait for the crest of an oncoming wave to rise up below the ramp, then it would lurch forward into the water. Even when it was done properly, it was rather dangerous." Sometimes the timing was not perfect enough. Loaded with men or equipment, the heavy amtracs could drop and take on water as they met the ocean. While the majority of amtracs hit the water as planned, some sank with their crews. Roush watched an amtrac go down: "I was horrified as I watched the amtrac drop about 20 feet through mid-air to the bottom trough of the wave. It plummeted below the surface like a brick and never came up again—taking the driver and crew down with it."[7]

To protect the marines, other armed vehicles preceded the amtracs as they moved toward the island. In front of the line were the twenty-four LCI(G)s (landing craft, infantry, gunboat) that would rush toward the reef "firing their 4.5-inch rockets and 20- and 40-millimeter guns at point-blank range onto the beach."[8] Behind them were the armored amphibious tanks, the LVT(A)4s (landing vehicle, tracked, armored, Model 4). This vehicle was basically an LVT with a turret-mounted 75-millimeter howitzer. As described by Colonel Joseph Alexander: "The top-of-the-line LVT-A4 weighed nineteen tons and featured half-inch frontal and turret armor—enough to deflect small-arms fire, but the vehicle proved vulnerable to every larger Japanese weapon."[9] The amphibious tanks were "to precede the infantry waves ashore and provide maximum gunfire on the landing area as the Navy shore bombardment lifted."[10] The tanks had to be light enough to float even when fully loaded, so they were not provided with a lot of armor and "could not absorb much punishment." According to crew member Marshall Harris, "Our armored amphibian tanks weren't up to slugging it out with a determined and skilled enemy land tank because of our lack of protective armor."[11] Following the amphibious tanks were the troop-carrying LVTs.

Early on the morning of D-Day the armored amphibian battalions disembarked from their LSTs and moved into position. By 0812 the headlong rush toward the waiting Japanese was under way. Company A of the 2nd Armored Amphibian Tank Battalion blazed a trail for the 2nd Battalion of the 6th Marines headed for Red Beach 2; Company B led the 3rd Battalion of the 6th Marines going to Red Beach 1; Company C was in front of the 3rd Battalion, 8th Marines, aiming for Green Beach 1; and Company D led the way for the 2nd Battalion, 8th Marines, on its way to Green Beach 2.

Crossing the reef was the first challenge the amphibious tanks encountered that day. Private Shirley in Company D recalled: "As we approached the reef, our Driver, Allen, had the good sense to down shift all the way to first gear and sure enough we hit that reef at the ebb of the wave. We had to climb that reef before the big wave coming behind us broke down on us and swamped us. An engine stall here would be disastrous. . . . Our

Driver had our lives in his hands trying to make it safely across the edge of that barrier reef."[12] Once safely on the other side, the tanks entered the lagoon between the reef and the beach. They were now even closer to the Japanese guns.

As they approached the beach the LVT(A)4s were to fire their 75-millimeter howitzers at Japanese gun emplacements, knocking out whatever enemy guns they could as well as diverting attention away from the marines approaching on LVTs. In order for the amphibious tanks to continue to fire as they moved toward the landing beaches, a straight line had to be maintained with the LVTs behind the LVT(A)4s. In practice this proved impossible, as "incoming fire, bouncing off the coral heads in the shallow lagoon, tide shift to the north, and faster speeds of the LVT's over the LVTA4's" all led to many breaks in the line. Japanese fire was intense, and the amphibious tanks paid the price. The 2nd Armored Amphibian Battalion suffered twenty-six deaths on D-Day.[13]

Some of the vehicles made it over the reef but submerged and suffered a failure of their electrical system. Others got through the water due to new fording equipment—intake and exhaust ducts that saved the crew from drowning.[14] And still others crawled onto the beach, only to be derailed by obstacles there or hit by enemy fire. When an amphibious tank went out of service, the crew jumped out, dug in, and joined the infantry. Despite these problems, for the most part the tanks performed well, clearing a path for the troops that followed them onto the beaches.

Intense Japanese artillery and mortar fire was one significant issue for the amphibious tanks, and finally beach obstacles, trees, trenches, shell holes, and mechanical failures all contributed to the variety of problems. Eventually, disabled LVT(A)4s were scattered in the water, on the beach, and farther inland. At the end of D-Day only thirteen of the seventy tanks assigned to the 2nd Marine Division were still operational.[15]

Volunteer runner R. J. Lee in Company A made it ashore, but his LVT(A)4 could not move beyond "a deep trench . . . just behind the beach shrubs or foliage." The tank backed out into the water, only to be hit by Japanese fire. Three men were killed, and the rest of the crew jumped out and headed back to the beach. One man "was shot in the face and killed instantly." Lee himself was wounded and evacuated.[16]

Driver S. A. Balsano remembered being stuck in a tank trench: "That June 15 was some day . . . and it was hot as Hades and our worst day in battle." After his tank hit the trench, two other vehicles also stopped. "The tank commander of the tank behind ours was hooking up the tow cable to the tank behind him. He was killed by a sniper. Lt. Pease went to finish the hook up and the same sniper killed him."[17]

Behind the amphibious tanks were the LVTs carrying the marines. As the marines moved forward the big navy guns targeted the beaches, but the firing ceased when the landing vehicles were a thousand yards off-shore. Naval bombardment was replaced by air attacks that started on the beach and moved inland as the amtracs approached. The navy carefully coordinated all of these actions in order to prevent hitting its own lines, but despite all of these efforts there would be casualties from friendly fire on Saipan.

As the amtracs moved toward the beach the Japanese used their marker flags in the water between the reef and the beach to target the landing vehicles. Due to the confusion created by enemy fire and the need to take evasive action around burning equipment, as well as the fast-moving tides, many amtracs carrying the marines in the 2nd Division landed too far north.

Enemy artillery and mortar fire intensified as the marines crossed the reef. Marines quickly learned to keep as low as possible in their amtracs. "In our coming ashore, our jeep driver stuck his head up to see how close to shore we were and had his head taken off as we watched. A lot of us in the amtrac were covered with blood and brains," recalled Corporal Charles Porter of Ticonderoga, New York.[18] Nevertheless, the first marines landed only three minutes after H-Hour (0840).

To the average marine on the beach, things did not appear to be going well. Some of the amtracs and LVTs had drifted to the north after they crossed the reef. They were reacting to strong tides, the crowding of the landing vehicles all rushing the beach at the same time, and the intensity of Japanese fire. This situation especially affected the 2nd Marine Division heading for Red and Green beaches. Several units of the 2nd Division came ashore in the wrong place, creating a crush of troops on one beachhead. The 2nd and 3rd Battalions of the 6th Marines were supposed to land on Red 2 and 3, but they came ashore on Red 1 and 2, about four hundred yards north of their targets. Both the 2nd and 3rd Battalions of the 8th Marines, instead of taking Green 1 and 2, landed together on Green 1. As Private First Class L. H. Van Antwerp recalled: "We were supposed to hit Green Beach II. . . . There was no way of really telling where one designated landing beach zone ended and another started. Anyway we all wound up landing off to the left (north) of our assigned beaches. . . . We hit Green I instead of Green II." Japanese gunners took advantage of the situation and killed or wounded large numbers of marines: "The Japs had open season on incoming amtracs all morning and they could see clear up the landing beaches and fire at us direct. There were so many of us and so many vehicles that it was hard to miss hitting something."[19]

The 6th and 8th Marines of the 2nd Division were the first to land, and they suffered the consequences of the initial crowding. Instead of being spread out across Red 2 and 3 and Green 1 and 2, the 6th Marines were on Red 1 and 2 while the 8th Marines found themselves on Green 1. The results were deadly. The Japanese waited for the first few waves of marines to land and then concentrated their artillery and mortar fire on the crammed beaches, inflicting high casualties. Corporal David Kinder remembered that "on landing we were under fire and lost one man to shrapnel. It ripped out his throat—we were shook up."[20] Many of the initial casualties were officers who were trying to gather and organize their battalions for the planned advance. As Hoffman noted, "all four assault battalion commanders of the 2nd Marine Division became casualties during the early hours of the battle." According to Johnston, Lieutenant Colonel John C. Miller "was hit first by mortar fragments, on the way to his amtrac. At the beach a Jap grenade caught him between the feet, and stripped much of the flesh from his limbs." Lieutenant Colonel Henry P. Crowe, Lieutenant Colonel John W. Easley, and Lieutenant Colonel Raymond L. Murray were also wounded on D-Day. That meant that the 2nd and 3rd Battalions of the 6th Marines and the 2nd and 3rd Battalions of the 8th Marines quickly needed new commanding officers, and the 1st Battalion, 8th Marines, lost Lieutenant Colonel Lawrence C. Hays Jr. shortly after it landed. In total, five of the first seven combat battalions of the 2nd Division replaced their commanders on the first day.[21]

Loss of officers added to the confusion of battle, even as other marines stepped forward to take command. Fortunately, marines had been trained for this eventuality. As Corporal Graf commented: "unlike the Japanese troops, we were trained to take over in case of the loss of leaders. A 'buck private' in the rear ranks could easily find himself acting as a Platoon Leader as our ranks were 'thinned' by casualties."[22] Landing on the wrong beach also meant that officers and men could not find the landmarks they had studied on maps and expected to capture. Further, bombardments by the navy and air force had inadvertently destroyed some of the landmarks, and other markers and guideposts were eliminated as the approaching marines and Japanese defenders exchanged fire. The confusion added to the expected chaos of battle as marines found themselves in an ever-changing landscape in which exploding landing vehicles and equipment and body parts littered the once pristine beach. Amidst the turmoil, marines remembered snippets and scenes that exemplified their tenuous existence.

Some marines were just happy to be dropped off on the beach rather than in the water. Corporal M. F. Leggett remembered the disaster at Tarawa when the landing vehicles stuck on the reef and they had to wade ashore in the face of devastating Japanese fire. At Saipan the improved amtracs and landing vehicles crossed the reef and drove right onto the island. Nevertheless, heavy Japanese shelling prevented most of the landing vehicles from advancing as far onto the beach as planned.[23] Once the marines scrambled out of the vehicles the fighting became intense. Private Reggie Dunbar described it as "pure hell."[24]

Sergeant Jim Evans was twenty years old in 1944, but with four years' service behind him he was an experienced marine. After basic training in San Diego, he was on Oahu at the Naval Air Station at Kaneohe Bay on 7 December 1941. By the time of the invasion of Saipan, Evans had already seen action at Guadalcanal and Tarawa. He landed about two hundred yards north of his target beach. On the beach, with land mines exploding and units all mixed up and marines wandering around looking for their platoons, marines simply engaged in one firefight after another. Evans confirmed the sense of confusion felt by so many marines: "All of the landmarks we had been trained to look for were not there." As a result, the first day was "horrendous. . . . We were getting the shit kicked out of us." Wherever two or three marines found each other they would form an informal squad until they could find their units and reestablish battalion cohesion. "You just gathered up people and tried to get something organized," remembered Evans. They also tried to help other marines find their units, but overall the situation was "very confusing." It would be two or three days before the situation improved.[25]

Private First Class Edward Skrabacz landed on Red Beach a few hundred yards from his intended location as well. The Japanese raked the beach with mortars and machine-gun fire, pinning down the marines. Skrabacz dug into a foxhole, sharing it with red ants that crawled over him while a Japanese tank prevented him from changing locations. Fortunately, the tank had a weak spot on its underside where the armor was thin, and several marines were able to hit the vehicle there and stop it. When the tank crew emerged to escape the burning vehicle, the marines finished them off. Under these grueling conditions, Skrabacz recalled that some marines froze or snapped and had to be sent back to the ships. "I can't blame them because of the pressure. I just did what I was told. I wasn't one of the bravest guys. I was scared from the day I landed until the day I left." Nevertheless, Skrabacz "did what I had to do."[26] In the resulting chaos the marines were able to move only 100–200 feet forward, far short of their intended goal for the day.

Despite being "scared to death," corpsman Chester Szech had to tend to the wounded in the face of withering Japanese fire. As Szech observed, all marines who have been in battle appreciate the contribution of corpsmen: "Most marines who have been in combat love corpsmen. Most marines who have never been in combat think corpsmen are queer." Szech wore a regular marine uniform without special insignia and carried a .45-caliber pistol and a carbine "just in case," although he had not been trained to use either. As one marine went down, another would call out "Corpsman!" and Szech would race toward the spot. There he would pour sulfa on the wound, bandage it as quickly as possible, and dispense morphine to kill the pain. Then he sent the marine back to the aid station.[27] It is obvious why marines loved the corpsmen and equally clear why they were favorite targets of Japanese snipers. Corpsmen saved wounded marines who might fight another day; targeting corpsmen meant that more marines would die.

Lieutenant Byron Bird was out of reach of any corpsman, so he was forced to operate as his own surgeon. A college football star in Stillwater, Oklahoma, Bird joined the Marine Corps after Pearl Harbor and received a Silver Star for his actions on Tarawa. According to his Silver Star citation, Bird "led his platoon to the rescue of another platoon which had been pinned down . . . he personally put an enemy machine gun out of action." He was twenty-two years old when his unit hit the beach at Saipan and a Japanese artillery shell ripped through his ankle, leaving the bone crushed and his foot dangling only by a piece of flesh. Because the battle was raging and medical help was not available, Bird took matters into his own hands. After the event, Bird described his ordeal matter-of-factly: "No one could assist me when that shell hit. I was losing a lot of blood and, because of the dirt and insects, I was afraid of gangrene. So I just amputated my foot with a trench knife. . . . It was the only thing left to do." He was evacuated from Saipan seven hours later.[28]

Bird was lucky to get off the island. Many marines died that first day because the incoming traffic and congestion and Japanese fire made it difficult to evacuate the wounded. Private Van Antwerp recalled that "amtracs bringing in Marines, ammo, water, etc. were supposed to take wounded back out to the LCVP's and boats standing off the reef. The first day it was hard to get wounded aboard outgoing amtracs before they were unloaded and departed quickly from the beach to get away from the awful shellfire raining down all along the beach. The wounded being collected along the beaches were constantly exposed to all this shelling. Many wounded inland were killed on the beach awaiting evacuation to a hospital ship."[29]

Marines who landed in the afternoon had to contend with enemy fire, destroyed machinery, dead bodies in the water and on the beach, and the smell of death. Scout Guy Gabaldon observed, "On the way to the beachheads everyone noticed and commented on the horrible 'sweet stink' coming from shore. The Jap bodies were already starting to rot and putrefy. The enemy did not have time to bury those who had been killed. . . . If I were to live a thousand years I would never get over that sweet stink. There is nothing else like it. No other putrid meat emits the horrible odor than does a rotting human."[30]

Most marines exemplified the toughness and endurance for which the Corps was famous. A few, however, could not handle the intensity of battle. Private First Class Ralph Browner, who received the Navy Cross for killing approximately forty Japanese soldiers, recalled several cases of what he considered "cowardice."[31] "Shell shock" might be a better term. A marine might freeze, but in some cases he just needed some time in the rear to recover and return ready for action. Occasionally the fear was more debilitating. According to Sergeant David Dempsey, "The shell-shock cases began to come in, too—boys who had 'cracked up' under very heavy fire at the front and had to be led or carried in. They hid behind trees and cowered at each new shell burst. Some could not remember their names."[32] Browner recalled that everyone in battle was "scared shitless" but that a marine can be scared "without being a coward . . . there wasn't a man alive who wasn't scared, but you'd rather die than be a coward." Absolute trust of the men to their right and left was essential in marine training, and all had been taught to be prepared "to die for your buddies."[33]

Corporal Steve Judd landed with the second wave and also recognized what the stress of battle can do to a marine. He recalled one sergeant who retreated to headquarters and did not return, and another who ordered the men forward but went in the other direction. When a regular marine froze and could not advance, the rest of the platoon just went around him. Like Browner, Judd performed well under these difficult conditions. He did not feel any fear at first, but as he moved on the beach his buddy turned to him and said, "Goddamn it Steve, I've got a terrible headache." Judd noticed a bullet hole in his friend's helmet. "That's when I got a little nervous."[34]

Fortunately, most of the marines were like Browner and Judd and able to perform under extreme stress. Corporal Jim Montgomery from North Dakota was part of an 81-millimeter mortar platoon attached to the 6th Marines. Shortly after setting up on the beach, Montgomery's battery faced serious problems—normally they mortar-fired out of four tubes, but almost immediately the fourth lost its sight and the squad was using only three. Firing as quickly as possible, Montgomery and his team discovered that the tubes were overheating, creating the danger that the powder charge could ignite when a shell was loaded. Nevertheless, the mortar squad, wearing asbestos gloves to protect themselves from the heat of the tubes, continued to hit the enemy. As more marines landed, the squad was ordered to move its gun forward. While that procedure was being carried out, Montgomery and Private Bill Martin went back toward the beach for more ammunition, and as they were returning to their platoon Japanese artillery hit the new location and killed four of their buddies.[35]

Despite intense Japanese fire, marines continued to pour onto the beach. Slowly they scratched out a space for themselves in the sand and then moved forward relentlessly. In the chaos of the first hours of battle, marines were forced to improvise. Sergeant Jerry Wachsmuth landed early on D-Day with the situation chaotic and unsettled. The worst part, according to Wachsmuth, was the anticipation while waiting in the landing vehicle before the battle started. Once a marine hit the beach, "even with bullets whizzing by his head," he would operate without conscious fear as adrenaline took over. "You'd become oblivious. Fear was a given. Sometimes you'd wonder if you'd make it. You accepted where you were and what might happen and you just did the best you could. You get so scared that you're not scared any more. Fear helps you stay alert."[36]

Within minutes, Wachsmuth's squad leader, Russell "Jake" Jacobs, was killed, shot through the forehead. Mortar fire killed three other marines as they filled their canteens. Wachsmuth indicated that as a result of the loss of officers and general battle confusion, many marines basically "did their own thing." Fortunately, their discipline and training allowed them to succeed. They had to, as the Japanese were planning to drive them off the beach before the day was out.

The 2nd Division continued to add to its strength as the day went on. The 1st Battalion of the 10th Marines moved into the woods in front of Red Beach 2, while the 2nd Battalion of the same regiment advanced across Green Beach 1 close to Charan Kanoa. The 10th Marines, with 75-millimeter howitzers and 105-millimeter guns, played an important supporting role in the early going. Colonel Raphael Griffin, commander of the 10th Marines, came ashore at about 1730. The 2nd Division's commanding general, Thomas E. Watson, landed at 1800 and moved into the divisional command post in the trees in front of where Red Beach 1 met Red Beach 2.[37]

According to National Archives documents, from midnight to dawn on that first night "the left flank of the 2nd Marine Division was under continuous attack."[38] Two companies of the 6th Marines bore the brunt of the Japanese assault. F Company and I Company of the 6th Marines were on Red Beach 1, on the far left or north end of the marine lines. While there were small-scale encounters throughout the night, the major Japanese effort came at about 0300 when a bugle sounded the charge. The Japanese attacked, screaming and waving flags and swords. Three American destroyers fired illumination star shells that lit up the beach and gave the marines excellent vision and a clear line of fire toward the approaching Japanese. The frontline marine companies devastated the Japanese offensive. American tanks and shells from the battleship *California* supplied important support to the marines, although the battleship often had to adjust its range to avoid hitting the marines themselves. "We spent the night penned down and watched the shells coming in and exploding behind us," recalled Corporal David Kinder. "We could overhear the spotter calling for corrections and hear the shells 'walking' closer to us. Every time he called for lowering the range, more of the sand fell on our shallow foxholes."[39]

While the marines loved the illumination, they were concerned about one side effect, as Private Dodson Smith noted: "One thing we feared more than the Japs were the star shells that the ships would fire to light up the area at night. The shells did a good job at lighting up the night. The bad thing was when it exploded there was a large cap from the shell that would come down with a thud and bury in the ground. Our foxholes were open."[40] Nevertheless the star shells greatly aided the marines, and the Japanese lost approximately seven hundred soldiers in this fruitless effort, providing an early example of the offensive strategy that would slowly decimate the Japanese Saipan garrison. While the Japanese lost this encounter, the marines also experienced stress and anxiety. As Corporal Kinder recalled, "a tank had been hit and was about burnt out on the small road just above us. There was a slight breeze that kept it glowing and we could hear the steel hulk moaning, twisting, ammo going off—all the dying sounds of machines and mortals alike. I'll always remember that night."[41]

Other units of the 2nd Division also fought Japanese attacks during the first night. Private First Class Jim Monroe from Brownwood, Texas, had been a marine since the age of sixteen. He entered the Corps in 1942 and turned eighteen on the eve of the Saipan invasion. Monroe fired a tank grenade and hit a Japanese tank about thirty-five yards from his position. In fact, several marines sent a barrage of tank grenades and bazooka fire into the tank at the same time. When the tank driver opened the hatch, "everyone had a bead on him. I don't know how many bullets he took." That night Monroe and a fellow marine prepared for action. "The first night we had a nice ditch to bed down in. You know if you pop up and look in front and then set back down, it's like taking a picture, your mind's eye tells you if there is anyone coming at you. Well my buddy and I were doing this all night. Here is one of the things about the war I will think about forever. Why him and not me. We were less than three feet apart, and he took one right through the head."[42]

Fire team leader Robert Groves of Fort Towson, Oklahoma, was also sixteen when he joined the Marine Corps, having altered his birth certificate in order to enlist. Two years later at Saipan, this young battle veteran of Guadalcanal and Tarawa manned a .50-caliber machine gun. After being hit by shrapnel on his amtrac during the landing, Groves had his right shoulder bandaged and continued to fight. After the Japanese tank offensive had been repulsed, Groves found that his "right leg was numb and bleeding so bad the corpsman placed a tourniquet to stop the artery that was pumping blood so hard that I thought I was through. But the Doc gave me a shot of the morphine we carried on our belts and all pain and care seemed to disappear until they loaded my stretcher on an amtrac to return to the hospital ship. I remember very vividly the amtrac nosing into the breakwater where the reef ended and the ocean began, seawater covered me and another marine with a leg wound, and my thought was immediately, how will I swim with one leg. When the coxswain announced that we were safely off the reef and at sea, that was the best news I had that day." The Battle of Saipan was over for Groves.[43]

Although the landing had placed thousands of marines on the island, not all had gone well. By the end of the first day the beach was littered with wrecked and twisted machinery, and the 2nd Marine Division had paid for its beachfront with heavy casualties—238 men killed and 1,022 wounded. It was already evident that the price of victory would be far greater than anticipated by General Holland Smith and Admiral Kelly Turner.

CHAPTER SIX

THE 4TH MARINE DIVISION LANDS

Each marine confronted his private thoughts and fears as he approached the beach. Some were ill from seasickness while others just prayed quietly. Others wondered if they were ready for the task ahead: "Can we do this? Am I going to live through it? Suppose I get my balls shot off? Am I going to piss in my pants going over the side? Do I look as scared as I feel? What about the other guys? Are they as scared as I am? They don't look it."[1]

Fortunately, the 4th Division's landing on Blue and Yellow beaches was a little different than it had been for the 2nd Division. The regiments of the 4th Division hit the correct beaches and did not suffer the crowding that the 2nd Division had. Lieutenant Colonels John J. Cosgrove and Edward J. Dillon led the 23rd Marines onto Blue 1 and Blue 2, while the 25th Marines, under Lieutenant Colonels Lewis C. Hudson and Hollis U. Mustain, landed on Yellow 1 and 2.[2] Blue 1, on the northern end of the 23rd Marines' beaches, lined up almost directly with the little town of Charan Kanoa. On Blue 2 and Yellow 1, in the middle of the southern beaches, most of the LVTs were able to ramble ashore, dropping marines between one hundred and seven hundred yards inland. On Yellow 2, at the southern end of the 25th Marines, heavy Japanese fire forced many marines out of their landing vehicles in shallow water where they had to race for shore and cover. Needless to say, the difficulty of running through water slowed the marine advance and provided ready targets for Japanese gunners. Of all the landing beaches used by the 4th Division, Yellow 2 was the

Figure 6. U.S. marine first assault wave hits Saipan beach on D-Day; courtesy of Private Rod Sandburg (USMC).

most difficult, with "heavy resistance" continuing throughout the morning. According to American intelligence reports: "As LVTs moved inland from Yellow Two enemy artillery fired on them and by 1052, the 4th Division was receiving minor enemy counter-attacks on its right flank."[3]

The army's 708th Amphibian Tank Battalion led the way for the 4th Marine Division. The 534th and 773rd Amtrac Battalions (U.S. Army) then brought the marines to the beach on three hundred landing vehicles. These amtracs had better luck hitting their targeted beach than those leading the 2nd Marine Division, but they too came under withering mortar and artillery attack. Nevertheless, they delivered four thousand marines from the 4th Division in approximately twenty minutes.[4]

Platoon leader Earl Guy of Montgomery, Alabama, was a member of the 10th Amphibian Tractor Battalion, part of the 4th Marine Division. Like other amtracs, Guy's vehicle had a three-man crew and carried three machine guns. The amtracs moved through the water at only five or six miles per hour and provided ready targets for the Japanese gunners.

After dropping the marines on the beach, the amtracs would pick up the wounded, return to the navy ships, and load more troops for another run at the island. At night the amtracs would sit on the reef, guns pointed toward the ocean, watching for an enemy attack from the rear. As Guy observed, "in the pitch black darkness, having the ocean water slapping into the sides of the tractor, being without sleep for a possible 24 hours or more, it was easy to think you could see rubber boats in the darkness and the enemy trying to quietly reach the side of the tractor and pitch in grenades to eliminate the crew."[5]

Also serving with the 10th Amphibian Tractor Battalion was amtrac driver R. P. Willson, who had been involved in the landing on Roi-Namur, the first landing of the 4th Division. At Saipan the amtrac attack waves left their larger ships in five-minute intervals. Willson followed the amphibious tanks onto Blue Beach 2. Although he was supposed to look for a specific spot, like other drivers he basically looked for any open ground on the beach after he crossed the reef. He saw amphibious tanks on the beach and noticed an apparent vacant area where he could unload on the port (left) side of a tank. As he approached the tank he wondered why its turret was pointed at a 2:00 angle when enemy fire was coming from 11:00. He backed up and moved to the other side of the tank and saw that the entire starboard (right) side had been blown away. The crew was dead. Willson's marines quickly jumped out of his vehicle, and at the same time Willson noticed the Japanese gun emplacement that had also been destroyed in the exchange of fire with the disabled tank. He speculated that the tank and Japanese gunners had fired simultaneously and destroyed each other. Willson took his amtrac back into the water to pick up more troops. As he approached the reef, Japanese mortars chased him and landed right behind him. He got to the reef and bounced hard. Out of reach of the Japanese gunners, Willson went back to check his amtrac and found numerous small holes in the stern. Despite being hit by fragments of two mortar rounds, he escaped and continued on his mission.[6]

Corporal R. B. Roberts of the 11th Amphibian Tractor Battalion had a similar experience. He was the operator of an amtrac, also manned by a crew of three with .30-caliber machine guns mounted on the sides. Roberts drove a 37-millimeter cannon and gun crew from the 4th Division onto the beach, unloading under "considerable enemy fire. The 37mm gun was destroyed and several of the crew wounded" before he could head back into the water for another run. His amtrac picked up wounded marines as well as a few local women and children, called Chamorros, who had given themselves up to the Americans.[7]

The 4th Division's original plan anticipated that on the first day the LVTs would drive the marines onto the beach and all the way to their objective (called the O-1 line), about twelve hundred yards inland. If successful, that would place them on the slopes of Mt. Fina Susu, approximately three hundred feet in elevation. Few of the amtracs made it that far, however. Saipan had been a Japanese possession since the end of World War I, and despite several reconnaissance missions, the United States knew little about its topography. The few photographic missions flown in the months preceding the invasion had revealed some major features of the terrain but not its essential details. In some places heavy vegetation on the beach stopped the amtracs and forced the marines to debark sooner than they had expected.[8] The LVTs that did approach the O-1 line were forced to drive in single file due to the narrow or obstructed road condition, making them vulnerable to attack from front and rear. Fortunately for the marines, the Japanese were unable to launch a full-scale counterattack and the LVTs were mainly harassed by small-arms fire that the marines quickly neutralized. Nevertheless, the LVTs could not make it to the O-1 line as anticipated, and their inability to achieve this objective on D-Day set an unfortunate pattern, with the marines always falling short of their objectives as the battle progressed.

Some confusion resulted because, while several amtracs advanced toward the O-1 line, others, under heavy fire, had to unload and race back to the water. As a result, a few marines actually landed more than once. Private First Class Paul Beverly of Richmond, Virginia, serving with the 2nd Battalion, 14th Marines, sat in his amtrac as it hit the beach but was sent back out into the water because of the heavy fire. After three tries, and still unable to unload, "the tractor driver decided that he had made enough landings. I looked out and the tractor people were tossing the disassembled parts of our weapon onto the beach . . . we manhandled the gun down the beach to our battery position."[9]

Other marines also made the run to the beach more than once. Lieutenant Alan Taylor of Spencer, Idaho, was serving as an ordnance officer (first lieutenant) with Headquarters and Service Company for the 25th Marines. His landing in the second wave was interrupted when the driver of his amtrac hit the reef and "lost his guts and froze." A wave turned the landing vehicle upside down, trapping Taylor and three other marines underneath. After working their way out of the stranded vehicle, they were picked up by an amtrac returning from the beach and taken back to their ship for new equipment. Taylor's main regret was losing the "good bottle of whiskey and the Colt 45 automatic" that went down when the amtrac overturned. On his return to his ship Taylor received a new rifle, but he complained that he was only given a "carbine that's no damned good." As an ordnance officer in a service company, Taylor was supposedly non-combat, but the distinction between his company and the other marines disappeared as soon as he landed.[10]

As a result of the confusion on the beach, companies were split up and marines had a hard time finding their units. One group that suffered as a result of this chaotic situation was Private First Class Orvel Johnson's unit (1st Battalion, 23rd Marines). They landed near Charan Kanoa, but on the first day of battle, four members of C Company were killed. Ralph Linaweaver was the first casualty of the day, shot as he left his amtrac and "dead before he hit the ground."[11]

Private Carl Matthews of G Company, 2nd Battalion, 23rd Marines, recalled that "the beach was a madhouse with individual marines trying to find cover, artillery shells landing, snipers picking off marines before they could leave the amphibious tractors. John Winnekins was fatally hit by a sniper a few feet from his amphibious tractor. One little marine, Tony Mar-riro from the Bronx, New York, didn't move quickly enough from where he lay in the sand and one of the amphibious tractors ran over his legs." Although Marriro survived, his war was over.[12]

Private First Class Don Swindle, born in Tennessee but raised in Indiana, had seen action on Roi-Namur before landing on Saipan on D-Day. His amtrac pushed forward about 250 yards inland until it was stopped by a ditch that served as an antitank obstacle. Rolling out of the vehicle, Swindle sought shelter from the steady stream of Japanese machine-gun fire, mortars, and artillery. Despite his efforts, Swindle acknowledged that he could not dodge the fire: "You just went in shaking and praying." After destroying a Japanese machine-gun emplacement, Swindle and his platoon continued to advance. By nightfall his platoon—part of F Company, 2nd Battalion, 23rd Marines—had suffered 40 percent casualties; it took three days to reach the objective for the first day.[13]

Although marines continued to pour onto the beaches, the Japanese had not given up their plan to stop the invasion, and enemy artillery and mortar fire continued throughout the day. Sergeant Norman Gertz, who would eventually retire as a colonel in the Marine Corps, called Saipan "probably the most violently opposed landing that we ever had." Intelligence Sergeant Bill More considered the landing on Blue Beach 2 on D-Day just as intense as the first day at Iwo Jima in 1945. Private First Class Joe E. Ojeda corroborated More's sentiments: "The landing was disastrous. The Japanese waited for us to land and then laid down an artillery barrage on the beach. There were slain Marines all around us. There were bodies and body parts all over, with everyone yelling for a corpsman. Some were cut by shrapnel or had a head cut off." Before the end of the day Ojeda had been quickly promoted to corporal because "others had been killed." Some marines, like Private First Class Jasper Smith in the 3rd Battalion, 23rd Marines, were wounded soon after they arrived on the beach. Smith was hit by artillery fire and his hip was shattered. He crawled into a hole for protection and was evacuated on a stretcher later that afternoon. He would spend the next year in the hospital.[14]

Of course, many marines were not as fortunate as Smith. First Lieutenant Harrison "Harry" Blaine, born in Boston in 1920, was one of the numerous officers who did not survive the first day. As his commanding officer, Captain William Weinstein of B Company, 23rd Marines, wrote to Blaine's parents in August 1944:

> As we took cover, we discovered that we were surrounded by infiltrating enemy that were attempting to capture our [amphibious] tractors for the reason that our tractors were all armed with machine guns. If the enemy captured the tractors our situation would have been precarious. I, therefore, called Harry and informed him to send out an 8-man patrol in charge of an N.C.O. to strip all tractors in the vicinity of our assembly area of guns and ammunition, since the tractor crews had abandoned their tractors. Harry, being the officer he was, instead of sending out the patrol in charge of an N.C.O., led the patrol himself. As he had stripped the last tractor an enemy sniper shot him in the chest. He was immediately evacuated to the beach and treatment was given him, but he never rallied.[15]

The chaos of the first day made it difficult to evacuate the wounded. One factor was the shortage of corpsmen. For Tibor Torok, who served in radio communications in the 4th Battalion, 14th Marines, the first night was particularly difficult: "During the night, I heard the cry of 'Corpsman! Corpsman!' a dozen times. There was no Corpsman. There was no help for the wounded and dying. I heard a man crying for his mother, 'Mama, oh Mama!' I found the man crying, 'My leg, oh, my leg.' I felt for his leg, and there was nothing there. He bled to death before I could take his belt off for a tourniquet."[16]

Some marines in the 4th Division had to be removed from battle for other reasons. On D-Day, with artillery and mortar rounds relentlessly hitting the beach, Torok saw a marine running on the beach. Torok warned him to get into the trench for safety. "I hollered, 'Are you crazy, man? Stay in the trench!' He said, 'I'm getting the hell out of here!' and he ran toward the beach. I guess he had cracked up."[17] Other marines continued to function but nevertheless reacted to the tension and fear in different ways. Private First Class Marvin Scott recalled being asked by a buddy if Scott had wet his pants. Scott felt his pants and replied that the dampness was "just sweat." His friend declared, "Oh yeah, mine is sweat too."[18]

Most marines adjusted to the chaos and kept going regardless of the situation. Corporal Paul Schwartz of Philadelphia volunteered to serve as a BAR man, which involved carrying a Browning automatic rifle (a one-man light machine gun that weighed nearly twenty pounds) in addition to his regular equipment. Despite the extra weight, Schwartz and other BAR men were glad to have such a lethal weapon at their command. For example, while a Browning fired between five hundred and six hundred rounds per minute, a .30-caliber rifle fired one hundred, and a .30-caliber carbine fired only forty-five. Schwartz recalled that although the landing for the 25th Marines was "very bad," they were able to push toward higher ground. The first night, as his company was repelling a Japanese attack, Schwartz was hit by shrapnel. Although a corpsman quickly patched him up, the wound became infected and he was moved to a field hospital for treatment. The next morning, without waiting for permission to rejoin his unit, Schwartz left the hospital and returned to battle.[19] Like Schwartz, many wounded marines refused to be evacuated and continued to fight alongside their buddies.

In addition to laying down sustained mortar and artillery fire, the Japanese pursued an offensive tactic of running directly at the American lines. "Banzai" was the Japanese battle cry that signaled the start of an attack. The expression means "ten thousand years" and was a salute to the longevity of the emperor ("May he live ten thousand years"). Most of these attacks resulted in far more Japanese than marine losses. After one such attack ended at dusk, Schwartz tried to get some rest. "Meanwhile, in my foxhole, I had leaned my head against what I thought was the root of a tree. At daybreak it turned out to be the elbow of a dead Japanese."[20]

Like the 2nd Division, the 4th improvised as necessary. With officers wounded and landing vehicles overturned or on fire, individual marines proceeded with the attack as best they could. According to Private First

Class Bob Verna, who landed on Yellow Beach 1, "as soon as you land plans don't mean a thing. You have to react and adrenaline keeps you going." Instead of being dropped at the O-1 line, Verna and most of his battalion jumped out of their landing vehicles onto the beach to escape Japanese fire. Their goal was then to advance on their own to the spot where they should have been dropped. By the time Verna and his company had achieved their objective, almost three-quarters of his company (G) had been wounded or killed.[21]

One of the most interesting and often-repeated stories about the initial days of the invasion involved a tall brick smokestack of a sugarcane refinery in Charan Kanoa. Although the American naval barrage had destroyed most of the town, many marines, such as Private Orvel Johnson, believed the smokestack had been intentionally spared as a "visual guide for the incoming amtracs."[22] Robert Sherrod of *Time* magazine disputed this view and suggested that the smokestack stood despite efforts to bring it down: "The big smokestack had been pierced a thousand times, but it still stood." Only later did the marines discover that the Japanese were using the smokestack to direct artillery fire against the American forces.[23] As Major James A. Donovan noted, "We didn't know it at the time, but in a tall smokestack nearby was a Japanese forward observer. He was directing the fire, looking right down on us." All of the marines in the vicinity "experienced extremely heavy damage from the Japanese mortars for two and a half days, until someone discovered a spotter was on top of the smokestack. That discovery brought about the total demise of the smokestack."[24]

Before the smokestack had been destroyed, and unaware of the threat it posed, Private Johnson's amtrac drove right into the town of Charan Kanoa. "The street was full of Japanese soldiers and civilians," Johnson recalled. "They appeared to be without leadership. . . . They had taken no defensive position but were firing wildly and attempting to stop us with grenades and small arms weapons." When Sergeant David Utley told Johnson to open up with his BAR, his "call to action was answered with several bursts into the crowded masses on the street of Charan-Kanoa." After the amtrac moved through the town it drove toward some trees for protection, but Japanese snipers were waiting. "At least some of them were tied to the branches and when they were shot or killed . . . [they] fell only the length of the rope."[25]

Realizing their perilous situation, Johnson and his buddies abandoned the amtrac and moved cautiously back through Charan Kanoa toward the beach in an attempt to find the rest of their company. Back on the beach the marines hastily dug foxholes, preparing for a long day and longer night. Two marines shared each foxhole, one trying to sleep for a couple of hours while the other watched the darkness. "Enemy infiltrators . . . with blackened nude bodies, armed with stilettos, were still able to creep stealthily toward our lines," so if an exhausted marine fell asleep during his watch, he and his buddy could quickly become casualties. At the same time, Japanese artillery continued to fall on all parts of the beach. "It appeared their guns were zeroed in on every inch of terrain that we occupied," Johnson recalled. "Airbursts rained shrapnel down over a wide area and other shells exploded upon impact. The sounds alone of exploding shells were terrifying. . . . We believed that if you heard the artillery shell, it most likely had already passed you by and you would not hear the one with your name on it, because the shell arrived before the sound did."[26]

That bit of conventional wisdom did not work for all marines. Private First Class Richard A. Hertensteiner of Sheboygan, Wisconsin, had joined the marines when he was seventeen, and Saipan was his first battle. As a member of an artillery battery, he had probably been told that if a marine heard a shell he didn't have to worry about it. On the beach, Hertensteiner met up with two other marines, and "as we were talking, we heard incoming rounds and we dived into a shell crater. I was the last person to fall into the hole when the first round hit. After the shelling, I got up off the other two men and began talking to them. It was at this time that I learned that both of them were killed while I never got so much as a small scratch. That was my first experience in combat."[27] Before the day was out the marines knew the difference between artillery and mortar. "When we got back to the landing beach it was receiving heavy shelling by both mortars and artillery. We all learned that morning to tell the difference between the two sounds and I'll never forget it," recalled Richard Pederson.[28] According to Private Rod Sandburg of the 10th Marines, 2nd Marine Division:

> As for the sounds of different shells there is a difference, however it is hard to explain. The only shells one can hear are those that go over your position. The ones that fall short one cannot hear. Each type of gun makes a different sound as it goes through the air. One can tell what is shooting the shell but to describe the sound would be difficult as each type of gun is different and one just naturally recognizes the type sending the shell whether it be a Mortar, 75mm, 105mm, 155mm, or a Naval gun, only if it goes past your position. We have had shells land between the trails of one of our guns but didn't go off. Like the Jap firecrackers before the war they had many duds. Thank God. I would like to meet anyone who can accurately describe what different sounds the shells make. They definitely make different sounds.[29]

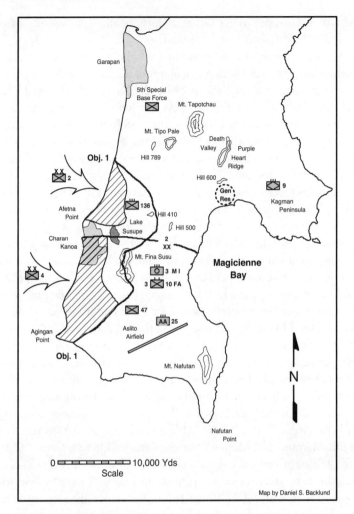

Map 5. Positions at close of D-Day

By the afternoon of the first day the marines were unloading their heavy equipment on the island. The first American tanks arrived, as did artillery and mortars. Unlike the armored amphibious tanks (LVT(A)4s) that had suffered losses in the initial assault, most M4 Sherman tanks made it ashore in good shape. Although a few tanks succumbed to Japanese artillery, high tides, saltwater short circuits, or other difficulties, their presence added a necessary boost to American firepower. Finally, at about 1930, 4th

Division commander Major General Harry Schmidt arrived on Yellow Beach 2 at the division's new command post.

As soon as the command post was created, the issue of communications became essential. Due to the inability of the Japanese to translate the Navajo language or break their special code, Navajos often played a role in communications units. Private First Class John Dickinson, who served with the Communications Platoon in the 23rd Marines, recalled several Navajos who served as radiomen: "We had three of them with us all of the time. They were a real asset to our platoon. We would give them messages to send to a fellow Indian using their code talk."[30] Another radioman, Pete Cypher, remembered two Navajo code talkers as well: "They took basic training with all Marines. They were on the front lines with other radiomen. They carried all regular gear—rifles grenades bullets, etc. One was on the front line with the radioman and the other was in the message center. I was the radioman and carried the radio and the Navajo code messenger was with me to take any special codes." Most Navajo code talkers operated on the division or regiment level for top-secret messages, while a radioman or a runner handled communications for a platoon or company.[31] Radio operator David Dowdakin, who served in the 3rd Battalion, 2nd Marines, 2nd Division, explained that "the commanding officer of a rifle company had a permanent radioman by his side but not a code talker. On that level it was not necessary. The radioman could communicate with battalion command and other company commanding officers. Company to platoon communications was done by new walkie-talkies. Unfortunately these were highly unreliable."[32] Ray "Chick" Hill, a machine-gun platoon runner in the 6th Marines, 2nd Marine Division, explained the problem: "All the walkie-talkies of that era did not work very well with thirty-six radios all using the same frequencies so many of our messages were by field telephone or by runner."[33] Unfortunately for a radioman like Dodson Smith from Winston-Salem, North Carolina, his SCR-300 (Signal Corps Radio model 300) took up most of his backpack, so he was unable to carry the same gear that other marines hauled into battle.[34] The most frightening experience for communications personnel occurred at night. Sometimes tanks would run over and destroy telephone wires unintentionally, but more commonly the Japanese would cut the wires. Dickinson hated going "out in the middle of the night to repair broken lines since you didn't know if there were snipers waiting when you spliced the lines together again." Japanese soldiers liked to operate at night, and they often waited in areas where they knew the marines would return—near broken communica-

Figure 7. U.S. marines move to secure Saipan beaches on D-Day; courtesy of Private Rod Sandburg (USMC).

tions lines or near dead or wounded Americans whom the marines tried to retrieve.[35]

Despite the increasing American presence on the island, the Japanese were determined to destroy them on the beaches. The defenders were willing to pursue their goal day or night. As nightfall approached on D-Day, the marines were forced to dig in, although they remained short of their objective for day one. In the few cases where marines had made it to the O-1 line they were ordered to pull back to establish a solid defensive perimeter for the night. Those portions of K Company and L Company of the 3rd Battalion, 23rd Marines, that had pushed farther inland than the rest of their regiment had to give up their positions, but they waited until dark before moving back.

As intense as the fighting had been during the landing, darkness brought special problems. Unable to establish a clear line of fire in the dark, exhausted marines had to stay awake and react to every noise coming from the trees and ridges. Corporal Robert R. Montgomery of the 6th Marines recalled that "this first night was probably our worst, but even the best nights were bad enough." Anxious marines might fire at any sound or rustling in the bushes—sometimes it was a Japanese sniper, sometimes it was an animal, and sometimes it was another marine answering the call of nature. Without access to a latrine, some marines used the cardboard tubes that 75-millimeter artillery shells came in; in an emergency, some had to use their helmets.[36] As Private First Class Calvin E. Orr of the 2nd Armored Amphibian Battalion recalled, "One of our guys got his rear end shot off one night because he was where he shouldn't be after dark."[37]

The 24th Marines, which had participated in the demonstration at Tanapag Harbor earlier in the day, landed on Blue Beach 1 that afternoon and suffered heavy casualties. As night approached, F Company, 2nd Battalion, 24th Marines, was sent forward to relieve another unit, with Scout Joe Risener of Piggott, Arkansas, leading the way:

> Night had fallen and this operation was carried out in the dark. . . . I was one of the 4 scouts that were sent out to make contact with the unit we were relieving. In their advance they had left pockets of enemy soldiers behind, which we encountered on our way to the front line. Two of my fellow scouts were killed in this action. Since we were in danger of coming under fire from the unit we were sent to relieve, the officers instructed us to shout out the words: "Marines coming through." That, my friend, was a terrifying experience.[38]

That same night, Lieutenant John C. Chapin of the 3rd Battalion, 24th Marines, sat in his shallow two-man foxhole watching for the enemy. After completing his watch, he changed places with his fellow marine and then went to sleep. Awakened at dawn, Chapin turned to his buddy, who seemed to be asleep: "He didn't stir. I shook him. He still didn't move. He was dead. With the callousness that war demands, I rolled him over, reached for his canteen, and poured the precious water into my own canteen. Then I left him lying there."[39]

During the first night and early the next morning the Japanese launched offensive actions against the 4th Division on Blue and Yellow beaches. The 23rd Marines on Blue 1 were unable to close a gap between their lines and those of the 8th Marines, 2nd Division, where Blue 1 met Green 3. According to marine historian Hoffman, at 0530 "about 200 Japanese moved from Lake Susupe through the 'no-man's land' between divisions and struck for the Charan Kanoa pier."[40] The 3rd Battalion, 23rd Marines, was able to hold its position and killed most of the Japanese intruders. A little earlier that morning, but farther south on Yellow beaches, the 25th Marines had faced a difficult situation. At 0430, after an artillery barrage to soften the American lines, the Japanese sent a group of civilians, including women and children, toward the marines. Some marines believed that the civilians were coming to surrender and held their fire. As the Japanese force moved closer, however, the marines recognized the trick and destroyed the attackers.

Nevertheless, the Japanese were able to inflict serious damage on the marines, especially targeting officers whenever they could. The 1st Battalion, 24th Marines, quickly lost its commander, Lieutenant Colonel Maynard C. Schultz of San Diego. The battalion's command post was located in a "clump of trees," and an artillery exchange proceeded even as officers discussed the battle situation. Captain Frederic Stott described the subsequent events: "Lt. Col. Schultz neglected to take cover and despite the severity of the shelling, he remained atop the hole. It was a deadly position as a close round sent a piece of shrapnel into his head, and he died in a matter of seconds. His death stripped the Battalion of its most-needed man, for good battalion commanders are practically indispensable." Stott recalled that Captain Gene Mundy of Mt. Carmel, Illinois, took over and "responded magnificently." Other sources indicate that Major Robert N. Fricke replaced Schultz.[41]

Official Marine Corps accounts assert that by the end of the first day of the Battle of Saipan, the outcome was certain. By several measures that was true, partly because of what the marines had already accomplished and partly because of the mistakes that the Japanese had made. The marines fought heroically, successfully landing on the beaches in the face of withering enemy fire. Amtracs delivered eight thousand marines from the 2nd and 4th Divisions in approximately twenty minutes. By the end of the day, twenty thousand marines were onshore, including more than two of the 2nd Division's three regiments and all three of the 4th Division's regiments. In addition, supporting artillery and tanks had arrived in sufficient quantity to counter any Japanese attacks. The marines had the support of scores of navy ships, big guns, and transports with supplies that could keep them in the field for a very long time. Further, the 27th Infantry Division was still in reserve if needed. In short, the battle was quickly tilting in favor of the United States. American commanders saw the invasion as the beginning of a fast and inevitable victory. Admiral Turner was pleased with the day's action, which he praised as having proceeded "on the button."[42]

Despite Turner's positive response to the punctuality of the landing, individual marines would continue to confront brutality and horror on a daily basis. The 4th Marine Division suffered eight hundred casualties by the end of the first day, and two thousand casualties after only twenty-four hours of battle. The Japanese defenders were exacting a price for American success.

For their part, the Japanese remained committed to Lieutenant General Saito's command to "demolish the enemy landing units at the water's edge."[43] This concept was not Saito's own creation, as the offensive policy reflected the wishes of Japan's high command. The policy was unsuccessful, and by 16 June, 31st Army Headquarters reported to Tokyo that "the counterattack which has been carried out since the afternoon of the 15th has failed because of the enemy's tanks and firepower. We are reorganizing and will attack again." The Japanese chief of staff responded by simply demanding further sacrifice: "Because the fate of the Japanese Empire depends on the result of your operations, inspire the spirit of the officers and men and to the very end continue to destroy the enemy gallantly and persistently; thus alleviate the anxiety of our Emperor." The Japanese forces in the Marianas could not refuse such a request and answered with a promise to die for the emperor: "Have received your honorable Imperial words and we are grateful for boundless magnanimity of Imperial favor. By becom[ing] the bulwark of the Pacific with 10,000 deaths we hope to requite the Imperial favor."[44]

Taking the offensive already appeared to be a serious mistake for the troops defending Saipan. The Japanese launched a series of attacks against the American lines, sometimes with infantry and sometimes with tanks, and were unable to mass sufficient forces to challenge the invaders. Whether the small units they sent against marine positions involved Japanese soldiers on foot or a few Japanese tanks, the marines successfully repelled them. Foolishly, the Japanese depleted their forces without inflicting significant damage on the marines. Saito's forces failed to use the tactical advantage that a purely defensive war would have given them. When the Japanese soldiers emerged from their strongholds, they did so in numbers too small to affect the outcome of the battle. Unfortunately for the marines, the Japanese did learn some lessons from their failure on Saipan, forcing the marines to attack against strong defensive positions later on Iwo Jima and Okinawa. The marines suffered even greater casualties on those islands than in the Marianas.

On Saipan, the Japanese undermined their own goals by employing the wrong tactics. Their commitment to stopping the marines on the beach negated their best weapon, the topography of the island. Instead of remaining in their defensive redoubts, they charged the American lines. These attacks gave the advantage to the marines, who had superior firepower, concentration of forces, and renewable supplies. A few Japanese soldiers at a time, screaming and waving swords and charging the American lines, could never win this battle. Similarly, an attack by a handful of Japanese tanks could not break through the American forces. The tanks were quickly destroyed, their military value wasted.

Without additional assistance, the Japanese were engaged in a brave but ultimately futile struggle. They were isolated on an island in the middle of the Pacific Ocean. Regardless of how long the battle lasted, the defending soldiers would have to fight only with whatever weapons and ammunition they possessed on 15 June and nothing more. They could not expect new tanks, more ammunition, better rifles, more food, or any other assistance. In this situation, they were doomed, as they could not win a war of attrition with the Americans. The Japanese could anticipate only one outcome—to die honorably—an acceptable conclusion to the battle within their culture.

A second possibility, however, provided some hope for the Japanese soldiers. In this scenario, the Japanese navy would confront and defeat the American fleet. Following a successful naval battle, the Imperial Navy would deliver the extra men and supplies that would lead to victory. The navy provided the only remaining hope for Japan's garrison on Saipan.

On 15 June, the Imperial Navy left the Philippines and sailed toward the Mariana Islands.

CHAPTER SEVEN

THE GREAT MARIANAS TURKEY SHOOT

Admiral Yamamoto Isoroku, commander in chief of the Imperial Japanese Navy at the start of World War II, had always promoted the idea of engaging the Americans in one large and decisive battle. The implementation of this plan had failed with Japan's defeat at Midway in 1942. Nevertheless, Japanese naval commanders still hoped that a major confrontation with the American navy would turn the tide in their favor. Realizing that the American fleet was now larger than the Japanese navy and that the Americans had more carrier planes available, the Imperial Staff developed a plan to counter this growing inequity. In addition to the planes operating off of Japanese aircraft carriers, the Imperial Navy counted on its land-based planes spread throughout the Pacific on Japan's island possessions. The islands, so-called unsinkable carriers, would provide the extra aircraft needed to defeat the United States by neutralizing its numerical superiority.

The plan seemed to make strategic sense. The Japanese navy was still large and formidable. The number of planes available for flying off carriers, added to the number of land-based craft, gave Japan the theoretical possibility of negating the American advantage. Because Japan viewed Saipan as a crucial defensive outpost, the American invasion triggered the Japanese navy's Operation A-Go, the plan for a showdown with the American Fifth Fleet. The Imperial Staff could not allow the landing on Saipan, within Japan's inner defense zone, to go unchallenged. Imperial Headquarters Directive no. 373 ordered the navy and army to prepare "for decisive action" by the end of May.[1] Further, with the American fleet exposed off the Marianas, the Japanese navy was prepared to engage in that large-scale battle that was intended to stop the American offensive. From Japan's perspective, everything was in place. While success depended on the land-based aircraft, Japanese admirals did not realize that Mitscher's Task Force 58, by hitting Truk, then the Marianas, then the Palaus, and then Saipan again, had already destroyed many of the planes that were essential to Operation A-Go.

Japanese naval commanders typically underestimated and underreported their losses after encounters with American forces, and they had replicated this problem on Guam, Truk, and Saipan as well as other locations in the Pacific. Further, due to Japan's significant losses in 1943 and the first half of 1944, few experienced pilots were available to replace the high-quality flyers who had participated and who had been lost in missions at the beginning of the war. Japanese pilots now had less battle experience than their American counterparts. When Japan launched Operation A-Go, naval commanders thought that they had more planes available than was the case in reality. Nevertheless, Japanese military leaders, unaware of these problems and other flaws in their plans, joined the confrontation enthusiastically.

Admiral Yamamoto was killed in 1943, and his successor as commander in chief of the Imperial Navy was Admiral Koga Mineichi. Like Admiral King, Koga understood the importance of the Marianas to the Japanese war effort. According to the U.S. Strategic Bombing Survey, Koga "announced his decision to hold the Marianas-Palau line until death, feeling that once this inner defense line was broken there could be no further hope for Japan."[2] At the end of March 1944 Koga was killed when his plane disappeared in bad weather. His replacement was Admiral Toyoda Soemu, a graduate of Japan's Imperial Naval Academy. Promoted to admiral in 1941, Toyoda served as a member of the Supreme War Council from May 1943 and then became commander in chief of the navy in May 1944.[3] He assumed his new position at a crucial moment in the war, with the Americans pushing relentlessly across New Guinea toward the Philippines and northwest across the central Pacific toward Japan's essential defense line in the Marianas. Japan had to stop the United States, and a decisive naval battle seemed to offer some hope of success. The Imperial Staff could not allow the attack on Saipan to go unchallenged, and they issued the order to implement Operation A-Go, unaware of the extent of Japan's air losses.

By destroying hundreds of Japanese land-based planes during the first half of 1944, Mitscher had helped to assure an American victory before the two navies ever met on the seas. Driven out of Truk by these American attacks, the Japanese navy moved to the Palaus and then to Tawitawi, located off the southwestern Philippines in the Sulu Archipelago. Fortunately for the Japanese, this last transfer, which occurred shortly before Mitscher's task force attacked the Palaus again at the end of March, saved many of their ships. The Imperial Fleet, though not its land-based airplanes, remained largely intact.

In April 1944 MacArthur took Hollandia in New Guinea and destroyed Japanese planes there. The following month his forces attacked Biak Island off northwestern New Guinea, and although his expectations of a quick victory turned into a difficult battle for the island, the Americans had effectively neutralized another Japanese air base. When Mitscher's task force bombed the Marianas on 11 and 12 June, Japan lost almost 150 planes essential to Operation A-Go.

American success also had its costs. On 13 June Lieutenant Commander Robert Isely was leading his squadron of Avengers in attacks on Aslito Airfield when his plane and two others were hit by antiaircraft fire. Although one of the planes was only damaged, two, including Isely's, were lost. According to historian Samuel Eliot Morison, "Isely was one of the most distinguished pilots in the Navy, having performed brilliantly in an escort carrier killer group in the Atlantic." The U.S. Navy later renamed Aslito Airfield in his honor. Despite the loss, American carrier strikes continued over Saipan on 14 and 15 June as well.[4]

In addition to Mitscher's task force, American submarines provided another crucial advantage for the United States. On 13 June the submarine *Redfin* spotted a large part of the Japanese fleet, including "6 carriers, 4 battleships, 8 cruisers, and numerous destroyers heading north from Tawitawi."[5] This information was radioed to Pearl Harbor and then to Admiral Spruance. Recalling the Battle of Midway in 1942, Spruance understood the implications of this report. While the Saipan landing proceeded, he paced the deck of his flagship, *Indianapolis*, and contemplated the possibility of a Japanese naval response. In preparation for a possible battle he ordered Task Force 58 to refuel ahead of schedule; at the same time, Admiral Nimitz, operating from his headquarters at Pearl Harbor, increased submarine and air surveillance of the area near the Philippines.[6] This additional action paid off on the early evening of 15 June when the submarine *Flying Fish* reported the movement of the Japanese fleet out of San Bernadino Strait in the Philippines. Shortly thereafter the submarine

Sea Horse detected another Japanese fleet about "200 miles east of Surigao Strait" and moving in the direction of the Marianas. The distance and speed of Japan's Imperial Navy indicated a Japanese attack by 18 June, the target date for the invasion of Guam. Clearly, that invasion would have to be postponed.[7]

At the same time, the raid by parts of Task Force 58 already scheduled against Japanese land bases on Iwo Jima and neighboring islands was allowed to proceed, as the ships involved would have enough time to strike and to return to meet the new Japanese threat. Those attacks were successful, and, as indicated in the U.S. Strategic Bombing Survey, "the area was left in poor condition to stage planes into the Marianas."[8]

With the invasion of Saipan in progress, Spruance confronted several issues. First, he had to counter the Japanese naval offensive while protecting the marines and soldiers on Saipan. Simultaneously, he had to deal with his own staff controversies, as Mitscher pressed for a more aggressive pursuit of the Japanese navy than Spruance considered prudent. As the encounter with the Imperial Navy developed, the rift between Spruance and Mitscher grew. Spruance considered protecting the troops on Saipan his primary obligation, while Mitscher favored taking the offensive and pursuing the Japanese fleet. Spruance feared that such a policy would pull American ships too far from the Marianas and open the islands to a Japanese flanking maneuver that would jeopardize the entire amphibious operation—reminiscent of how the Japanese had split their fleet at Midway. The possibility of a Japanese "end run" around the American fleet haunted Spruance and would affect his decisions in the upcoming battle. His greatest fear was that enemy ships would "sneak behind him."[9] Mitscher did not accept that argument, and the two admirals disagreed during the battle.

On 16 June, Spruance left his flagship and boarded the *Rocky Mount*, Turner's command ship, in order to inform Turner and Holland Smith of the situation. "The Japs are coming after us," he told them. When Smith asked if "the Japs will turn tail and run," Spruance emphatically asserted, "No, not now. They are out after big game . . . the attack on the Marianas is too great a challenge for the Japanese Navy to ignore."[10] Spruance indicated that protecting the Saipan operation was his primary goal and that he and Mitscher would interdict the Japanese First Mobile Fleet to prevent its interference with the Marianas invasion. Turner admitted that the Saipan offensive was not going as well as anticipated, but he agreed to move all nonessential transport ships to the eastern side of the island, away from the approach of the Japanese navy, for safety. At the same time, he directed the "transports of the Southern Attack Force, carrying the Guam invasion troops, . . . to remain at sea some 200 miles east of the Marianas."[11] Fortunately for the American forces, the Japanese submarine fleet was not capable of hitting all of these ships sitting in the water to the east of the island.

Spruance and Mitscher led a formidable navy in search of the First Mobile Fleet. Mitscher's Task Force 58 already included fifteen carriers with 819 planes, seven battleships, thirteen cruisers, and fifty-two destroyers. Spruance attached additional ships from the Fifth Fleet to Mitscher's task force, so his totals ultimately included twenty-one cruisers and sixty-nine destroyers, and of course Spruance's flagship, *Indianapolis*. At the same time, Spruance had to leave some ships near Saipan to protect the marines. Rear Admiral Harry Hill remained twenty-five miles off the island with seven older and slower battleships, three cruisers, and five destroyers in case, as Dyer noted, "a fast detachment of the Japanese First Mobile Fleet might do an end run around TF 58 and seek to attack the cargo ships and disrupt the logistic support of the troops on Saipan."[12]

By 17 June, Spruance and Mitscher were prepared to meet the Japanese if they could find the enemy ships. Throughout the ensuing battle, Spruance's primary goal continued to be the defense of the Marianas invasion forces; he also hoped to sink as many Japanese ships as possible if such an opportunity arose. Nevertheless, throughout the battle he was unwilling to sail too far from Saipan in pursuit of the Japanese fleet. According to Forrestel, his orders were clear: "Task Force 58 must cover Saipan and the forces engaged there and this can be done best by proceeding west in daylight and towards Saipan at night." In other words, the American ships would sail toward the Japanese navy during the day but away from it at night. Mitscher wanted to continue to sail west and go after the Japanese ships, even if it meant moving his task force farther from Saipan.[13] Spruance refused the request, and he was in overall command.

Vice Admiral Ozawa Jisaburo led Japan's First Mobile Fleet. He had attended Japan's Imperial Naval Academy, becoming a rear admiral in 1936 and a vice admiral in 1940. At the beginning of the war he led the Japanese navy in the South China Sea. In early 1942 he served at Sumatra and Java, and at the end of 1942 he replaced Nagumo as head of Japan's carriers. Americans considered Ozawa one of Japan's best naval commanders.[14]

In June 1944, while Spruance's major goal was protecting the marines on Saipan, Ozawa's primary objective was stopping the American invasion of the Marianas. While Admiral Toyoda remained on his flagship in the

Inland Sea to coordinate the attack, Ozawa sailed in a northeasterly direction on the flagship *Taiho*, Japan's largest aircraft carrier. In accordance with Operation A-Go, the Japanese divided their ships into two forces, with Vice Admiral Kurita Takeo's three aircraft carriers serving as a decoy force to attract the Americans while Ozawa's six aircraft carriers and five battleships launched the main attack. Ozawa's fleet also included thirteen cruisers and twenty-eight destroyers, impressive but inferior to the Americans in every category.[15]

Toyoda and Ozawa believed they had a solid tactical plan in place. If the Americans attacked first, they would have to fly through intense antiaircraft fire to get to Ozawa's carriers. Japanese antiaircraft fire would then destroy the American planes. If the Americans hesitated, Ozawa would not drive his ships directly toward the American fleet but rather would use the planes on his carriers and land-based aircraft to launch long-range attacks on Task Force 58. The Japanese enjoyed an advantage in this area, as their planes could attack at three hundred miles, while the better-armored American planes could attack from 150 to 200 miles. According to the Japanese plan, the First Mobile Fleet carriers would launch their planes from a distance beyond the reach of American planes, strike the U.S. ships, and then refuel on Guam and other islands before the return flight to their base carriers.[16]

The American fleet had superior numbers, with 956 planes compared to 473 in Ozawa's fleet.[17] To counterbalance this discrepancy in the number of carrier planes available, Ozawa was counting on his unsinkable carriers, that is, the estimated five hundred land-based aircraft that he did not realize no longer existed as a significant force. In May he distributed the Combined Fleet Ultrasecret Operation Order 76, in which he listed the air assets he believed he possessed in the Marianas: 100 planes on Saipan, 192 on Tinian, 170 on Guam, and 16 on Rota.[18] In reality, most of those planes had been destroyed before Operation A-Go could be implemented. Even as the battle progressed, Ozawa believed, due to exaggerated claims by Japanese officers on Guam and other islands, that land-based air support would materialize. While Operation A-Go had anticipated the assistance of five hundred land-based planes for Ozawa, in reality this air support never materialized, and Ozawa was not at fault in believing that these reserves existed when his ships moved into battle formation. Even as the battle progressed, Japanese officers on the islands continued to report that they controlled planes that did not exist and that they were inflicting heavy losses on the Americans.[19] Like most of the decisive naval battles of World

War II, and unfortunately for Japan, this confrontation would be decided in the air.

Spruance was handicapped by his desire to remain within three hundred miles of Saipan. In addition to having a shorter range than their Japanese counterparts, American planes did not have bases near the First Mobile Fleet and had to return to their carriers to refuel. Despite this disadvantage, the Americans had the advantage in the number of planes and the experience of their pilots. On 17 June Ozawa's fleet had been spotted by the American submarine *Cavalla*, and based on this information the four American submarines in the area moved into position between the Japanese and American ships. Nevertheless, Spruance refused to take his ships in Ozawa's direction. "If I were the Japanese admiral in this situation," he told his staff, "I would split my forces and hope that the ships remaining to the west were sighted in order to decoy the main forces of the American Fleet away from Saipan. Then I would slip behind with my separated strike force in order to get into Saipan and if possible destroy the transports."[20] American submarine sightings indicated that Ozawa had indeed split his fleet, and this strengthened Spruance's determination to remain close to Saipan. Mitscher persisted in pushing for permission to pursue the Japanese fleet to the west, and Spruance continued to resist that more aggressive approach.

By 18–19 June the enemy fleets were three hundred miles apart, with Spruance two hundred miles west of Saipan and Ozawa five hundred miles west of the Marianas. The First Mobile Fleet was divided into two parts, with three carriers protected by four battleships, nine cruisers, and eight destroyers sailing about one hundred miles ahead of Ozawa's six larger carriers. Attacking American planes would have had to fly through the protective screen of the vanguard ships before being able to approach the main Japanese force. But an American attack never came, as Hellcats could not fly three hundred miles to the target and return safely. In addition, despite submarine sightings of the Japanese fleet, American spotter planes could not establish the exact location of the Japanese navy. Although at least one American plane made radar contact with the Japanese fleet, the plane was unable to establish radio contact with Spruance.[21]

Fortunately for the Americans, these factors did not prove significant as the Japanese took the offensive. Before launching his attack, Ozawa invoked the memory of one of history's greatest naval victories, Japan's defeat of the Russian fleet in 1905: "This operation has immense bearing on the fate of the Empire. It is hoped that the forces will exert their utmost and achieve as magnificent results as in the Battle of Tsushima." Ironically, Spruance used the same analogy to explain his strategy: "The way Togo waited at Tsushima for the Russian Fleet to come to him has always been in my mind. We had somewhat the same basic situation." The two admirals also had a similar defensive concept: Spruance arranged his carriers into task forces so that Japanese planes would have to fly through intense antiaircraft fire in order to approach the American carriers.[22]

As Taylor stated in his biography of Mitscher, "There was nothing to indicate this was really the beginning of such a robust day as June 19, 1944—the day of the 'Marianas Turkey Shoot'." At approximately 0730, Hellcats flying off American carriers one hundred miles to the west of Guam attacked Japanese air reinforcements flying to that island's Orote Field. The result was totally one-sided: "Thirty Navy fighter planes knocked down thirty-five enemy aircraft. Mitscher's loss was one Hellcat."[23] An hour later, unaware of his losses at Guam, Ozawa launched the first of four air strikes against the American fleet.

Ozawa's first attack sent sixty-nine planes toward Task Force 58. American radar spotted the Japanese planes in midmorning, and Hellcats were in the air before 1040. Japanese planes fell from the sky as Mitscher's Hellcats exacted their toll, and the few attacking planes that approached the American ships met a wall of antiaircraft fire. Several pilots emerged as aces that day as they finished off the Japanese planes. Despite some mechanical problems that kept his plane from attaining full speed, Lieutenant Alexander Vraciu dove toward thirty enemy planes two thousand feet below his. As Vraciu fired, he announced on the radio, "scratch one Judy."[24] He continued to shoot until he called in "splash number six." Low on fuel, an exultant Vraciu returned to his carrier, having shot down all six enemy planes in just eight minutes while using only 360 rounds of ammunition. Ensign Wilbur "Spider" Webb spotted a large patrol of Japanese planes over Guam and brazenly radioed to the carrier *Hornet*, "I've got 40 Japs surrounded." Webb also scored six kills. Up to this point the American plan had worked perfectly, as the Japanese never got close to the American aircraft carriers and lost more than forty planes in this first encounter. While Mitscher directed the battle, a seemingly detached Spruance sat on the bridge and read as the fighting raged.[25]

At about 0900 Ozawa sent a second wave of 110 planes toward the American fleet, and this time the American pilots destroyed even more enemy planes, with 79 Japanese planes lost. Ozawa's third launch, of forty-seven planes, sent up shortly after 1000, also failed, with seven shot down.

Finally, at 1130, Ozawa sent a fourth strike of eighty-two planes, many of which were destroyed as they tried to land at Guam's Orote Field for refueling. The Japanese lost seventy-three planes in this final phase of the air assault.[26] The battle, which started at dawn with Ozawa's first air strike, was virtually over early in the afternoon on the same day. The Japanese lost well over three hundred planes, more than 60 percent of their original total, and more importantly a large number of pilots. Finally, Japan lost about fifty additional planes on Guam.

Estimates of Japanese plane losses vary. Mitscher claimed 383 Japanese planes shot down, while Admiral King in Washington declared the number to be 402. Historian Samuel Eliot Morison, adding all Japanese carrier losses, float planes, and land-based planes, arrived at a figure of 476. Discrepancies exist in the figures according to whether the claimant is reporting the first day of battle, the entire battle, only planes off aircraft carriers or land-based planes as well, and other factors. By any estimate, Japan suffered a devastating defeat.[27] Ozawa, who cannot be faulted for lack of courage or aggressiveness, left the scene without damaging a single American aircraft carrier. American pilots, who added so many kills to their records, referred to the battle as the "Great Marianas Turkey Shoot."[28] Officially the encounter is called the First Battle of the Philippine Sea.

While the battle's primary air phase ended with a decisive American victory, additional action took place later that day and the next day. Shortly after sending the second group of planes toward the American fleet at 0900 on 19 June, Ozawa's flagship, the *Taiho*, was hit by one of six torpedoes fired from the submarine *Albacore*. Ozawa was unaware that gas fumes were accumulating in the sealed-off area where the torpedo had damaged the hull even as the *Taiho* continued to sail without apparent impairment.

Shortly after noon, at about the same time that Japan's fourth air strike was being decimated, another American submarine, the *Cavalla*, hit the carrier *Shokaku* with three of six torpedoes fired. The *Cavalla*, under Commander Herman J. Kossler, was the same sub that had warned Spruance that the Japanese fleet was leaving its harbor at Tawitawi. From that moment on the *Cavalla* began to shadow the enemy ships. Kossler described the subsequent events: "At 10:52 I raised periscope and the picture was too good to be true. I could see four ships, a large juicy carrier, with two cruisers ahead on the port bow and a destroyer about 1,000 yards on their starboard beam. . . . The problem was developing so fast that I had to concentrate on the carrier and take my chances with the destroyer. . . . We fired a spread of six torpedoes. . . . By the time the fifth torpedo was leaving the tubes, we already had nosed down for a deep dive." The

Japanese destroyer hunted the *Cavalla* for three hours, but the sub escaped. The Japanese carrier did not get away. At 1510 the *Shokaku* blew up and sank, and half an hour later the gas fumes inside the *Taiho* also exploded and sent Ozawa's flagship to the bottom of the sea with a loss of 1,650 crew members.[29]

With Japan's defeat becoming apparent, Spruance told Mitscher that he was now prepared to take the offensive: "Desire to attack enemy tomorrow if we know his position with sufficient accuracy." No longer fearing an end run by the Japanese fleet, Spruance and Mitscher decided to launch an air attack late on 20 June. It was midafternoon when Mitscher learned of the location of the First Mobile Fleet. Ozawa was sailing toward the northwest, away from Task Force 58, but preparing to resume the battle on 21 June. Unfortunately, resuming the attack so late in the day would create two problems for American pilots. First, with the Japanese fleet between two hundred and three hundred miles to the northwest, the American planes would stretch their range and might not have enough fuel for a return trip. Also, the mission probably could not be completed before nightfall, and night landings on aircraft carriers were always dangerous. Nevertheless, Spruance and Mitscher felt that they could not allow the First Mobile Fleet to escape and, as Forrestel reported, "accepted the risk and responsibility in view of the utmost importance of the mission and permitted the strike to proceed, while the force steamed at top speed towards the target, to lessen the distance of the return flight."[30]

Mitscher's 216 planes were in the air by 1636, but the Japanese fleet was already farther away than Mitscher had hoped. Nevertheless, he decided to proceed with the attack. "The new position would strain the last ounce of fuel, and make night landings inevitable. If Mitscher didn't recall the planes, the casualty list was sure to be heavy. After rechecking the charts, Mitscher decided not to recall them."[31] American flyers knew they might be on a one-way mission. Pilots in the air discussed the navigation situation when one volunteered, "No sense working this out both ways!"[32] American planes found the Japanese ships just before dusk, and Ozawa launched his remaining eighty planes to defend his ships.

Lieutenant George P. Brown led one of the American attack squadrons. As he dove toward the Japanese carrier *Hiyo*, he flew through a barrage of Japanese antiaircraft fire. His friend Lieutenant J. D. Walker described to the compilers of *Battle Report* what happened next: "Brown's plane took the brunt of the Japanese fire; shell after shell struck home and suddenly it began to burn." Brown's two crewmen bailed out because of the intense heat, but Brown continued to fly toward the carrier. "Brownie pushed on, and pretty soon the flames went out, leaving his plane black and his recognition marks burned away. He reached the dropping point and released the torpedo straight and true." At this point Brown could have flown away from the antiaircraft fire, but instead he aimed straight toward the carrier to draw fire to himself as a diversion so other planes could come in undeterred. When one of the other American planes flew by to check on him, "Brownie waved a shattered arm to his friend. His khaki shirt was splattered with blood. Then his plane wavered and plunged nose first into the blackness below." Brown died in this action, and shortly thereafter the carrier *Hiyo* went down. Brown's two crewmen floated in the ocean and watched the entire battle until rescued by search crews several hours later. Lieutenant H. H. Moyers called the scene reminiscent of "Fourth of July fireworks around the Washington Monument."[33] Other than the *Hiyo*, the carriers *Zuikaku, Junyo,* and *Chiyoda* were damaged but escaped. Japan lost sixty-five more planes, while only twenty of the American planes did not return.

As American planes made their way back to Task Force 58 after dark, they began to run out of fuel. Mitscher sailed his carriers as fast as possible in the direction of the returning planes, well aware that he was "facing the worst disaster in naval-aviation history" if all the planes were lost. Despite the fear that there might be Japanese submarines in the area, Mitscher decided to violate the navy's "lights out" rule to help guide the planes back to the carriers: "As the planes approached, he directed the lights be turned on to facilitate recovery and as running lights, truck lights and deck lights went on, star shells were fired in the air and vertical searchlight beams served as homing beacons." As pilot Lieutenant Commander Robert A. Winston observed: "The effect on the pilots left behind was magnetic. They stood open mouthed for the sheer audacity of asking the Japs to come and get us. Then a spontaneous cheer went up. To hell with the Japs around us. Our pilots were not to be expendable."[34]

Fortunately, no Japanese submarines were in the area. While many of the returning American planes ran out of fuel and had to ditch in the ocean, the United States lost only twenty planes in combat and perhaps eighty more because of the night return.[35] Of the 209 crew members who had participated in the action of 20 June, 49 were lost, "a fair price to pay" according to Admiral King.[36] On 21 June, with Ozawa's ships out of range, Spruance ordered Task Force 58 back to Saipan.

Although Mitscher criticized Spruance for lack of aggressiveness, the United States had won a major victory and protected the Saipan invasion at the same time. The Japanese had suffered a defeat from which they would never recover. Ozawa lost three carriers and almost all of his airplanes. Early in the battle Mitscher wanted to pursue Ozawa and sink his carriers, but Spruance's defensive strategy paid off. Ironically, Mitscher, an aviator, did not consider the battle a total success despite the massive losses in Japanese aviation. Japan lost approximately 400 planes and 445 crewmen, including most of its remaining experienced pilots. Ozawa was left with only thirty-five carrier planes and virtually no seasoned flyers.[37] In practice, the remaining aircraft carriers were worthless without airplanes and skilled pilots.

The argument between Spruance and Mitscher never ended. Mitscher's report, as noted by Taylor, asserted that "the enemy had escaped. He had been badly hurt by one aggressive carrier strike at the one time he was within range. His fleet was not sunk."[38] According to Taylor, Mitscher's biographer and one of his defenders, "hindsight indicated that Admiral Spruance made a mistake." Taylor also quoted Admiral Frederick C. Sherman's support for Mitscher: "[Spruance] did not grasp the tremendous power of our air weapons or their ability to strike in any direction to the limit of their fuel. There were no end runs in aerial warfare."[39] In contrast, both King and Nimitz defended Spruance. King insisted that "the Saipan amphibious operations had to be protected from enemy interference at all costs. In his plans for what developed into the battle of the Philippine Sea, Spruance was rightly guided by this basic obligation. He therefore operated aggressively to the westward of the Marianas, but did not draw his carriers and battleships so far away that they could not protect the amphibious units from any possible Japanese 'end run' that might develop."[40] For his part, Nimitz noted: "There may be disappointment to some in the fact that in addition to the successful accomplishment of our purpose—the occupation of the Southern Marianas—there was not also a decisive 'fleet action,' in which we would naturally hope to have been victorious, and to have thereby shortened the war materially. . . . There is no restriction on surmising how a hand might have been played and how much could have been won had the cards fallen differently from the way they did." Taylor acknowledged: "Nimitz, too, felt that Admiral Spruance had played his hand properly.[41]

Ironically, Spruance had analyzed the battle correctly: "As a matter of tactics, I think that going after the Japanese and knocking their carriers out would have been much better and more satisfactory than waiting for them to attack us; but we were at the start of a very important and large amphibious operation and we could not afford to gamble and place it in jeopardy."[42] His obligation was to the thousands of troops on Saipan. If he had chased the Japanese fleet and lost, or if he had pursued the fleet and it turned out that other elements of the Imperial Navy were making an end run toward the eastern side of Saipan, those troops would have faced a potentially tragic situation. Finally, attacking the Japanese fleet directly would have required American planes to fly through the Japanese antiaircraft screen, causing much greater American losses. In the end, Ozawa lost three aircraft carriers, and while his remaining carriers escaped physically, they lost their effectiveness as offensive weapons without the needed airplanes and pilots. Mitscher should have celebrated his victory and congratulated Spruance for a well-balanced plan.

In any case, the defeat was not Ozawa's fault, as the United States had already ruined Operation A-Go by eliminating nearly all of Japan's land-based airplanes. Throughout the battle Ozawa received erroneous information about a fleet of planes that did not exist. His offer to resign after the battle was not accepted by Admiral Toyoda, and the remnants of his fleet would play a role at Leyte Gulf later that year. Significantly, it had been the reduction in Japan's air strength at the First Battle of the Philippine Sea that paved the way for the destruction of Japan's surface ships at Leyte Gulf. Japan would continue to fight for another fourteen months after Saipan, but the failure to stop the Americans, on the sea near the Marianas and on the land at Saipan, settled Japan's fate. It was not a surprise that Japan lost the war; it was more amazing that the Japanese were able to resist as tenaciously as they did for another year.

But one incident from the Battle of the Philippine Sea might provide some insight into why and how a crippled Japanese military fought on. At about 0900 on 19 June, Admiral Ozawa launched his second air strike of 110 planes. A few minutes later the American submarine *Albacore* fired several torpedoes at Ozawa's flagship, the *Taiho*. Komatsu Sakio, one of the Japanese pilots, spotted one of the torpedoes in the water racing toward *Taiho* and flew his plane straight down into the sea in an attempt to stop it. He was unsuccessful, and one torpedo did hit *Taiho*. Ozawa's flagship eventually exploded. Nevertheless, Komatsu's voluntary martyrdom demonstrated the dedication of the Japanese fighters and explains how Japan continued the war even when defeat was inevitable. In the meantime, the American invaders on Saipan faced nearly thirty thousand Komatsu Sakios. Holland Smith was correct: "Saipan could only mean one thing: a savage battle of annihilation."[43]

CHAPTER EIGHT

THE 2ND MARINE DIVISION MOVES FORWARD

Japanese battle tactics called for stopping the marines on the beach, but the landing on D-Day had quickly placed more than twenty thousand Americans on the island. Still hopeful that they could push the Americans back into the ocean, the Japanese soldiers, beginning the first day, launched a series of late-night and early-morning attacks. Surprisingly, they did not attempt to use darkness to disguise an impending offensive; Japanese soldiers often made a lot of noise or announced their charge by sounding a bugle. On D-Day the Japanese moved down the beach from Garapan and prepared to move forward at 2200. Under the command of Major LeRoy P. Hunt Jr., the 2nd Battalion, 6th Marines, on the far left (north) side of the American landing forces, faced the main Japanese counterattack. When the Japanese charged, marines waited in their foxholes while naval vessels illuminated the darkness with star shells. The artificial light helped the marines separate the enemy from other night shadows, and this first enemy offensive was repulsed by steady fire from M1 rifles, machine guns, and antitank guns. Despite their losses, the Japanese continued to employ the strategy of night attacks. Although the marines ultimately won these encounters, they too suffered from certain problems and shortages. As Hoffman's official history reported: "The supply of star shells was limited, however, and after the first night it was necessary to ration their expenditure to six per hour except in cases of emergency."[1] While they stopped the Japanese attacks, the marines paid a steep price for their beachhead. The 2nd Marine Division lost 238 men killed and 1,022 wounded on D-Day.

At 0545 on 16 June, enemy soldiers again moved down the beach from Garapan. This time the 6th Marines came under a full-scale tank attack, with the 1st Battalion being hit immediately and the 3rd Battalion moving up to help reinforce the line. At first the marines were overwhelmed by the enemy tanks and were forced back about fifty yards. When A Company, 1st Battalion, was hit and forced to pull back, K Company, 3rd Battalion, was alerted and pushed forward to offer support. Soon the marines were able to employ their tanks and antitank bazookas in the engagement, and these weapons turned the tide of battle. K Company helped destroy at least seven tanks in relief of the beleaguered but determined marines of the 1st Battalion.

Sergeant Jim Evans recalled the chaotic situation, with marines shooting in all directions (especially when enemy tanks overran marine positions) and relying on their bazookas to disable Japanese tanks. "You don't know what's going on" in the middle of a raging battle, Evans confessed. With star shells again lighting the sky, the marines had difficulty distinguishing the enemy in the ever-changing shadows. When a Japanese tank stopped and the hatch opened so the driver could see where he was going amid the smoke, Evans shot the enemy soldier and threw a phosphorous grenade into the tank. "I'm looking at these damned tanks. This tank stops. The hatch comes open and an officer sticks his head up. I blew his head off with my carbine and dropped my phosphorous grenade in the hatch."[2]

This first Japanese tank attack, launched against the 6th Marines, failed to drive the marines back into the sea. Indeed, the pattern for the rest of the battle was set—the Japanese continued to attack, often fruitlessly, and suffered high losses, while the marines took high but ever-decreasing casualties. For the 2nd Marine Division, 16 June did not match the carnage on D-Day, as it lost 54 men killed and 484 wounded.

As the G-2 Intelligence Report indicated, the night of 16 June and the early morning of 17 June saw another Japanese attempt to stop the marines at the water's edge and "drive our forces into the sea. The 2nd Marine Division received counter-attacks throughout the night." Rather than attacking straight down the road from Garapan, the Japanese approached at 0330 from the ridges and hills in the direction of Mt. Tapotchau. This time the enemy committed five hundred ground troops and more than thirty tanks to the battle.[3] Nevertheless the 6th Marines were better prepared, with even more firepower at their disposal than they had the previous night. Additional American equipment had been landing continuously. Now American tanks, as well as grenade and rocket launchers, 75-millimeter guns, and artillery shells, met the Japanese attackers. Again the 6th Marines were hit by a frontal assault, but rather than A Company, 1st Battalion, taking the punishment, B Company was hit the hardest. Corporal M. F. Leggett, who served in C Company near the center of the battle, called the situation "hell on wheels for B Company."[4] In some cases Japanese tanks rolled over marine foxholes, with the marines ducking down under the tanks and then emerging to fire, as Sherrod reported, at the "vulnerable rears with bazooka rockets and anti-tank grenades."[5]

Corporal William "Jeff" Jefferies also served in the 6th Marines, and he was a member of A Company, 1st Battalion, which had been hit so hard the night before. For the second night in a row he found himself in the middle of the action. His partner, Bob Reed, fired his bazooka with Jefferies as his loader. As the battle continued, Reed and Jefferies ran across an open field. Jefferies fired his carbine and killed an enemy soldier. At that moment a Japanese officer ran toward Reed with his sword drawn; Jefferies attempted to defend his friend, but his carbine jammed. Jefferies used his carbine to block the officer's sword thrust and then shot the officer with his rifle, which was suddenly working again. The two marines fired their bazooka shells and knocked out four enemy tanks. Jefferies, nearly deaf due to the proximity of exploding shells, took off to find more ammunition. Reed could not wait for Jefferies to return. He jumped on top of a Japanese tank, hoping that the driver would open the hatch. When the driver did so, Reed dropped a hand grenade into the tank and slammed the lid shut. Reed received a Navy Cross for his actions that day, having made "four hits on four different tanks with his rocket launcher, and, then after running out of rockets, climbed upon a fifth tank and, with utter disregard for his own personal safety, dropped an incendiary grenade in the turret, thereby disabling the tank." For his part in the tank battle, Jefferies earned the Silver Star.[6]

Reed's and Jefferies's bravery was matched by other marines: Privates John Kounk and Horace Narveson "hit three tanks with four bazooka charges," Alex Smith stopped three tanks with his grenade launcher, and Charles Merritt and Herbert Hodges fired seven shots at seven tanks and hit all of them.[7] Major James A. Donovan, executive officer of the 1st Battalion, 6th Marines, recalled: "The battle evolved itself into a madhouse of noise, tracers, and flashing lights. As tanks were hit and set afire, they silhouetted other tanks coming out of the flickering shadows to the front or already on top of the squads."[8] One marine pointed out to Sherrod that the Japanese often wasted their own resources: "The Nips would halt, then jump out of their tanks. Then they would sing songs and wave swords. Finally, one of them would blow a bugle, jump back into the tanks, if they hadn't been hit already. Then we would let them have it with a bazooka."[9] When this confrontation ended after only forty-five minutes—"the largest tank battle of the Pacific War up to that time"—twenty-nine of the Japanese tanks had been destroyed, twenty-four of them by the 6th Marines alone.[10] While the marines would confront individual enemy tanks later in the battle, this encounter on 17 June eliminated the Japanese tank as a significant threat. Once again the Japanese had wasted resources by attacking without a chance of success, and this time they dissipated almost all of their tank reserves. Although the Japanese were unable to mass sufficient force to stop the Americans, they persisted in their offensive strategy.

At almost the same moment that this crucial tank battle was taking place, Admiral Spruance made the decision to confront the Japanese fleet moving out of the Philippine Sea toward the Marianas. As the U.S. Navy left the Marianas, Holland Smith and his chief of staff, Brigadier General Graves B. "Bobby" Erskine, came ashore and established their headquarters in Charan Kanoa. Erskine was the youngest brigadier general in the Marine Corps and, like Smith, an expert on amphibious warfare. Erskine remained in constant contact with officers in the 2nd and 4th Marine Divisions, and all communication flowed through his hands. According to Smith, Erskine was "a brilliant staff officer. His office buzzed with activity and his only regret was that he could not get away more frequently to visit the front. For nearly two weeks, his personal knowledge of Saipan was limited to the area immediately adjacent to our quarters. Duty tied him to his desk." Holland Smith did not visit the front lines; he received his information from Erskine. They met two or three times a day to discuss the current situation and make plans for the next day. Other staff personnel would be called in as necessary to report on various aspects of the battle. Smith considered these meetings "excellent examples of inter-staff cooperation." At all of these conferences Smith made his goals clear: "I was determined to take Saipan and take it quickly."[11]

On 17 June the marines were ready to take the offensive, but their goal remained the O-1 line for D-Day. Smith's goal of a quick victory could not be achieved. According to plan, the 2nd Marines turned north along the coast toward Garapan while the battle-tested and weary 6th Marines drove northeast in the direction of Mt. Tipo Pale. They immediately fought a "bloody battle for Hill 790, a limestone table-top cliff."[12] Along the way a marine walking on Corporal Leggett's left stepped on a mine and lost a leg; Leggett lost his hearing for forty-eight hours.[13]

Figure 8. Destruction in Charan Kanoa, 18 June 1944; courtesy of Private Rod Sandburg (USMC).

At the same time, the 8th Marines were pushing east into the swampland around Lake Susupe, where "men carrying machine guns, mortars and ammunition found themselves sinking waist deep into the muck. The swamp—extending one thousand yards north and south of Lake Susupe, much larger than it had appeared on the map—was infested with snipers."[14] Japanese soldiers held positions around the swamp, in the hills directly to the east of the swamp, and in a coconut grove south of the hills. Unfortunately for the marines, the Japanese held the high ground. As the 8th Marines attempted to eliminate the enemy in the lake area, withering enemy fire from the coconut grove slowed the 1st Battalion, 29th Marines, which was attached to the 8th Marines.

Activated on 1 February 1944 as a reserve battalion of the 2nd Marine Division, the 1st Battalion, 29th Marines, was one of the more interesting units on Saipan. When the battalion was first organized its members did not know what their affiliation would be or where they might be sent, and for that reason they called themselves the "bastard" battalion. Eventually they were attached to the 2nd Marine Division, with Lieutenant Colonel Guy Tannyhill in command. On 17 June, Tannyhill was wounded in the fight through the marsh around Lake Susupe and evacuated from Saipan.[15]

When Tannyhill was wounded, Lieutenant Colonel Rathvon McClure "Tommy" Tompkins took over the battalion. They were being "held up by a swamp heavily infested with Japanese snipers, a cliff honeycombed with powerful hostile gun emplacements, and an elaborate trench system in a coconut grove." Determined to capture the position before dusk, Tompkins rallied the troops and "risked his life to make a hasty reconnaissance of the front lines." He then deployed tanks against the enemy and "led his men in a brilliantly executed attack against these vital objectives, waging battle with relentless fury and reducing the Japanese strongpoints according to plan."[16] Tompkins's leadership and four tanks of the 2nd Tank Battalion were instrumental in diminishing enemy resistance from the hill in front of the marines. Tompkins earned the Navy Cross for his actions. Following this success, the 8th Marines halted its eastward drive and took the next couple of days to pivot and move north toward Mt. Tapotchau.

While the intense battle in and around Lake Susupe continued, the 2nd Marines moved up the coast toward Garapan and the 6th Marines pushed northeast in the direction of the heavily defended hills. As nightfall approached on 17 June the marines dug in, but they continued to be harassed during the night by small groups of enemy soldiers. In a couple of areas the Japanese enjoyed limited success, breaking through where thin lines from one marine unit had not quite tied in with another. Given the terrain, the connection between companies could be tenuous, and the Japanese often hit at those weak points. Such an attack occurred toward 0100 on 18 June when twenty enemy soldiers charged between the 6th and 8th Marines and overran two machine guns. Nevertheless, the marines quickly rallied and killed the attackers.[17]

Early on the morning of 18 June, the marines gazed at the ocean and wondered where their naval support had gone. Of course, they had not been told of the impending naval confrontation between the U.S. and Japanese fleets. From their perspective, an ocean devoid of support ships was an ominous sign. Despite their fears, the marines moved back into action. From this point forward the 2nd Marine Division set its sights on two goals: the city of Garapan and Mt. Tapotchau. Garapan was a town of between ten and fifteen thousand inhabitants and would provide the marines' first experience with house-to-house warfare. Mt. Tapotchau was the highest point on Saipan.

On 19 June, navy battleships and cruisers that had not accompanied

Figure 9. Garapan after U.S. Navy shelling, 25 June 1944; courtesy of Private Joe DeLeo (USMC).

Spruance and Mitscher to the Philippine Sea began to bombard Garapan. While the town was soon leveled, the marines still faced the difficult task of moving through the rubble and checking every house and hiding place. Most of the buildings in the center of the town were made of concrete and most dwellings had tin roofs, neither of which could stand up to the shelling of the big naval guns. Pharmacist's Mate Chester Szech remembered that "the city was gone by the time we occupied it." The entire population had moved to the hills or nearby caves.[18]

On 23 June the 2nd Marines were on the outskirts of Garapan, and the next morning the 1st and 3rd Battalions moved into the city. Sporadic enemy resistance was quickly overcome, but the Japanese launched one major attack that afternoon behind seven tanks. The marines countered with grenades and bazookas, and when the fighting ended the Japanese had lost six precious tanks and control of the capital city of Garapan. By evening the marines had moved up to the street they called Radio Road. This success put them at the O-5 line—despite all of their heroic efforts, the marines remained behind schedule.

After taking the city, the 2nd Marines enjoyed a few days of well-

Figure 10. Marines engage in house-to-house fighting in Garapan, 23 June 1944; courtesy of Private Joe DeLeo (USMC).

deserved rest. Many marines collected souvenirs, while a few of the officers were allowed the luxury of spending their nights sleeping on real mattresses. Several marines paraded the streets in colorful Japanese clothing, some of which had been liberated from the "comfort houses" where women from Korea, the Philippines, and other Japanese colonies had been forced to serve as prostitutes. Radioman Dodson Smith recalled the "red building in town that had been a house for the 'comfort' girls." It had a long hallway with little compartments down each side with a sheet for a door on each one. "We found some coins with a man and woman in a well known position. These must have been issued to the soldiers to use at the house."[19] In addition, the marines discovered the island's main bank and were able to blow the safe open. Celebrating troops used the money to light cigarettes, only to discover during their occupation of Japan the following year that the money they had burned so freely was legal currency. Several marines lamented their loss of potential wealth.

The 6th Marines operated directly to the east of the 2nd Marines. Twenty-seven-year-old Lieutenant Colonel William K. Jones, who led the 1st Battalion, 6th Marines, was the youngest commanding officer of a marine battalion. On 15 June his battalion was in reserve for the 2nd and

3rd Battalions, 6th Marines. Due to the situation on the beach, however, reserve status did not last long, and at 1015, shortly after the 2nd and 3rd Battalions landed, Jones's men went ashore. In the confusion of D-Day, each of Jones's three companies landed on different Red beaches, but they quickly regrouped. Jones told Sherrod how proud he was of the effort: "The speed with which these three company commanders reorganized and attacked indicated the initiative and guts shown by every officer and man in my outfit."[20]

On the morning of 17 June, the 1st Battalion, especially B Company, "bore the full weight of the tank attack."[21] During the next few days the 6th Marines crossed very difficult ground, "fighting along a plateau constantly furrowed by ravines and ridges running from the high mountain down to the sea."[22] By 19 June they were approaching the hills leading to Mt. Tapotchau in a formation that placed the 1st Battalion on the left (west) next to the 3rd Battalion on the right, but before they could advance they suffered from a friendly fire incident. According to Colonel Jim Riseley, commanding officer of the 6th Marines: "We had some bad luck this morning. One of our best company commanders was killed by rockets from one of our own planes. The pilot must have been crazy. He came smashing into our front lines, and got a direct hit, then he fired wild, then he fired again, killed the captain. The artillery has been off, too. One of our 105's hit a bunch of our own men, killing three and wounding seven or eight." By this time Jones's 1st Battalion alone had lost 287 men, more than 30 percent of its original strength.[23]

The targeting of artillery was always difficult in this terrain, and the use of mortars presented its own unique problems. On 22 June, Corporal Jim Montgomery prevented a major disaster in the 3rd Battalion, 6th Marines. Montgomery was part of an 81-millimeter mortar platoon, and when a "burning increment [powder charge] from an expended round started an intense fire," he and another marine put out the fire with dirt. Despite their efforts, the situation became more serious: "A series of increments attached to a stack of mortar rounds piled in the gun pit close to the Battalion Command Post had been ignited." As other marines ran for cover "like stripe-assed apes," Montgomery "stayed at his post despite the danger and intense heat and removed all the shells." He received the Navy and Marine Corps Medal for his action.[24]

On 21 June, after nearly one solid week of fighting, the 2nd and 4th Marine Divisions had suffered 6,165 casualties. Despite this heavy toll, they were planning a major offensive to begin the next day. Eighteen artillery

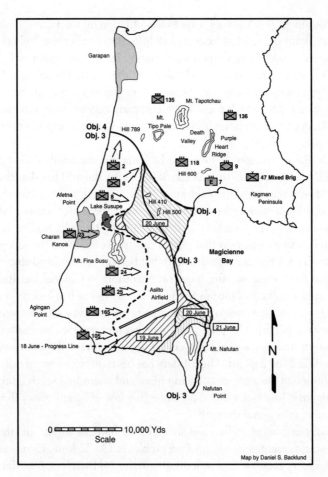

Map 6. Positions on 18–21 June

battalions prepared to support the offensive, and on 22 June the marines attacked in a line across the island. The 8th Marines continued their push toward Mt. Tapotchau while the 6th Marines drove in the direction of nearby Mt. Tipo Pale. In both areas the terrain was extremely rugged, with caves, ravines, gullies, and ridges scattered over the landscape. The topography played to the advantage of the Japanese, and the American offensive needed all possible units to participate in the attack. The next day, in order to assist the operation, the 27th Infantry Division moved between the 2nd and 4th Marine Divisions, but due to the difficult terrain they arrived late in some sectors and slowed the advance.

Between 20 and 22 June, the 6th Marines were forced to pause briefly while the 8th Marines on their right, which had been slowed earlier by Lake Susupe, tried to straighten the attack line. As the 8th Marines moved up, they were forced to wait for the 4th Division on their right on the east coast of the island. At the same time, elements of the 27th Infantry Division were also moving forward.

At 0600 on 22 June the 8th Marines began one of the most important actions of the entire battle. From their vantage on top of 1,554-foot-high Mt. Tapotchau, the Japanese had been able to see the entire island and target American forces. In the "Battle of the Mountain," the 1st and 3rd Battalions, 8th Marines, and the 1st Battalion, 29th Marines, led the assault over the rugged ground:

> Tapotchau rose almost vertically, in a long, sheer, seldom-indented line on the east, dropping 1,000 feet to the Magicienne Bay coastal slope, and in a series of scallops on the west. Between these ultimates, the cliffs approaching the coruscated peak resembled a handful of rusty razor blades, jumbled in a box. And they were just as sharp—needled coral and lava heads, and limestone crags with a thousand cutting edges on every rocky knob. It was no country for tanks, or even jeeps. Here, in these heady heights of a lost continent, the battle would be won or lost by foot soldiers.[25]

Fighting continued throughout the next two days. On 23 June, F Company of the army's 106th Infantry (27th Infantry Division) linked up with the 2nd Battalion, 8th Marines, and the two units fought side by side. According to Marine Corps historian Richard Johnston, "for several days the Army company fought on the ridge with the Marines and gave an excellent account of itself."[26]

On 20 June the 1st Battalion, 29th Marines ("bastard" battalion), had learned that its assignment, along with the 8th Marines, was to capture Mt. Tapotchau. On 21 and 22 June the battalion moved toward the mountain, hiking mostly uphill through the hills and valleys, as well as across sharp coral outcroppings leading to their target. While settled down for the night of 23 June the battalion was hit by artillery fire. At first the marines assumed that the Japanese had focused on the American lines, but soon a more depressing realization took place. According to Sergeant John Orsock, "the first salvo hit directly on our line. They kept pounding us. A lot of people were being killed by direct hits. Finally someone sent up a green flare, the signal for shells landing short on friendly troops, and the firing stopped. It was so called 'friendly fire.' I never found out if it was Marine, Army or Naval gun fire."[27] These errors occurred too often. According to

Corporal Bob Parker of Los Angeles, "It was fairly common to have rounds of 105mm howitzer fall short and somebody would fire a green star shell into the air to alert our gunners that they needed a little more range on their settings."[28] Of course, Japanese shelling also took its toll on the men. As Private Earl Lingerfelt, who carried a BAR, recalled: "A lot of things happen to you while in battle that you try to forget. You try to block them out of your mind, to no avail. Such as your very best friends getting killed right beside you and you wonder why it was him and not you. My friend Lt. Passons was killed in his foxhole right beside mine on the night of the shelling. . . . Someone, I can't remember his name, lost his left foot just above his ankle. I put a tourniquet on his leg. When day light came, there was Lt. Passons with his head laid back and a hole in his neck right under his chin."[29]

Lieutenant Colonel Tommy Tompkins, leading the 1st Battalion, 29th Marines, vowed to Lieutenant Colonel Marion M. Drake that he would "take the mountain come hell or high water." Twenty-eight-year-old Major William C. Chamberlin led the 2nd Battalion, 8th Marines, up the eastern ridge while the 3rd Battalion, 6th Marines, pushed across Mt. Tipo Pale to the west.[30] A determined Tompkins led his men "directly toward the summit," and on Mt. Tapotchau the equally dedicated Japanese defended their positions. Fighting was fierce and Tompkins's men were temporarily stopped. "Our advance was thwarted for three days by intense Japanese resistance," recalled Corporal Bob Parker, "until one of the senior commanders suggested that a frontal assault was never going to be successful and some of our battalion moved east and then around and basically attacked the Japanese defenders from their left flank."[31] Moving east through Chamberlin's lines, Tompkins deployed one platoon of the Division Reconnaissance Company—twenty-two men—to climb to the top of the mountain. After this successful occupation of the summit, Tompkins had to move back down to find the rest of his battalion for reinforcements; he asked the Division Reconnaissance platoon leader, Marion Drake, if he could hold the top until dark. Drake answered honestly: "We could sure try." The Japanese attempted a counterattack, but now it was their turn to fight uphill and they suffered heavy losses. As Japanese soldiers fell wounded, "they all seemed to have a grenade that they pulled the pin on and blew themselves up."[32] Against strong Japanese opposition, the Division Reconnaissance Company held its position.

With dusk approaching, Tompkins used mortar fire and smoke to cover his return to the top of the mountain, and A Company arrived at the summit as night fell on 25 June. Despite the darkness and treacherous terrain, "the battalion did not lose a single man in scaling the cliff and managed to set up their defenses before midnight."[33] Realizing that they had lost the advantage of holding the high ground, Japanese troops became increasingly desperate to drive the Americans off the mountain. Despite shelling the summit and trying several counterattacks, the Japanese suffered greater losses than the Americans. Nevertheless, many marines died in these Japanese attempts to retake the heights. According to Marion Drake, "If you were on the mountain that night you will remember that it was a long night with the Japs coming back with bayonets and attempting to dislodge the Marine battalion with bayonets and knives."[34] On the second day on Mt. Tapotchau, as Private Frank Borta recalled, Japanese mortars killed one marine, "blew out his guts, ripped off his hand, etc. He was still living, but just groaning. We covered him with a poncho to keep the flies off, and 15 minutes later buried him there."[35]

Despite these losses, the marines were on Mt. Tapotchau to stay. As military historian Crowl stated: "Honors for the capture of the summit of Tapotchau, the highest point of the island, were shared by the 2nd Battalion, 8th Marines, and the 1st Battalion, 29th Marines."[36] In order to get a good look at the entire island, as well as to provide a boost to the morale of the marines, Brigadier General Merritt A. "Red Mike" Edson, assistant commander of the 2nd Marine Division, came up to the top of the mountain on 26 June. Edson's visit to Mt. Tapotchau included a rather unpleasant and scary moment. On his way down the mountain, Edson and his staff came under friendly fire from either marine or army artillery. To the relief of the shocked marines watching this action, Edson escaped unharmed.[37] In any case, the marines now had the advantage of the superior vantage point, and they held Mt. Tapotchau from then on. Enjoying their moment on top of the island, Corporal Bob Parker remembered that the marines of the "bastard" battalion enjoyed watching "the naval bombardment of Garapan in a block by block and street by street walking grid pattern."[38] The 29th Marines had taken a lot of casualties in capturing Mt. Tapotchau, and they were soon relieved and given some well-earned rest.[39]

By 23 June, Lieutenant Bill Jones and the 1st Battalion, 6th Marines, had progressed only a few hundred yards in three days. Jones was frustrated by the poor quality of the maps in his possession and angrily swore: "These God damn inaccurate maps . . . look at this; we're on top of a hill 600 feet high, but the contour map shows us on a rolling plain."[40] Unfortunately, neither the maps nor the battle situation improved immediately, with 25 June (D+10) proving to be an especially difficult day in the area on and around Mt. Tipo Pale. The 6th Marines continued to face tough enemy resistance.

Sergeant Jerry Wachsmuth and Private First Class Bob Thatcher, both with E Company, 2nd Battalion, 6th Marines, remembered losing six men from their platoon that day. The stress was too much for some of the marines, and the next day one marine said he could not continue in battle. As was the usual practice, he was allowed to move to the rear for a while; this marine eventually rejoined the company. The practice of allowing a marine to "regroup" himself was not uncommon, and usually after a brief rest most marines returned to battle. Only a few refused or were unable to continue in combat. "There were guys in our company who said they just couldn't go anymore. If you say you weren't frightened you're lying."[41]

Frightened or not, Private First Class Harold Glenn Epperson from Akron, Ohio, took charge of a deadly situation. On 25 June, a few weeks before his twenty-first birthday, Epperson was serving in the 1st Battalion, 6th Marines, when he found his machine-gun emplacement under the "full brunt of a fanatic assault initiated by the Japanese under cover of predawn darkness." He fired his weapon "with determined aggressiveness, fighting furiously in the defense of his battalion's position and maintaining a steady stream of devastating fire." Epperson killed several Japanese soldiers before one enemy soldier, "assumed to be dead," jumped up and threw a grenade into the American machine-gun emplacement. "Determined to save his comrades," Epperson threw himself onto the grenade and "absorbed the shattering violence of the exploding charge in his own body." According to his Medal of Honor citation, "Epperson fearlessly yielded his own life that his able comrades might carry on the relentless battle against a ruthless enemy."[42]

Just as the "bastard" battalion had done at Mt. Tapotchau, the 6th Marines needed to take and hold the high ground on Mt. Tipo Pale in order to dislodge the Japanese artillery and mortar observers who used their altitude advantage to target the marines. Staff Sergeant S. E. "Gene" Brenner recalled advancing toward the mountain when a Japanese mortar attack hit his position: "We learned that the forward observer for the [Japanese] mortar crew was on top of Mt. Tapotchau looking down on us and had four mortar crews firing on us."[43] Approximately sixty to eighty marines in the 3rd Battalion's command post near the south base of the mountain came under fire.

> Just after dusk we were all in foxholes when all Hell broke loose. It started raining mortar shells over the area with cries for corpsman coming from all directions. Mortars explode on contact and many were exploding on tree branches. Shrapnel was flying all over. It was like a hailstorm. I heard one drop about sixty feet to my left and then another thirty feet away. I knew they were searching and traversing and I felt the next one would land in the middle of my back and I would meet my Maker in short order. You can bet I was saying what I thought would be my last prayers. The next one landed about a couple of feet off the foot of my foxhole and covered me with rocks and dirt. With that I jumped up and ran with three others over to the base of the mountain and we stood with our rifles at the ready for any attack. In the midst of this battle, Les Gutzman, a navy corpsman, ran from one wounded marine to the next. He spent the whole night wrapping men up while he also caught some lead. He should have had a Navy Cross for what he went through.[44]

Despite the Japanese resistance, the 6th Marines finally took possession of Mt. Tipo Pale.

As a result of the slow but steady American advance, Lieutenant General Saito realized that the situation was desperate. On 20 June he had reported to Tokyo: "Having lost the influence of the Emperor due to the weakness of our representatives, we are not able to work at our best here. Please apologize deeply to the Emperor that we cannot do better than we are doing . . . the army will defend its positions to the very end, though that be death. . . . There is no hope for victory in places where we do not have control of the air and we are still hoping here for aerial reinforcements. . . . Praying for the good health of the Emperor, we all cry Banzai."[45]

By the end of June, the 6th and 8th Marines controlled the high ground between Garapan and Mt. Tapotchau in the center of the island. The 2nd Marines had fought their way into Garapan, but there Japanese resistance continued. On 29 June near the southeastern sector of the city, a Japanese unit was hiding in the caves on "Flame Tree Hill," named for its colorful vegetation. In order to force the Japanese out of their caves, the marines hit the hill with artillery, machine-gun fire, and finally a smoke screen that normally signaled a marine attack. The Japanese fell for the ruse and charged out of their caves, anticipating hand-to-hand combat. Instead, the marines held back and allowed their artillery and mortars to complete the job. According to Captain John C. Chapin, "The enemy,

Figure 11. Marines moving through Garapan, 2 July 1944; courtesy of Private
Ralph Browner (USMC).

caught in the open, was wiped out almost to a man."[46] By 2 July, Flame
Tree Hill was under marine control. With their missions accomplished on
Mt. Tapotchau, on Mt. Tipo Pale, and in Garapan, the entire 2nd Marine
Division prepared to move into reserve. Holland Smith's plan called for the
27th Infantry Division and the 4th Marine Division to move west, cutting
to the north side of the 2nd Marine Division, which would be allowed to
recuperate before the invasion of Tinian. Their rest was well deserved, as
the 2nd Division had lost 4,488 men by the end of June.

CHAPTER NINE

THE 4TH MARINE DIVISION MOVES FORWARD

Not surprisingly, all marines were ecstatic when their tank battalions drove ashore on Saipan, and the tanks were sent immediately into action. Realizing the threat that this weapon posed to their control of the island, the Japanese quickly targeted the American tanks with artillery. On 16 June a battery of enemy 77-millimeter guns disabled the tank of Gunnery Sergeant Robert Howard McCard of Syracuse, New York, who served with A Company, 4th Tank Battalion. Despite his perilous situation in an immobile tank, McCard continued to fire at the Japanese gun emplacements. Under an intense barrage, he ordered his crew to escape through the hatch while he used his grenades to cover their retreat. Seriously wounded and out of grenades, "McCard then dismantled one of the tank's machineguns and faced the Japanese for the second time to deliver vigorous fire into their positions, destroying 16 of the enemy but sacrificing himself to insure the safety of his crew." McCard died protecting his men and was awarded a Medal of Honor for his heroic actions.[1]

Throughout the battle for Saipan, the 23rd Marines were involved in some of the most intense fighting on the island. Under the command of Captain Fred Eberhardt, C Company, 1st Battalion, moved from the beach through Charan Kanoa and then toward Mt. Fina Susu on the second day. As the marines climbed one side of the hill, the Japanese moved about two hundred feet down the reverse slope so that they would have a clear shot as the marines came over the crest. As Private John Seymour recalled, "Every one of us who came over the top was a sitting duck waiting to be shot. We were sent over in waves of 20 (plus or minus) men about two minutes apart." The Japanese were waiting. Seymour continued: "Our plan had been anticipated and their guns of all kinds had been zeroed in on every inch of this battlefield . . . all hell broke loose." Private Orvel Johnson and several other marines moved forward, "firing our weapons, dodging, dropping, rolling, and jumping up firing as bullets tore through the air." Johnson, carrying a Browning automatic rifle, continued in this manner—running, firing, dropping, rolling, and then starting the process again. Realizing that the Japanese had set a trap, the marines pulled back in order to allow their own mortars to hit the enemy positions. Moses "Moe" Iadanza, another C Company BAR man, refused to withdraw as ordered and stood on the ridge, continuing to fire as he hurled obscenities at the enemy until he ran out of ammunition and was killed. June 17 was C Company's worst day on Saipan, with forty-five wounded and four killed. The company had landed with 244 men on 15 June, but by the end of the third day they had lost 95 marines wounded or killed, a casualty rate of nearly 40 percent.[2]

The men of C Company were allowed to rest on 18 June due to their heavy losses, but they were ordered to resume the attack the following day. The situation was not much better as they moved north toward the center of the island through hilly terrain overgrown with thick brush. As Seymour remembered, "It was a heavy firefight with lead zinging everywhere." While American shelling had disabled many Japanese mortars, enemy soldiers continued to offer stiff resistance, killing six and wounding ten more marines from C Company on 19 June. Nevertheless the marines advanced, only to be ordered to pull back at night to establish a solid defensive line. While C Company had lost 48 percent of its original strength by this time, leaving only 116 marines in combat, it had also destroyed most of the Japanese resistance in its sector. As a result, its losses over the ensuing two weeks were relatively light compared to the first days of combat. Nevertheless, by the end of the battle C Company counted 29 men killed and 113 wounded, a casualty rate of more than 55 percent.[3]

Another unit of the 23rd Marines, G Company, also experienced intense combat throughout the battle. Lieutenant James Stanley Leary Jr. of Ahoskie, North Carolina, served as leader of the 2nd Platoon. Private First Class Carl Matthews, who grew up in Dawson and Hubbard, Texas, served as his "runner." In this capacity Matthews carried a radio, semaphore flags, and pencil and paper and tried to stay nearby in case Leary needed him. In this process Leary and Matthews also developed a close friendship, forged by their common experiences. As the 2nd Platoon moved off the beach and through Charan Kanoa on 15 June, Japanese snipers waited in the trees. Frank D. Witte from Desdemona, Texas, was hit and killed immediately. The marines "pushed on without stopping, pausing only for a glance and private grief. We had been trained not to attempt to assist those who had fallen. Snipers expected comrades to rush to the fallen and the comrades then became targets for the sniper." As they moved forward the marines sprayed the tops of trees with gunfire, and occasionally a sniper would tumble out of his perch. Marines in the 2nd Platoon forced themselves to press ahead, then back, then forward once more as the battle raged. They passed the body of Witte, "still lying where he had been hit."[4] By evening the 2nd Platoon had advanced only two or three hundred yards, far short of the day one objective (O-1 line). They dug in for the night, but as they tried to sleep their rest was interrupted by the sound of a banzai attack on their right flank against the 3rd Platoon.

On the morning of 16 June, Lieutenant Leary gave the order for the men to move out across a sugarcane field in the direction of Aslito Airfield. While there were some firefights and a few casualties, the day went fairly well and the platoon dug in on a hillside for the night. Most of the marines had not slept for two days, and they set up a rotation system so they could take turns resting. Nevertheless, their sleep was disturbed by the sound of a wounded Japanese soldier not far away who "moaned and screamed throughout the night. . . . A man in our platoon yelled, 'Will someone please shoot that SOB so I can get some sleep.' The screaming and moaning ceased before dawn and we assumed that the poor soul had died."[5] Some marines could not sleep in any case. Corporal John "Jack" Rempke operated a .30-caliber water-cooled machine gun. Well aware that the Japanese preferred night attacks, he and the other machine gunners set up after dark and waited. They were rarely disappointed, as the enemy usually emerged close to midnight. Based on his experience, Rempke learned that his gun had a tendency to rise as it fired, so he would keep his cheek against the gun breach in order to maintain a steady firing level.[6] Gunnery Sergeant Keith Renstrom instructed his machine gunners to aim at knee level, so that as the enemy dropped to the ground the fire would be targeted on their helmets.[7]

By the end of the second day, the bodies of the dead were piling up on the island. *Time* magazine reporter Robert Sherrod passed by such an area: "As we neared the beach, in what had been the hard-hit 23rd Marines D-Day sector, we saw about 50 dead who were now becoming heavily covered with dust. Their bodies were hugely bloated, and they were turning black in the hot sun. The only way to distinguish Jap from American was by the helmets, leggings (Jap, wrap-around; American, canvas), or belts (black leather or khaki web). There were about two dead Marines for three dead Japs."[8]

A few marines barely escaped joining the pile of dead bodies. On the morning of 16 June, Private Bob Verna's company awoke in view of a road and a sugarcane field. A Japanese patrol marched in the open toward the marines, and while most marines waited for the enemy to close the distance, a marine machine gunner started shooting too soon and a firefight broke out. Eventually the marines killed almost all the enemy. Verna and his comrades then started toward Aslito Airfield. They had to cross fields with sugarcane about eighteen inches high, perfect cover for the defenders. As they moved across the open field, Verna spotted an enemy machine gun ahead. He "hit the deck" too late and was shot in the shoulder. He "felt no pain" because he had lost all feeling in his left side. When the rest of his company was forced to withdraw from the field, Verna was left alone and spent the next six hours crawling back toward American lines before being evacuated to the USS *James O'Hara*.[9]

The 23rd Marines' mission changed on 17 June after the 27th Infantry Division landed on Saipan with the objective of taking Aslito Airfield. Rather than moving south toward the airfield, a target now assigned to the army, the 23rd Marines were ordered to move north toward thick vegetation and hills in the center of the island. G Company would push along the area that they called the Devil's Backbone, running from one end of the island to the other. After a day's rest to allow all of the units to move into position, G Company started its drive forward on 19 June. The fighting remained fierce as the Japanese used their defensive positions to inflict significant casualties on the 23rd Marines. The Japanese held a line to the southeast of Lake Susupe, near the meeting point of the 2nd and 4th Divisions. There was always some confusion about which division was responsible for closing that gap, and the enemy was able to take advantage of the disarray on the American side. Unfortunately for the marines, artillery could not be used in the area because the close lines of combat increased the danger of friendly fire.

By 19 June the 23rd Marines had moved about four hundred yards beyond Lake Susupe. At the same time, solid contact was finally established with the 2nd Division, and it would be maintained as both divisions pushed through the center of the island. In this drive northward, Carl Matthews and the 2nd Platoon were ordered to move across an open field approximately two hundred yards from a grove of palm trees. The field provided no cover for the troops. When withering enemy fire suddenly tore into the men, everyone except those who had already been hit retreated toward a small ravine that offered some protection. Wendell Nightengale, a BAR man in the 2nd Platoon, was wounded and attempted to crawl in the direction of the ravine. Another member of the platoon, Richard Freeby, ran through a "hail of bullets" and tried to drag Nightengale to safety. In support of Freeby and Nightengale, every weapon in G Company targeted the brush. The two marines, now out in the open, were subjected to intense Japanese fire, and Nightengale was killed. "Freeby dropped Nightengale and began to race back to the gulley" in what Matthews called "the greatest act of bravery I had ever seen or ever hope to see. He [Freeby] had risked his own life in an attempt to save the life of his friend. And he cried when he realized he had failed." Freeby received a Silver Star for his act of courage. G Company did not learn until later that as they moved across that open field they were advancing directly against a major enemy command post. All the platoons of G Company suffered high casualties that day. In retaliation, artillery and mortars saturated the palm grove with shells, "tears mixing with sweat as men of the mortar squad cursed and dropped the mortar rounds into the tubes."[10] At about 1500 the entire company was ordered to finish the job by advancing on the palm trees. Matthews recalled:

> The remaining men of G Company raced over the bodies of their dead comrades who lay on the open field, swearing vengeance with every step, determined to make the Japanese pay dearly for what had happened. Every bush that moved became the recipient of hundreds of rounds of small arms fire. Any warm body exposed was met with a hail of bullets fired by angry marines. One older man, emerging from a hole in the ground, was shoved back into the hole by the force of bullets hitting his body. Concussion grenades were tossed into the hole. It was over in a few minutes, but we had all aged a lifetime.[11]

When the firing finally ended in that sector, Lieutenant Leary and Private Matthews returned to find Nightengale's body. "Lt. Leary removed one of Nightengale's dogtags, the other was left for the burial detail," Matthews recalled. "We placed a bayonet attached to a rifle into the ground and hung Nightengale's steel helmet on the butt of the rifle. We had performed the procedure as we had been instructed and raced to catch up with the 2nd Platoon. Several days later we were given a day of rest and on our way to the beach passed the area where Nightengale had been killed. His body was still there, waiting for the burial detail."[12] On 20 June the 25th Marines replaced the 23rd Marines on the left flank of the 4th Division. At the same time, the 24th Marines drove forward past Magicienne Bay along the east coast of Saipan.

The frontline companies of the 24th Marines that had taken the north ridgeline of Magicienne Bay had no tanks or support vehicles, because the steep cart path with hairpin turns prevented military vehicles from reaching the top. The marines were being held up by heavy fire from rifles and machine guns, and needed tanks and artillery. Corporal Frank Britt served as a combat engineer with B Company, 1st Battalion, 20th Marines. The mission of this engineer battalion was to use bulldozers to assist the combat units of the 4th Marine Division. Britt was ordered to "volunteer" to take his bulldozer up to the ridge, and after three hours he had cut a trail as wide as the bulldozer blade and widened the hairpin turns sufficiently to allow several tanks to proceed up the ridge.[13] As a result, the marines were able to continue their offensive.

Although the 4th Division had performed well and had accomplished its goal of driving east across the island and then wheeling north, conditions were deteriorating for both sides. The first couple of days had depleted marine combat units, some by 40 percent or more. Individual marines were exhausted from lack of sleep, the heat, and the harsh conditions caused by the island's terrain. Finally, supplies had begun to run down as transports had been withdrawn due to the threat from the Japanese fleet. For one week, from 17 to 24 June, the marines and soldiers used whatever supplies had been landed in the first two days of the operation. By 20 June even artillery shells were being carefully parceled out. The situation was not militarily threatening at that point, but the long-term outcome of the battle depended upon the result of the Battle of the Philippine Sea and the return of the supply ships.

On 22 June, still awaiting the conclusion of the sea battle and the anticipated return of the American fleet, the entire 4th Division attacked north toward the Kagman Peninsula, making good progress and advancing about twenty-five hundred yards. Nevertheless, after a week of combat the division was still short of the O-4 line. The next day, the 27th Infantry Division took over the left flank of the 4th Division in the center of the island while the marines turned east to mop up the Kagman Peninsula.

While the ground was relatively flat, especially compared to the terrain in the sectors of the 2nd Marine Division and the 27th Infantry Division, the Kagman Peninsula had its own disadvantages. Sugarcane fields dominated the area. According to Chapin, one platoon leader indicated that "in every field the company would lose a man or two. . . . The Jap snipers who were doing the damage were dug in so deeply, and camouflaged so well, that it was impossible to locate them before they fired. And then it was too late; you were right on top of them, and they had nailed another one of your men."[14]

In addition to the sugarcane fields, the marines in this area had to clear out the caves along the shore. Corporal Robert Graf, a radio operator with E Company, 2nd Battalion, described the method for dealing with enemy inside the caves: "Quite often there would be multi cave openings, each protecting another. Laying down heavy cover fire, our specialist would advance to near the mouth of the cave. A satchel charge would then be heaved into the mouth of the cave, followed by a loud blast as the dynamite exploded. Other times it might be grenades thrown inside the cave, both fragment type which exploded sending bits of metal all throughout the cave, and other times phosphorous grenades that burned the enemy."[15]

Marine procedure involved shouting into a cave with a promise of food and water; if the enemy responded with hostility, the troops would throw a grenade into the opening. Marines knew that the caves often housed civilians as well as enemy soldiers. As Sergeant Jerry Wachsmuth noted, the enemy's use of caves forced the marines to throw TNT into holes or openings they passed, "not concerned with who might be hiding in there."[16] While seemingly hardened to the realities and consequences of war, many marines risked their own lives to try to save children and babies in these situations. Corporal M. F. Leggett could not suppress his emotion when he pulled a six-month-old baby out of a cave: "That's what makes you want to throw your weapon down."[17]

Another method of clearing caves involved flamethrowers. Graf described their use: "Also the flamethrower was used, sending a sheet of flame into the cave, burning anyone that was in its path. Screams could be heard and on occasions the enemy would emerge from the caves, near the entrance, we would call upon the tanks, and these monsters would get in real close and pump shells into the opening."[18] Carl Matthews "always felt bad when the Japanese would run out of their hole, almost naked, but with fuel and fire from the flamethrowers covering their bodies, scream-ing and dying. But if we gave them half a chance we would have been the ones dying."[19]

Army private Clifford Howe also reacted emotionally to the use of flamethrowers at first, but he soon accepted them as necessary in war: "We

Figure 12. U.S. flamethrower tank in action; courtesy of Private Ralph Browner (USMC).

hadn't gone far when we ran into a cement pill box. An engineer came up with a flamethrower, and released a stream of fluid, and then ignited it. Three horribly burned Japanese soldiers came running out, and one of our soldiers shot and killed them. Being 18 I felt this to be extremely cruel, but then thinking it over, it was a mercy killing as they were burned to a crisp and were undoubtedly in such excruciating pain."[20]

Corporal Steve Judd belonged to an assault demolition team that used dynamite (mostly TNT) and flamethrowers to clean out caves and other Japanese strongholds. If a squad of marines ran into trouble or was held up by pillboxes or caves, the demolition team was called in with napalm and TNT. After the team sent a blast of napalm into a cave, an assistant would then throw in a demolition charge. Judd volunteered as a flamethrower's assistant, "the last man in and the last man out." While all jobs in the marines were difficult and dangerous, demolition was especially risky, since enemy fire could explode the flamethrower's napalm supply. "Man, but that tank was heavy to carry on your back and it made a perfect target." Judd recalled losing a good friend who was killed by a bullet in the neck while

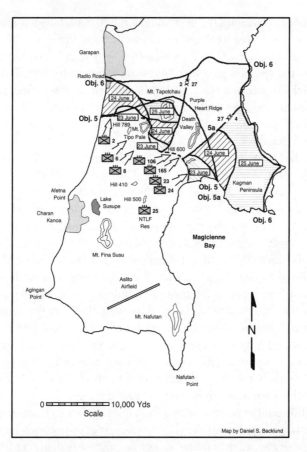

Map 7. Positions on 23–26 June

approaching a cave. Despite the loss, Judd moved forward because he had "a job I had to do." Wounded in the arm on 2 July, the day after his birthday, Judd had his arm wrapped; despite its limited utility he returned to the front lines. He reiterated the same theme: "The job had to be done."[21]

The 4th Division continued to advance on 24, 25, and 26 June, with parts of the O-6 line finally reached on 25 June and the rest on 26 June. At the same time, the 25th Marines, temporarily in reserve, fought off three hundred Japanese soldiers who had passed through army lines near Nafutan Point in the south and moved toward Hill 500. The Japanese expected to link up with their own troops but unexpectedly found U.S. marines instead, and the Japanese force was eliminated.

From 27 June until the beginning of July, the 4th Division made slow progress as it waited for the army to advance and straighten the combat line across the island. The 27th Infantry Division had been hindered by some of the roughest terrain on the island. The combat battalions of the 4th Division used the time to consolidate their position, clear Japanese strong points, and get a little rest. The rest was well deserved and necessary—by 1 July the 4th Division had suffered approximately forty-four hundred casualties.

By the end of June, G Company, 23rd Marines, was in the mountains, with the 25th Marines on their right. They were, as Matthews recalled, "in extremely difficult terrain, [and] the points between the two regiments widened until we were, perhaps, two to three hundred yards apart. Word came to close the existing gap, but we did not have sufficient manpower." Many marine companies had been reduced to 40 to 50 percent of their original strength by this time. Lieutenant Leary ordered Private Matthews to use his semaphore flags to contact the 25th Marines to alert them to the dangerous gap between the regiments, but as soon as Matthews started waving the flags, enemy fire targeted his position. Leary then sent a five-man patrol, led by Matthews, to make personal contact with the other regiment and inform them of the gap between their lines. Despite the harrowing assignment, which took men down a ravine and across an open field through hostile fire, all members of the patrol made it to the other side, and reserve troops moved up and closed the gap.[22]

While positioned on a ridge a short distance from a Japanese unit, G Company prepared an artillery barrage against an enemy unit. Lieutenant Buck Finney joined the marines to act as a spotter, to call in coordinates for an artillery strike against the enemy location. Finney was on his stomach, using a field telephone to contact the artillery units, and Leary and Matthews were seated nearby. As the Japanese were only a few yards in front of the marines, the artillery was at first hitting closer to the marines than to the Japanese. Finney kept moving ("walking") the artillery strikes closer to the enemy. One artillery round failed to clear the crest of the ridge and landed in the middle of the marines. Matthews reported: "My ears rang, I was dazed. My entire body felt as if a giant firecracker had exploded and slammed against me." Matthews was lucky. "One young Marine, lay near the crest of the ridge on the left flank. He didn't move and never would. A small shrapnel had gone through his helmet and into his head. He had died instantly." Despite the impact of friendly fire, Finney stayed at his post and

Figure 13. Marines in 4th Division throwing grenades toward Japanese position;
U.S. Marine Corps photo.

continued with his job: "The artillery spotter had not moved, his dungaree
jacket in shreds, the flesh of his back slashed open and bleeding, but he
continued to direct artillery fire." Within minutes the Japanese position
had been destroyed.[23]

Japanese defenders continued to exact a price from the marines. In
early July, as A Company, 1st Battalion, 24th Marines, moved forward they
came to an open field about a hundred yards long. The battalion had to run
down the first part of the field and then uphill on the other end. As they ran
they encountered Japanese sniper fire, and one marine was hit. After the
entire battalion made it to the top of the hill, another marine started back
down to pull the wounded marine to safety. As Private Alva Perry recalled,
the rest of the marines started cheering for them, "just like a high school
football game." As the two marines struggled back up the hill, snipers hit
both of them and they fell "like a sack of potatoes. . . . We know they are
finished as the snipers keep up their fire. The cheering stops, a voice sounds
out, 'scouts out, don't bunch up.'"[24] It was time to move on.

Shortly after that incident, on 6 July, A Company was pinned down by
intense Japanese fire. Perry "fearlessly rose to his feet and walked forward

firing his automatic rifle, personally accounting for twenty-seven Japanese soldiers." Following Perry's example, his platoon charged ahead and "broke the enemy counterattack."[25] Perry received a Silver Star for his actions.

Despite Perry's bravery, A Company suffered many losses during the campaign. The original company of 246 men was reduced to approximately 155, a casualty rate of 37 percent, by the end of the battle. In C Company, 23rd Marines, 29 members were killed or died of wounds on Saipan, and another 111 were wounded.[26] Many combat units lost more than half of their officers and enlisted men. By the end of June the 4th Marine Division counted approximately 4,450 casualties. These high casualty figures continued throughout the war. When it left the United States in 1943 the 4th Marine Division included almost 19,500 men; by the end of the war, 17,000 of them were casualties.

CHAPTER TEN

MARINES UNDER FIRE

Although the marines advanced steadily northward across the island, the fighting remained extremely difficult. The Japanese defended every hill and cave. Private Orvel Johnson recalled how marines continued to plod ahead: "I didn't know where I was most days except who was in command, who was on our left flank and right flank. One hill was pretty much the same as any other."[1] Private Alva Perry agreed with that assessment: "When you are fighting for your life you don't know exactly where you are at. I scouted nearly every day for my company and fought the entire length of Saipan and I was never told that you are fighting near the bay or on the plain. All a frontline person knows is that it's hilly, flat, or heavily wooded." Even as a scout, Perry never saw a map with place-names on it—it was just Hill 410 or Hill 500: "We were just trying to fight our way up to the next phase line."[2]

Despite heavy losses and difficult obstacles, the marines kept pushing forward. It had taken only a few days for the burden of battle to begin to show. Marines wore the same clothes from the first day of the battle to the last. Private Rod Sandburg never forgot the daily difficulties they faced: "We ate, slept, and fought in clothes that became so rotten from perspiration and rain that they were very threadbare when the campaigns were over . . . our dungarees would rot, from body sweat, right on our bodies." A major obsession for many marines, who were sweating in their boots in

tropical heat, was having the time to wash their socks. A lucky marine fighting near the beach could take advantage of the supply of water. "We could
wash them out in the water at the bottom of shell holes on the beach,"
recalled Sandburg. "We would dig holes near the beach about a foot deep
and then we could wash our socks and hands and faces. This water would
not be salty even though it was sea water seeping into the hole."[3] Of course,
marines fighting for days inland through forest and jungle did not have the
opportunity to wash their socks. There was no place to shave or shower and
no toilet paper. Private "Chick" Hill with K Company, 3rd Battalion, 6th
Marines, remembered "twenty-one straight days without shower or shave
and without changing anything but socks."[4] If a marine unit crossed a
sugarcane field the situation became even more unpleasant. The Japanese
and local farmers used "night soil" (human waste) as fertilizer. As marines
hit the ground they would end up "covered with shit," and if incoming fire
was intense they would have to press their face and head down.[5] Occasionally in the middle of a firefight a marine would have to relieve himself in
his clothes. If there was a lull in the battle and it started to rain, marines
might strip down and lather with soap, and "most times the rain would pass
before we could rinse the soap off, which was not a good result," recalled
Corporal "Jerry" Goforth.[6]

After a few days of battle, marines looked quite frightening, especially
to the local population. The Japanese told the Chamorros, members of the
native population, that marines would rape and kill them, and some of the
Saipan natives and Japanese civilians were likely to attempt suicide rather
than risk capture by the hideous Americans. "We captured a Chamorro girl
about 17," recalled corpsman Jerome Baron, "and she grabbed a Marine's
knife and wanted to kill herself. We stopped her."[7] Many other Chamorros
and Japanese civilians could not be stopped in time.

In addition to nonexistent sanitation and the strain of battle, marines
endured the same food every day—C rations. Later in the struggle, after
advancing farther into enemy territory, they occasionally uncovered a cache
of Japanese provisions. Many marines particularly enjoyed the canned
crabmeat and other items provided to Japanese soldiers as a nice break from
the marine diet. After capturing a Japanese shelter, Guy Gabaldon, a scout
with the 2nd Marines, commented on some of the provisions available
from the enemy: "There are a lot of goodies in the shack, but I can't take
them all. What to choose? Rock candy, canned crab meat, lemon soda?
Man, did the Japs ever like rock candy and lemon soda! It was in every cave
and bunker. And many cases of Kirin beer."[8]

The marines subsisted on a variety of canned meats, such as meat and beans, meat and vegetable stew, meat and spaghetti, meat and noodles, pork and rice, franks and beans, pork and beans, and ham and lima beans. Often in combat the variety was even more limited, noted Tibor Torok— "either greasy beef stew or corned beef hash."[9] Private Sandburg mostly ate "pork and beans along with a box of soda crackers."[10] In addition the troops received several cigarettes a day.

The marines also craved fresh drinking water. Fighting nonstop in the island heat created a serious dehydration problem, so the navy distilled sea-water and sent giant drums of it to Saipan. Worried that the marines were not getting enough salt, the navy medics added salt to the distillation, but "it was so damned much that the water was almost undrinkable," recalled Private Paul Beverly.[11] In some cases the marines compensated for their lack of potable water by taking advantage of the sugarcane fields. Lieutenant John Chapin repeated a comment from a platoon leader: "With water so scarce, one of our chief sources of liquid sustenance was sugar cane juice. We'd whack off a segment of the cane with our combat knives, then chew and suck on it till only the dry fibers were left." Chapin also remembered the scene when water was delivered to his company: "Everyone crowded thirstily around, and we had to order the men to disperse. . . . Then each platoon leader rationed out a can of the precious liquid amongst his men. . . . The water was lukewarm, rusty, and oily as it came out of the cans, but it still tasted like nectar!"[12]

In addition to eating the same food day after day and drinking salty and oily water, the marines had to put up with the vast number of flies on the island. Flies were everywhere, and a marine could not get his spoon to his mouth without flies sharing his meal. They were a problem from the very beginning, as the bodies of Japanese soldiers killed by navy shelling even before the marines landed rotted where they lay, flies feasting on the corpses. On 16 June, Guy Gabaldon wanted to find the Japanese lines, and he worked his way north from the Lake Susupe area:

> I came to a trench in which there were quite a few Japanese bodies torn apart by a direct hit. It must have been a big naval shell. The stench was strong and maggots were having a field day all over the bloated bodies, crawling in and out off their eyes and bellies that had expanded and burst. That is an indication that they were undoubtedly killed several days ago during the initial naval shelling. In this tropical heat it does not take long for the flies to do their work. This is a stench that we're going to live with day and night for the next month because we won't have time to bury the enemy.[13]

For many marines the sight of dead bodies covered with flies remained one of their most powerful and unpleasant memories of Saipan. Corporal John Rempke called "dead bodies covered with maggots" the worst sight of the war. "What a terrible way to die."[14]

For the next month a steady supply of dead bodies would be rotting in the sun on the island. According to Sandburg, "There were more flies than any of us had ever seen. . . . It was impossible to keep them off our food. Our shit skillets [mess kits] would be covered with blow flies so deep one couldn't see the food."[15] Unfortunately, the flies had recently "feasted on the mutilated bodies and the garbage," noted Dodson Smith.[16] Marines used camouflage nets to cover their mouths as they ate. "I would put the can of rations and a spoon under my helmet net and tie the net around my neck," recalled Tibor Torok. "I held the can with one hand and used the spoon with the other. We did our best to avoid the damn flies, but several weeks later, we all got dysentery anyway."[17] Finally, the army decided to spray the island with insecticide. They started at the southern end of the island and drove the flies north into marine lines. Sandburg continued: "We had to cover our faces with hankies to keep from breathing the insects."[18] While the flies were the most serious irritant, many marines also complained about the land crabs that would share their foxholes near the beach.[19]

Marines were happy to find Japanese food stocks, and many of them also shared fond memories of Japanese sake. A few days after landing, Private M. Neil Mumford and some buddies from Company A, 2nd Armored Amphibian Battalion, "found a house that must have been used as a warehouse by the Japs. We found many cases of sake. After consuming as much as we could, we decided to hide the remaining. We dug a hole on the beach." To remember the spot, Mumford and his comrades lined it up with a destroyer, but when they returned a few days later the ship was gone and they never found the rest of the sake.[20]

Private First Class Herb Cracraft and his comrades in the 2nd Armored Amphibian Battalion were luckier and found a liquor warehouse in Garapan. They filled the compartments of their pontoon with alcohol, and Cracraft acknowledged that they were fortunate that they did not have to head back out into the water, since the extra weight created serious drag on their vehicles.[21] Sometimes a battle experience led to a surprise cache. After killing two Japanese soldiers in an old shack, Guy Gabaldon found a keg of sake inside: "I take several swigs of the stuff, pour the water out of my two canteens and fill up with Jap firewater."[22] Of course, marines had been warned to avoid Japanese alcohol. One caution claimed that some of the sake had been spiked with drugs in order to give the Japanese soldiers a feeling of bravado before a big battle. Torok recalled the warning "never to drink the sake if the seal was broken . . . it could have been poisoned."[23] Nevertheless, many marines were undeterred and continued their quest for fermented beverages, even making their own brew on occasion. Apparently, marine-supplied beer was too weak for battle veterans. "Jerry" Goforth, who was with Motor Transport, 2nd Marine Division, and helped clear the jungle with a bulldozer, admitted that "we made Apple Jack and Raisin Jack. We mixed it in wooden nail kegs, then dug holes in the coral with jackhammers, placed the kegs in the coral to ferment for a few days. We then poured the dynamite mixture into our canteens, mixed with 2 percent beer, and watched as smoke boiled up and our canteens turned black."[24] Fortunately, the marines were young and tough.

Several marines recalled that some Native Americans in their units had difficulty with alcohol. Corporal David E. Kinder remembered being happy to share his bottle of wine with a Native American, but "he returned less than half the bottle."[25] Private First Class John Dickinson, a marine who served in a communications platoon, remembered the results of stumbling upon some alcohol: "[Navajos'] work was always efficient until we ran into a cache of sake. Sorry to say they found some liquor on Saipan and got so drunk one night that if we had been over run by the Japs we would have had all kinds of trouble."[26] In the midst of general praise for the code talkers and for Native Americans' toughness as marines, the issue of inebriation remained a general theme among many marines. After praising the fighting ability of Navajo marines, Radioman Dodson Smith corroborated Dickinson's account: "The only problem we had with the code talkers is that if they got drunk, it took about six marines to hold them down and get them into the shower."[27]

Native American marines faced one humiliating situation based solely on race. According to Dodson Smith, "Most of them looked so much like the Japanese that they were always being captured by the marines and had a hard time explaining that they were U.S. Marines."[28] Corporal Kinder indicated that the situation was exacerbated by illness: "Soldiers from one regiment captured ¾ of the Indians and put them in the stockade with the Japs. Scared the hell out of those kids. Our Major had to go and vouch for them. They had been treated for malaria and their skin and eyes were yellow—they looked like Japs."[29] As a result of mistaken identity, some Native Americans became victims of friendly fire: "Their resemblance to the enemy made them vulnerable and several became casualties."[30] Despite these problems, all marines agreed that Native Americans, almost all of whom were called "chief" by other marines, made fine fighters and that their common enemy was the Japanese.

"Poisoned" sake was neither the only nor the most dangerous "trick" that the Japanese played on the marines. Private Sandburg recalled that on some occasions Japanese soldiers "would string wire from one tree to another at a height that would decapitate the people in a jeep. To keep this from happening we had to weld an upright angle iron on the front of the jeep to break the wires."[31] The Japanese also used spider traps, or camouflaged holes in the ground. Torok described the procedure: "The Jap snipers would hide in these holes, pop up to fire a few rounds off, then retreat into the hole again, and pull the covers over them." If the enemy soldier was fast enough, "no one could tell where the shot came from." Occasionally, Japanese soldiers would hide under leaves until a marine passed by them and then "spring up and kill the person that had walked on them."[32]

Corporal Basil Duncan from Cooper, Texas, served in the 3rd Battalion, 25th Marines, and uncovered a spider trap. He barely emerged unscathed from the encounter: "Out of the corner of my eye, I saw a piece of sheet metal that had been turned up at the corner and protruded from the sand about an inch. I knew exactly what it was. . . . I then stooped down and slowly placed my hand under the metal's edge and quickly jerked it away. . . . I saw a Japanese officer. . . . Quick as I was, he was just as fast and jammed the pistol under my chin and pulled the trigger." The officer's gun misfired and Duncan survived. The Japanese officer did not.[33]

Private First Class Marvin Scott remembered how an encounter with a spider trap turned a pacifist marine into a warrior: "We had this fellow in our company who was quite religious. He said he could not kill a man. He was sincere about it. About a half-hour after we landed a Japanese soldier came out of a spider hole and shot his best buddy. This guy got out a grenade and went over and lifted the lid and threw it in and killed his first man."[34] Corpsman Jerry Baron from Brooklyn, New York, serving with K Company, 3rd Battalion, 25th Marines, was also lucky. He carried a carbine, and when he saw a bush about ten feet away move he thought he might be "hallucinating after all the straight days of fighting." Then the bush moved again. "I knew it was a Jap and I fired an entire clip from the hip and killed him and a grenade went off when he died. He was ready to throw it at the six of us."[35]

Japanese soldiers were willing to die for their cause, and American

Figure 14. Marines in firefight on Saipan; courtesy of Private Paul Schwartz (USMC).

grenades gathered from dead marines sometimes played a role. Private Sandburg recalled that the Japanese "would steal our hand grenades and hold them under their arm pits with the pin pulled and pretend to give themselves up; when they lifted their arms the hand grenade would fall on the ground and explode killing them and those around them." They also used civilian women to perform the same stunt.[36] Private Scott remembered that on some occasions they would send a child out of a cave to ask for help, claiming there was a wounded woman or another child who needed assistance and wanted to surrender. Japanese soldiers would be waiting in the cave and attack the marines who entered.[37] Most marines learned to approach all caves with great caution, but even toward the end of the battle such tricks could take their toll on battle veterans with a lot of experience. Lieutenant Frederic Stott described a patrol from the 24th Marines on 5 July: "Using civilian men, women, and children as decoys, the Jap soldiers managed to entice a volunteer patrol forward into the open to collect additional civilian prisoners. A dozen men from A Company were riddled as the ruse succeeded."[38]

Despite the unfortunate results of that incident, Lieutenant Colonel Justice M. Chambers expressed his pride in marines who took these chances: "The thing that really got to me was watching those boys of mine; they'd take all kinds of risks; they'd go into a cave never knowing whether there would be soldiers in there, to bring out these civilians. The minute they got them out, they began to feed them, give them part of their rations, and offer their cigarettes to the men. It made you feel proud of the boys for doing this." Chambers himself was wounded in action on 22 June, but he returned to his unit—the 3rd Battalion, 25th Marines—the next day.[39]

The Japanese also utilized several kinds of decoys. Some were simple, some fairly elaborate. When marines came under attack originating from a dilapidated wooden building, they wondered why their return fire had no impact. When the outside of the building finally blew off, it revealed a concrete blockhouse inside that had simply deflected their bullets. Another time the marines noticed a Japanese scout with binoculars on a watchtower, but their fire had no effect. Later they discovered that the scout was a dummy, set up to draw fire to alert the Japanese to American positions. Sometimes a Japanese soldier himself was the decoy. When communications operator Tibor Torok awoke one morning, "lying about three feet away from me was a 'dead' Jap. His bayonet was about two feet from the edge of my foxhole. . . . From the corner of my eye, I saw his lips twitch. He was twitching to shoo a fly away from his mouth. . . . If I had slept for a few more minutes, I would have been bayoneted." Torok apprehended the soldier, "the first and only prisoner I ever captured!"[40]

While the marines took prisoners and sent them to a camp near Lake Susupe, the Japanese did not keep American prisoners of war. Gunnery Sergeant Keith Renstrom of Huntsville, Utah, served with F Company, 2nd Battalion, 25th Marines. He remembered watching a Japanese officer cut a marine in half with his sword. Renstrom was too far away to prevent that atrocity, but many marines reported similar actions by the enemy.[41] Of course, Japanese camps in the Philippines and other locations became notorious for their harsh and inhumane treatment of American prisoners.

Ironically, some marines appreciated Japanese aggressiveness, as it made the ultimate task of the Americans easier. While Sergeant Mike "Iron Mike" Mervosh considered the Japanese "excellent soldiers," he recognized that their determination not to be taken prisoner led them to fanatical and suicidal actions. If faced with death a Japanese soldier always tried to inflict injuries on the American forces, and usually to his own detriment. Some would tie explosives around their bodies and charge American tanks. As

Japanese soldiers emerged from caves and attacked marine machine guns, "we'd have a field day," exclaimed Mervosh.[42]

Often, when marines passed by Japanese bodies lying on the road they would fire a shot into them. What appears as gratuitous cruelty was in fact a necessary guarantee against Japanese soldiers who were pretending to be dead. Corporal M. F. Leggett made no apologies for these survival techniques: "Sorry, but that's the way life was. You shot first and done your thing to them before they done it to you."[43] Lieutenant Colonel Chambers encouraged his men to take those precautions: "Within the battalion my instructions were 'if it didn't stink, stick it.'" When passing this advice on to one of his officers, the response indicated that the situation had already been resolved: "[He] just laughed and said the Marines had bayoneted all the bodies. You had to do it!"[44]

Private First Class Bob Thatcher was fortunate to have followed that rule of war. As he passed a trench with two Japanese bodies in it, Thatcher sensed that something was wrong and shot one of them "through the head. He was playing possum."[45] Jerry Wachsmuth agreed: "when a situation didn't look right, you'd shoot them."[46] The Japanese also knew that the marines always returned to retrieve their dead buddies for burial. Marines had to check each dead body carefully for booby traps that might have been planted by enemy soldiers. In addition, as they retreated, the Japanese left mines that could be set as booby traps. In some cases, Japanese engineering units would tie a detonator into the ground so the mine would explode if pulled out. From the top the mine appeared to be safe, but any attempt to remove it would set off the special anchored detonator. The Japanese hoped that uninformed marines or soldiers would fall prey to this trick.

Collecting enemy souvenirs was one of the more popular—and dangerous—marine pursuits. Many marines coveted Japanese officers' swords, guns, flags, watches, and other items. Guy Gabaldon gained a reputation for capturing Japanese soldiers and also bragged about being a prodigious collector of Japanese memorabilia. He was successful in his first attempt to find souvenirs: "As I came down the hill I came across Japs and pieces thereof. I picked up two Seikosha watches for which the owners would no longer have use, two flags, crab meat, 'rock candy,' and two bottles of sake." One of Gabaldon's sergeants was not so fortunate: "Sgt. Ridgeway was bayoneted at the same trench I had been to. He and another marine were looking for sabers among the 'dead' Japs. Suddenly one of them comes alive and sticks his bayonet right into Ridgeway's gut." Ridgeway later died of his wound. Other souvenir pursuits were less dangerous but ultimately unjustifiable. The Japanese used a lot of gold in their dental work, and some marines collected gold fillings. "I was tempted to try to get some gold teeth I had spotted, but did not have anything to pull them with," recalled Gabaldon. "Maybe next time."[47] A few marines did perform this grisly action. When they entered Garapan, one member of the 6th Marines found a dentist's tool and used it to remove the gold from the teeth of dead Japanese soldiers. "He made some good money." Some souvenirs were even more gruesome—a few marines collected Japanese body parts: "We did some crazy things. We were only 18, 19, 20, so we didn't give a damn."[48]

As Gabaldon traveled across the island he continued to accumulate Japanese items. One night he and his buddy Lloyd Hurley were patrolling near a farmhouse with a cistern about eight feet deep. Three Japanese soldiers were hiding inside, but Gabaldon and Hurley killed them with grenades and gunfire. Gabaldon then jumped into the cistern in order to "get their diaries, watches, and stuff." Among the treasures was a lieutenant's .32-caliber sidearm. Gabaldon considered the pistol his most prized possession. "I used a shoulder holster and was the envy of one and all." Gabaldon also pinned on himself Japanese medals that he had taken off of dead soldiers: "What the hell, they didn't need them anymore."[49]

In any case, all of these items were considered war booty that would make nice trophies and impress friends and relatives back home. If a marine obtained several swords, he might sell them to the sailors on board ship. Occasionally a marine would create a collectible for a gullible sailor by shooting a bullet hole in a Japanese helmet and selling it as a battle memento. Navy corpsman Robert Winters remembered the value of those trophies: "We traded souvenirs to the pilots from the carriers, because they couldn't come ashore. We took Japanese helmets and shot a hole in the center. These were always good for meat, potatoes and bread."[50]

The marines who fought across the Pacific endured extraordinary daily hardships in addition to the tenacity of a determined enemy. Having grown up during the Great Depression, future marines had learned to deal with deprivation. Sandburg indicated that wearing the same clothes every day or using leaves for toilet paper was not unusual for his generation. While the physical and psychological toll on the individual marine was immense, most marines simply drove themselves forward. As Corporal Leggett observed, "we were all scared but you did what you were trained to do . . . we had a job to do and the only way to do it is to get it over with."[51]

CHAPTER ELEVEN

THE 27TH INFANTRY DIVISION ON SOUTHERN SAIPAN

The 27th Infantry Division was a New York National Guard unit until it was federalized in the fall of 1940. From that moment on, membership in the division diversified as draftees from other states were added to bring it to full strength. Following the attack on Pearl Harbor, the division was shipped to Hawaii to serve as a defense force on the outer islands. Originally composed of four regiments, the division was "triangularized" in 1942, divided into the 105th, 106th, and 165th Regiments. In 1943 the 165th Regiment led the assault on Makin in the Gilberts, and the next year two battalions of the 106th participated in the taking of Eniwetok in the Marshalls. As a result, only the 105th Regiment was mostly without battle experience at the time of the invasion of Saipan.[1] After November 1942, Major General Ralph Smith served as commander of the division.

The 27th Division left Hawaii early on 1 June 1944 and spent one week sailing to Kwajalein before the final debarkation for Saipan. As the floating reserve, the 27th faced a unique situation. While the marine divisions knew exactly what their mission would be, the army could find itself fighting on Saipan, Tinian, or Guam, depending on how each situation unfolded. As a result, "staff officers had to provide for a total of nineteen different operational plans."[2] Some sources claim that there were as many as twenty-two plans.[3] Not surprisingly, individual soldiers were confused by all of the contingencies they were forced to study. In the end, none of the tactical designs fit the actual deployment of the division.

Although American officers had discussed the problem of army versus marine tactics in advance, these issues had not been resolved before the ships left for the Marianas.[4] Holland Smith had expected a rapid victory that would not include the army, but when that quick conquest did not materialize the reserve forces had to be committed to the battle. Smith assumed that army officers would understand and execute his orders as if they were Marine Corps officers. When receiving orders from Smith, however, army officers implemented them in accordance with army training and principles. Smith never worked to resolve these differences. He was not pleased with the results, but he never understood his own role in the dispute.

As late as noon on 16 June, neither Smith nor naval command had determined whether the 27th would be deployed, but early in the afternoon the situation changed rapidly. The rushed decision to commit the 27th Division to Saipan was the result of two factors. First, while the marines fought valiantly on D-Day, they suffered heavy casualties and had not achieved their objectives for the first day. Committing the reserves to compensate for lost manpower was a logical action. Second, American submarines had sighted the Japanese fleet moving from the Philippines toward Saipan, and Admiral Spruance realized that a major sea battle was imminent. As a result, he felt that the troop transports holding the army regiments were vulnerable and had to unload their soldiers. On orders from navy officers, Ralph Smith sailed to the command ship, the *Cambria*, for a planning meeting. Unfortunately, confusing and incomplete communications between navy, marine, and army officers created a difficult situation. According to one of Ralph Smith's officers, Holland Smith was unprepared for the arrival of the army commanders and barked at the army leadership: "What the hell are you doing here?"[5]

Despite this rude welcome, Ralph Smith met with Rear Admiral Harry Hill, second in command under Turner, and with marine Graves Erskine, Holland Smith's chief of staff. They ordered the 27th Division artillery to move onto the island immediately to support the marines, with that action to be followed quickly by the landing of the 165th Regiment and then the 105th. Both regiments were ordered to assist the 4th Marine Division. For the moment the 106th Regiment would remain on ship as a possible reserve for the invasion of Guam. Reflecting the confusion prevalent at this moment, the order to land the 27th Division, minus the 106th Regiment, was sent to Ralph Smith's command ship, the *Fremont*, before Smith had returned to her. In addition, these broad instructions did not clarify or delineate the precise mission of the 27th. Nevertheless, Brigadier General Ogden Ross, the 27th Division's assistant commander, and Colonel Gerard Kelley, commander of the 165th Regiment, rapidly drew up plans to commit the 165th to battle. They decided that the 165th would land on Blue Beach 1, just south of Charan Kanoa, and then link up with the 4th Marine Division.[6]

General Ross left immediately for the beach to set up a command post and to find 4th Marine Division headquarters. Unfortunately, naval vessels between ship and shore had not been informed of his approach, and armed and potentially hostile American patrol boats stopped him several times. As a result it took him almost five hours to reach the beach. In addition, Ross had not been told exactly where 4th Division headquarters was located, and he spent several more hours before he found his destination. While Ross and his fellow army officers wandered the beach, the men of the 165th Regiment proceeded to climb down rope ladders onto their landing vehicles. The order to debark arrived at 1711, and the soldiers started over the sides within half an hour. The army planned to land the battalions of the 165th on Blue Beach 1 in waves, with the 2nd Battalion leading the way and the 1st and 3rd Battalions to follow.

The order to land came as a surprise to soldiers aboard ship. Private John Earley remembered cruising on his troop transport off the coast of Saipan on 16 June. He listened to the ship's public address system, which supposedly "kept us informed on the marines' progress. They kept telling us that all was well, and we did not expect to land." Of course, soldiers like Earley did not know that the marines were losing a lot of men in battle; nor were they aware of the pending Japanese naval action. Earley recalled that "all hell broke loose, horns blasting" at about 1800 on the evening of 16 June, and the soldiers were ordered to their landing stations. The result was "mass confusion" as the soldiers scrambled to gather their equipment and "go over the side down the heavy rope ladders" onto their landing vehicles. A rumor quickly spread that the marines were being pushed back and might lose the beachhead. Earley surmised that "their strategy of rush and bypass tactics leaving live armed Japs behind them backfired and they were being hit hard from the rear."[7]

Earley climbed down into his assault boat, crowded with other soldiers and mortars and shells. The landing vehicles moved away from the large ships and began to organize for the assault run toward the beach. Rather than move directly in the direction of the island, the boats moved in apparent circles late into the night. Shells from the naval batteries continued to slam into the island while flares overhead illuminated the chaotic scene. "I don't believe any of us thought we could survive this night." After seven hours in the water the landing vehicles hit the beaches, the soldiers already exhausted from this nerve-racking ordeal.

Two problems had impeded the progress of the soldiers. Due to the late start, it was dark by the time the soldiers were on the landing vehicles, and after the departure of the 2nd and 1st Battalions of the 165th, there were not enough amtracs available for the entire 3rd Battalion. Nevertheless, the 2nd and 1st Battalions started toward shore. Army historian Captain Edmund Love described the approach: "The three-mile voyage was made through almost total darkness, the only illumination being the gun flashes from naval support ships standing offshore."[8] Amtracs had to weave their way slowly through the dark sea and past hundreds of other ships and boats; many of them soon became lost. The darkness created another problem, as many amtracs could not find their way over or through the reef. "In most cases the coxswains finally tired of circling aimlessly, drove their boats up to the reef and ordered the troops into the water, where they waded ashore in water all the way from waist-to-neck-deep."[9] Instead of arriving as a unit on Blue Beach 1, the soldiers of the 165th Regiment were scattered all over the landing beaches in the middle of the night. The first few hours after landing were spent collecting and reassembling the men.

When Earley finally arrived on the beach, he immediately noticed all of the dead marines. "In the half light of the flares and exploding shells we could see the beach with bodies scattered all over. Dead Japs and Marines." Earley and his buddy Arthur "Red" Conlon scrambled onto land and jumped into a large shell hole. Falling asleep from exhaustion, Earley and Conlon awoke at daylight to discover that they had shared their refuge with two dead marines. Private Jack Cotton, another soldier with division artillery, had the same impression: "At dawn, it became apparent to me that we were surrounded by dead marines."[10]

Private Clifford Howe of Havre, Montana, served with C Company, 1st Battalion, 165th Regiment, and his first impression matched Earley's. After climbing into his landing vehicle, Howe expected to move toward Saipan immediately. Instead, his amtrac "circled for a couple of hours" and finally headed for the beach at about 0400 on 17 June. As he approached the battle, Howe "suddenly realized that I was at the very front of the boat, and when the ramp dropped, I was afraid that I was going to be the first casualty." Howe was lucky. He moved through the shallow surf until he could drop into the wet sand and advanced on his stomach. Howe served as a radio operator for Captain Paul Ryan, but Ryan was killed by a mortar that hit a rock next to him on the afternoon of 17 June.[11]

All units of the 165th Regiment were ordered to move to the far right (southern) side of the marine lines and prepare to attack in the direction of Aslito Airfield at 0730 on 17 June. Scattered as they were, the soldiers of the 165th made their way slowly down the beach, hugging the water line to avoid Japanese artillery as well as marine patrols that might mistake them for the enemy. After walking a few yards, the soldiers would drop to avoid incoming shelling; then they would repeat the process. The executive officer of the 165th, Lieutenant Colonel Joseph T. Hart, earned the nickname "Jumping Joe" because of "the number of times he led his men in dropping and getting up that night, and the name stayed with him for the rest of his career in the Pacific."[12] Despite these obstacles and a mostly sleepless night, the troops were in position and prepared to attack on command at 0530 on 17 June.

The 1st and 2nd Battalions of the 165th Regiment pressed the attack early that morning. Their goal was Aslito Airfield and Nafutan Point, the latter not far to the southeast of the airfield but across "heavy undergrowth and coral outcroppings."[13] The Japanese had almost fifteen hundred troops behind the airfield and another five hundred supporting them at Nafutan Point. While they conceded the airfield fairly quickly, the Japanese positioned themselves on the reverse slope of a ridge just to the south and east of Aslito. "This heavily defended ridge was the key to Aslito Airfield. As long as the ridge remained in Japanese hands, the airfield itself could not be safely captured or supplied."[14] While the landing strip was soon in American hands, the Japanese maintained a position that would allow them to shell American planes trying to use Aslito. The ridge and Nafutan had to be taken, but the Japanese had a lot of firepower in the Nafutan area: "A battery of four six-inch British Whitworth Armstrong guns was found on Nafutan Point. . . . A battery of three 140mm coastal defenses was found on the east slopes of Mt. Nafutan. . . . Like the six-inch guns on Nafutan Point, this battery had been effectively camouflaged with straw and painted canvas. . . . Three concrete revetments for Type 89 127mm dual purpose guns were found on Mt. Nafutan near a radar emplacement."[15]

Around noon on 17 June, an attack by the 165th Regiment against the ridge to the southeast of Aslito quickly stalled in the face of intense enemy fire. For two hours U.S. artillery bombarded the ridge from a distance. Like the naval barrage that preceded the invasion on 15 June, this artillery fire did little damage to the Japanese defense line. As in other confrontations, the Japanese should have held their defensive positions and forced the Americans to attack. Instead, consistent with their belief in taking the offensive, the Japanese counterattacked and absorbed heavy losses. Nevertheless, the 165th was forced to withdraw to establish a strong defense line for the night. The next morning the regiment resumed the attack and took the ridge with little difficulty, as the Japanese had already pulled back toward Nafutan Point to establish a defensive position there.[16]

As a result, Aslito Airfield was under American control on 18 June.[17] By 22 June army P-47 fighters started using the field, with seventy-four planes arriving within the next two days.[18] Without fear of enemy planes in the area, these P-47 Thunderbolts were able to provide important support for ground troops on Saipan. In the meantime, on 19 June the 165th Regiment and elements of the 4th Marine Division had reached Magicienne Bay on the east coast, effectively isolating the southern sector of the island.

On 17 June, while two battalions of the 165th Regiment were fighting for Aslito and Nafutan, the 105th Regiment and the remainder of the 165th landed. The 3rd Battalion of the 165th Regiment, previously stranded due to the lack of available amtracs, finally made it to the island, followed by artillery battalions and the 105th Regiment. The troops landed without incident, although once again many had to wade ashore in chest-deep water while trying to keep their equipment dry. Upon landing, the troops witnessed the carnage that had resulted from the previous days of fighting. Major Kenneth Dolan recalled that "what had once been the proud little town of Charan Kanoa was nothing but a shambles with twisted wreckage everywhere. There were plenty of dead Japs all around and the odor of the dead was beyond description."[19] Sergeant Felix Giuffre confirmed this view, remembering "bodies floating around in the water. Some of them were Japanese and some were marines and they were being evacuated from the beach."[20] In addition to the sights and smells of the casualties of war, the main problem was crowding on the beach, which prevented some of the supplies—especially communications equipment and vehicles—from arriving the same day as the troops. Then, due to the start of the Battle of the Philippine Sea on 18 June, all supply ships and transports were immediately ordered to leave the area. As a result, the 105th Regiment was left without essential equipment for one week.[21] Lieutenant John Armstrong from Troy, New York, executive officer of Headquarters Company of the 105th, remembered this difficult situation:

> Regimental Headquarters Company, 105th Infantry, was transported to Saipan on USS Cavalier, the ship that carried the 105th Infantry Regiment. The company disembarked in the late morning or early afternoon of June 17, 1944 (D-

Day+2). . . . During that evening of June 17th, the Cavalier put out to sea with our communications equipment, vehicles and some of our communications personnel still on board. We later found that the naval battle elements were heading toward the Battle of the Philippine Sea and the unprotected transports, as a safety measure, were ordered out to sea. I can remember 1st Lt. Walter Sluzas, Regimental Communications Officer, trying to beg, borrow or steal communications equipment. Despite Walt's efforts, we were seriously short of communications and other equipment, a situation that lasted for 8 days until Cavalier returned with the much needed cargo.[22]

The 1st Battalion, 105th Regiment, entered the battle for Saipan early in the afternoon on 18 June. Lieutenant Colonel William J. O'Brien of Troy, New York, commanded the battalion, and his previously inexperienced soldiers would eventually participate in some of the most intense fighting on Saipan. Remarkably, the untested 105th Regiment produced three Medal of Honor recipients during the Battle of Saipan.

As soon as they landed, the 1st Battalion, 105th Regiment, was ordered to fight its way eastward across the island. The soldiers made rapid progress on 18 June but ran into heavy Japanese defenses the next day. Concentrated in an area that the army called Ridge 300, the Japanese had dug several strong points and pillboxes that were dug into the hilly and rocky terrain. Soldiers had their own name for the area—"Bloody Ridge." On 19 June, in the face of withering enemy fire, soldiers of the 1st Battalion attempted to destroy those Japanese positions. Several soldiers volunteered to infiltrate enemy lines, only to become victims of machine-gun fire or grenades. Unfortunately, others were victims of friendly fire. Lieutenant Luke Hammond recalled that Lieutenant Norman Arnold's "head was sliced in half as if an ax fell on it" and that Private William Erbach had "his stomach torn up."[23] Toward the end of the day, Sergeant Thomas A. Baker of Troy, New York, attempted to clear the way forward as he moved along Ridge 300: "He then borrowed a bazooka from one of his comrades and, under heavy fire, walked boldly out into the fields that covered the ramp, and calmly knelt down and fired his weapon singlehanded into one of the dual-purpose-gun positions, knocking it out with his second round. Then he got up and walked back to his company with the bullets still landing around him."[24] Baker's subsequent Medal of Honor citation indicated that he had "dashed alone to within 100 yards of the enemy." His actions, "through heavy rifle and machinegun fire that was directed at him by the enemy," enabled his company to take this ridge.[25]

With the situation at the southern end of the island still unresolved,

Ralph Smith and his staff decided to commit three battalions—two from the 165th Regiment and one from the 105th—to the struggle for Nafutan Point. Another battalion of the 105th was also involved in the fighting but approaching from the south. Fighting raged all day on 20 June, with the soldiers moving steadily forward before halting for the night.

Both marine and army intelligence underestimated the number of Japanese defenders on the southern end of Saipan. An army report stated that there were no more than three hundred to five hundred enemy defenders left in that area. By the end of the day on 20 June, Holland Smith and his marine staff were convinced that the Japanese were nearly defeated in the Nafutan Point area. Based on erroneous information, Howlin' Mad issued Operation Order 9-44 on the morning of 21 June. The order called for one army battalion to "mop up remaining enemy detachments, maintain anti-sniper patrols within the garrison area [Nafutan Point] and along the coast line and protect installations within its zone of action with particular attention to Aslito Airfield." The rest of the 27th Infantry Division was to turn north to support the two marine divisions.[26] By the time Ralph Smith had received Holland Smith's order, the soldiers of the 165th and 105th Regiments were already on the move south to confront the Japanese in the Nafutan sector.

During the night of 20–21 June the Japanese used the cover of darkness to dig new fortifications, and at dawn the Americans saw "a formidable defensive position containing several machine guns and almost a company of riflemen that had not been in evidence the night before."[27] At first light the Japanese opened fire on the American lines, and several companies of the 165th were hit hard. The army responded with artillery, but the brief barrage did little damage to the Japanese defenses. Intense combat continued throughout the day, and American troops made little progress. The army called up tanks to support the 1st Battalion of the 105th, but again problems occurred. In the rugged terrain where battle lines were neither straight nor clear, at one point in the afternoon the tanks turned and began to fire toward their own men. Lieutenant Hammond "saw a dead corporal of A Company—later I learned killed by our own tanks."[28] Because Lieutenant Colonel O'Brien could not reach the tank crews by radio,

> [He] ran out through the hail of fire to meet them. He eventually stopped their movement by crawling up on the turret of the lead tank and banging on it with his pistol butt. This tank then called the other two on the radio and the movement and firing stopped. . . . Lt. O'Brien majestically sat up on the turret of the lead tank for the whole length of the advance, alternately firing his pistol, bang-

Figure 15. Combat troops taking cover behind tank; courtesy of Private Rod Sandburg (USMC).

ing down on the turret top with its butt to give directions to the men inside, and shouting encouragement to the infantrymen running along behind. The whole performance was carried out under considerable enemy fire.[29]

O'Brien's actions were matched by those of Sergeant Thomas Baker. Again acting alone, as he had on Ridge 300, Baker killed eighteen Japanese soldiers when he "took up a position in the rear to protect the company against surprise attack and came upon 2 heavily fortified enemy pockets manned by 2 officers and 10 enlisted men which had been bypassed. Without regard for such superior numbers, he unhesitatingly attacked and killed all of them. Five hundred yards farther, he discovered 6 men of the enemy who had concealed themselves behind our lines and destroyed all of them."[30]

Despite these events, Japanese resistance remained strong and determined. Finally in possession of Holland Smith's order, Ralph Smith realized that there was a problem because one battalion was not sufficient to clean out Nafutan Point. At 1700 on 21 June he called Holland Smith, explained the situation, and requested a modification in Order 9-44 that would leave all three battalions of the 105th Regiment in Nafutan while the 165th Regiment went north in support of the marines. Howlin' Mad agreed to leave two battalions of the 105th in combat with the third as a reserve. Following this conversation, as indicated by both Crowl and Love, Ralph Smith issued Order 45A, directing the 105th to "hold present front line facing Nafutan Point with two battalions," to reorganize the front lines by the next day, and then to continue "offensive operations against the enemy."[31] Several days later, Holland Smith criticized Ralph Smith for Order 45A, claiming that it mandated the troops to "hold" rather than attack. For Ralph Smith, the order to "hold" was a necessary transition in order to reorganize his lines.

During the night of 21–22 June the Japanese again dug new defenses, this time on the four-hundred-foot-tall Mt. Nafutan, whose "most prominent feature was the nose of Mount Nafutan, a sheer cliff splitting the battalion front like the bow of a ship. The cliff was not more than thirty feet high, but the approach to it was up a steep slope through the stubble of a cane field that offered no cover."[32] At dawn on 22 June the Japanese opened fire on G Company, 2nd Battalion, 105th Regiment: "The fury of the enemy concentration was almost unbelievable. Within the space of a few minutes Captain [Frank] Olander's company lost six men killed or mortally wounded and twenty-one other casualties."[33] As a result, the 105th lost ground. Army division headquarters then used most of the day to reorganize the front and reposition the 105th in an attempt to comply with Holland Smith's orders. Ralph Smith again consulted with the marine general. According to Ralph Smith, Howlin' Mad objected to the lack of progress in Nafutan and questioned the leadership ability of Colonel Leonard Bishop, commander of the 105th Regiment: "Colonel Bishop must not be permitted to delay. If he couldn't do it, to send somebody who could." The army general "pointed out difficult terrain and Jap positions in caves and said rapid advance was impracticable if undue losses were to be avoided and if Japs were to be really cleaned out. I said that continuing pressure would be applied and that I thought the Point could be cleaned up in a couple of days more."[34] After this conversation with Howlin' Mad, Ralph Smith ordered the 2nd Battalion, 105th Regiment, to continue its action against Nafutan Point. Shortly thereafter Holland Smith issued a similar order and then reprimanded Ralph Smith, telling the army general that the 2nd Battalion, 105th Regiment, was under marine jurisdiction and that Ralph Smith did not have the authority to give it any orders. The clash between the two generals was approaching a critical stage.

From this point on, the 2nd Battalion, 105th Regiment, had the task of clearing Nafutan Point—a terrain that was "mountainous, full of cliffs, crevices, and caves"—on its own.[35] Robert Sherrod, the *Time* magazine correspondent who visited the area, agreed with that description: "The southern end of the island was tough; the coral-rock formations provided natural caves, and the last 1,400 yards were laced with these jagged rocks and caves."[36] Thinly spread across twenty-five hundred yards, the army troops made little progress on 23 June. Again basing his orders on erroneous intelligence that indicated only a small Japanese presence in the area, Holland Smith ordered the battalion to move at dawn on 24 June and "to mop up remaining enemy detachments."[37] Howlin Mad's order to "mop up" suggested that he anticipated little difficulty for the army in this area.

At 0800 on 24 June, in response to Holland Smith's order, parts of the line pressed forward. In other areas company commanders waited until they had closed their lines and established closer contact with each other before proceeding, and in these sectors the advance did not start until 1130 or even 1330. Upset by this slow progress, Howlin' Mad personally called Colonel Bishop. Captain Mac Asbill Jr., aide to Holland Smith, reported on the conversation:

> "Colonel, this is General Smith. What's holding you up down there? Sure, the ground's rough but it's rough all over this island. That's no excuse. How many Japs are in front of you? Well, if there aren't any Japs, how the hell could you be held up?" Then the conversation changed to a monologue, "Now listen, Colonel. I want you to push ahead with your battalion and clean up that damned place. If you don't the Japs will break through and be all over the airfield. Now move out and take it. Do you understand."[38]

By the end of the day little headway had been made, but by then Ralph Smith was no longer in command of the 27th Division. On 24 June Howlin' Mad removed him from command of the 27th Division. Army major general Sanderford Jarman replaced Ralph Smith, and Jarman placed his own chief of staff, Colonel Geoffrey O'Connell, in charge of the attack on Nafutan Point. In order to accelerate the advance in the south, O'Connell quickly gave the 105th Regiment more firepower, placing two batteries of 90-millimeter antiaircraft guns and four 40-millimeter guns at the battalion's disposal. O'Connell also insisted on more aggressive tactics, and this approach was successful with the final clearing of Ridge 300 on 25 June.[39]

With Ridge 300 and Mt. Nafutan finally under American control, the defeat of the rest of the Japanese forces on the island's southern tip was imminent. Nevertheless, Captain Sasaki, the Japanese commander of the 317th Independent Infantry Battalion, a part of the 47th Independent Mixed Brigade, decided to attempt a dramatic breakout from his shrinking base. On 26 June he ordered his men to make a run for Hill 500, about six thousand yards north of his command post, where he hoped to find and join the rest of the 47th Brigade. Sasaki told his men: "The Battalion will carry out an attack at midnight tonight. After causing confusion at the airfield, we will advance to Brigade Headquarters in the Field [Hill 500]. . . . We will carry the maximum of weapons and supplies. The pass word for tonight will be 'Shichi Sei Hokoku' [Seven lives for one's country]." The wounded were ordered to stay behind and "defend Mount Nafutan," while soldiers too weak to "participate in combat must commit suicide."[40] Around midnight on 26–27 June, 409 Japanese soldiers moved forward in three columns. Under cover of darkness, all of the Japanese soldiers passed through the sparse army lines undetected, and at 0200 some of them attacked the command post of the 2nd Battalion, 105th Regiment. While the army troops suffered four killed and twenty wounded, they handled the attack well and killed twenty-seven Japanese soldiers. At 0400 another group of Japanese soldiers attacked Aslito Airfield and destroyed one P-47. A couple of other planes were damaged, but the Japanese soon retreated in the face of American fire. Several other American-controlled areas were hit, including Hill 500, where Captain Sasaki had expected to join his own units for a drive to the north. Instead, the Japanese ran into the 25th Marines of the 4th Marine Division and were wiped out in the ensuing skirmish.[41] By the evening of 27 June, Nafutan Point was in American hands. Rather than acknowledge the role and sacrifices of the army in this phase of the victory, Holland Smith gave all the credit to the Marine Corps: "The 14th and 25th Marines took care of Nafutan. Elsewhere my Marines were equally alert to enemy attack."[42]

The Japanese had been successful in inflicting casualties on the Americans as long as they used the rocky terrain and caves and waited for the Americans to take the offensive. Captain Sasaki had some good reasons for trying to break out of the Nafutan area. The Japanese position was clearly untenable, since reinforcements and supplies could not get through to his troops. American victory in the area was simply a matter of time. Nevertheless, once the Japanese emerged from their defensive outposts, they did not have a chance in the open against the superior numbers and firepower of the invaders. The American estimate of 300–500 defenders at

Nafutan had significantly underestimated Japanese strength, which had been closer to 2,000 at the beginning of the struggle and still approached 1,250 on 23 June. The Japanese breakout, combined with the mopping up of the southern end of Saipan by the 2nd Battalion, 105th Regiment, on 27 June, terminated the Japanese threat in this area. The speed of the army's advance, or lack thereof, has remained controversial. One army historian has judged the 105th Regiment harshly:

> Against these people [Japanese], the American drive was halting and slow. There was some justification for Holland Smith's lack of confidence in the leadership of the regiment, and later of the battalion, committed to cleaning up Nafutan. The attack of the infantry companies was frequently un-coordinated; units repeatedly withdrew from advanced positions to their previous nights' bivouacs; they repeatedly yielded ground they had gained. Whatever the extenuating circumstances, these facts could not fail to raise doubts about the aggressiveness and combat efficiency of the unit assigned to the mission.[43]

Another historian viewed the situation differently and did not criticize the 105th Regiment. Captain Edmund Love, who was with the 27th Division on Saipan and served as its official historian, emphasized the difficult terrain and the sacrifices of the previously untested troops. After assessing the number of Japanese defenders on Nafutan as well as the number of enemy dead, Love concluded: "These figures clearly refute the charge made against the battalion by one news magazine that it had failed dismally against a 'handful' of Japanese."[44]

Despite these allegations and the debate they engendered, army troops were on the verge of being deployed to one of the most hazardous areas on the island. The resulting battle would prove difficult, bloody, and again, controversial.

CHAPTER TWELVE

INTO DEATH VALLEY

While the battle for Nafutan Point was raging, army regiments were deployed as needed in support of the marines. When the 165th and 105th Regiments landed on Saipan on 16 and 17 June, the 106th Regiment, commanded by Colonel Russell G. Ayers, remained on board ship as a reserve. By 20 June the situation on Saipan warranted bringing the 106th ashore in anticipation of a major offensive in the center of the island. On 22 June Ralph Smith visited Marine Corps headquarters and met with Holland Smith's chief of staff, Graves Erskine. With the 105th still occupied on the southern end of the island, Smith and Erskine discussed a plan to move the 165th and 106th Regiments between the lines of the 2nd and 4th Marine Divisions. The army would take over the left (west) flank of the 4th Division and advance up the center of the island. Shortly thereafter, Ralph Smith explained the plan to his regimental commanders, Colonel Gerard Kelley of the 165th and Colonel Ayers of the 106th. The regiments of the 27th Division were to move forward on the morning of 23 June, find the 4th Division's front lines, which were approximately three miles north of the army base, and then attack from there at 1000.[1]

With the invasion of Guam postponed because of the Battle of the Philippine Sea, the 106th Regiment was released for deployment on Saipan. The regiment landed on 20 June and received orders to move toward marine lines. The 106th and 165th Regiments began their advance at 0530 on 23 June. The assault battalions of the 165th Regiment arrived

Figure 16. Admiral Raymond A. Spruance, Admiral Ernest J. King, Admiral Chester W. Nimitz, and Major General Sanderford Jarman on Saipan, 1944; U.S. Naval Historical Center photo.

on time, relieving the 24th Marines at 1000. Unfortunately, a problem developed with the deployment of the 106th Regiment toward its forward position. According to army historian Edmund Love, who accompanied the army troops at that time, the narrow roads were congested with 4th Marine Division supply traffic moving south while the 106th attempted to move north. The 3rd Battalion, 106th Regiment, under Lieutenant Colonel Harold Mizony, had mixed success as a result, with some of Mizony's companies on time and other companies arriving quite late. L Company, under Captain Charles N. Hallden, was half an hour early in relief of the sector held by the 25th Marines, but K Company, led by Captain William T. Heminway, arrived almost an hour late, at 1055. In addition to the confusion that had been caused by the few and narrow roads, another problem arose when army officers arrived at their line of departure and discovered that marine lines were at least three hundred yards behind the point indicated on their maps.[2] The soldiers had not been told that the marines had pulled back the previous evening to create a more defensible line during the night. Although marines had taken the correct action the previous night, the army companies were now in the difficult situation of being some three hundred yards behind their designated point of departure. Despite all of these problems, most of the attack companies of the 106th Regiment moved forward on time at 1000 (K or King Hour). Because K Company was almost an hour late, Lieutenant Colonel John McDonough's 2nd Battalion, 165th Regiment, had to wait before moving forward in order not to expose his unit's flank to enemy fire.[3]

The army confronted two major obstacles: the terrain and the Japanese. The soldiers had to advance into and across hazardous ground that they soon called "Death Valley," some of the most difficult territory the Americans faced on Saipan. Crowl described its features:

> The "valley" is really a terracelike depression on the eastern slope of the sprawling mountain mass that fills most of central Saipan and culminates in the towering peak of Mount Tapotchau. The floor of the valley, less than 1,000 yards in width, is dominated along its entire length by the rugged slopes of Mount Tapotchau on the west and a series of hills, the highest about 1,500 feet above the valley floor, on the east. This eastern hill system was to be called "Purple Heart Ridge" by the soldiers who fought there. Death Valley, then, was a sort of trough into which the men of the 27th Division were to advance. The valley itself was almost devoid of cover. . . . Obviously, this terrain was ideally suited for defense against any attack through the valley, and the Japanese made the most of it.[4]

As Love indicated, the Japanese held the high ground, and they could watch and anticipate American actions: "From his vantage point atop Mt. Tapotchau the enemy had excellent observation on the whole road network for a distance of two miles to the south."[5] Private John Munka of Akron, Ohio, remembered Death Valley as a kind of bowl about two or three hundred yards wide, with high mountains on one side and vertical cliffs on the other.[6]

This area in central Saipan was heavily defended by some of the best Japanese units remaining on the island. "Unknown to the American command, the Japanese had selected this area for one of their main defensive positions." The command post of the 31st Army under General Saito was situated at the northern end of Death Valley, and the 118th Infantry Regiment under Colonel Ito Takeshi, the 136th Infantry Regiment under Colonel Ogawa Yukimatsu, and the 9th Tank Regiment under Colonel Goto Takashi protected the valley. "Altogether a force of some four thousand men guarded the plateau. They had spent many weeks in placing their weapons and planning the battle that would be fought here."[7] The Japanese defenders used the caves and brush to conceal their weapons, and they employed this defensive advantage to wait for the American soldiers to reveal themselves before countering.

Colonel Albert Stebbins, the 27th Division's chief of staff, described the situation: "The cliffs and hillsides were pocketed with small caves and large caves. The wooded area was rough, filled with boulders, and excellent for defensive operations. . . . Well-placed, hostile guns fired only when lines passed and striking our forces in the rear disrupted the attack."[8] The Japanese were prepared for the American attack, and this time they wisely allowed the terrain to help their cause.

Holland Smith accommodated the Japanese by insisting that the army take the offensive and advance straight into the enemy stronghold. Army officers who were with their troops in Death Valley and saw the terrain privately questioned Howlin' Mad's tactics. Colonel Russell Ayers, commander of the 106th Regiment, believed that "if he had tried to advance rapidly across the open ground in front of him his regiment 'would have disappeared.'" Ralph Smith also felt that "any further pushing of troops in that zone would only lead to increased casualties, without accomplishing adequate results."[9] Nevertheless, the army was ordered to proceed. Eventually both Ayers and Ralph Smith lost their commands because of these differences with Holland Smith.

The alignment of the 27th Division placed the 106th Regiment on the west (Mt. Tapotchau) side of the valley next to the 2nd Marine Division, with the 165th Regiment to the east, closer to Purple Heart Ridge and tied into the 4th Marine Division. Despite their initial difficulties in relieving the marines on 23 June, the army moved ahead with its planned attack that same day and in most areas on time. The campaign did not go well and took an entire week to complete. L Company, 3rd Battalion, 106th Regiment, on the far left of the army lines (closest to the 2nd Marine Division), moved fifty yards ahead before it ran into enemy mortar fire coming from caves in a cliff wall a few hundred yards ahead. These caves "provided ideal spots for Japanese machine guns." Adding to the variety of descriptive names used by the soldiers, the troops called this cliff "Hell's Pocket." Despite incoming fire, the men continued forward until "an enemy mortar shell set off a Japanese ammunition dump and the flying debris kept the men pinned down for over an hour." L Company made little additional progress that day. Meanwhile, K Company, 3rd Battalion, 106th Regiment, which had arrived at 1055 and briefly held up part of the offensive, pushed ahead as soon as possible. By noon the company was stopped by machine-gun and mortar fire but continued to work its way forward into the shelter of some woods. Neither L nor K Company was able to advance to its goal or objective line that day.[10]

The situation was not much better along Purple Heart Ridge on the east (right) side of Death Valley. The first objective of the assault companies of the 165th Regiment was labeled "Hill Love," seven hundred feet tall, covered with trees, and, according to Crowl, "infested with Japanese." By the end of 23 June, A and C Companies (1st Battalion, 165th Regiment) had encircled Hill Love and then dug in for the night.[11] The two companies had basically moved back to where the marines had been the day before. Army historian Love noted the situation: "When the 27th Division took over the line next morning [23 June] they had to fight for the line of departure from which they were ordered to launch their attack. The fight took all day, and in the process the Division took heavy casualties. When the day's action concluded, Ralph Smith's men were in possession of the line from which they were supposed to have moved at 1000 that day, but they were not an inch farther."[12]

Hoping to push the Americans out of central Saipan, the Japanese launched an attack on the night of 23–24 June with two companies of infantry and six tanks. Soldiers quickly destroyed five of the tanks, but the lead tank continued to drive through American lines, as Love described it, "like a big, wounded, caged wild animal." Finally, a shot from its turret gun hit an ammunition dump close to the 3rd Battalion, 106th Regiment, and "as the shells began flying, the Japanese in the cliffs of Tapotchau unloosed a heavy concentration of mortar fire. Within twenty minutes the whole area occupied by the three line companies of the 3rd Battalion was an inferno. Four men were killed and 27 wounded."[13] A marine bazooka eventually knocked out the rogue tank.

Holland Smith was not satisfied with the army offensive on 23 June. In one sense, he was properly concerned. As the marines on the coasts advanced more rapidly than the army in the center, marine flanks became exposed. The marines were forced to slow down in order to maintain contact with army companies adjacent to them and prevent gaps from appearing in the American lines. "I considered the two Marine divisions on the flank were jeopardized by the sagging in the center of the line," Smith later wrote, "and I plugged the gaps between them and the Twenty-seventh. We made little headway that day. By nightfall my map showed our lines as a deep U, with the Twenty-seventh very little ahead of its departure point and still occupying the bottom of the U."[14]

While Smith was correct to worry about that configuration, in a more fundamental sense he did not live up to his obligation as head of the invasion force. He did not take the terrain into consideration as he looked at his map, and he made no effort to rethink his tactics in a creative way to account for the topography in the center of the island. Regardless of the situation faced by his troops, his tactics remained the same: direct assault into the face of the enemy's defensive position. Smith never reconsidered his strategic conception of how the battle might proceed, but instead blamed the army and especially its officers. Quoting his personal military hero, Smith observed: "As Napoleon has said, 'There are no bad regiments, only bad colonels.'"[15] Apparently Smith was not referring to his own leadership, but rather that of army officers. While the best generals develop contingency plans in case the situation on the ground necessitates flexibility, Howlin' Mad was not flexible.

Holland Smith ordered a general attack for 0800 on 24 June. Once again, the 165th Regiment was responsible for the series of hills that made up Purple Heart Ridge, while the 106th would move directly into Death Valley. The day did not go well, as the caves and ridges again provided excellent cover for Japanese defenders. Although some companies of the 165th advanced 150 yards on 24 June, others made less progress. The situation was similar for the 106th. Between 0800 and 0945 the troops had moved only fifty to one hundred yards against strong opposition, and as Crowl noted, "there was no sign of any abatement of enemy fire, especially from the cliffs of Tapotchau." Ralph Smith, feeling the pressure from Marine Corps headquarters but unaware that he was on the verge of dismissal, ordered his troops to push the attack: "Advance of 50 yards in one and a half hours is most unsatisfactory. Start moving at once." Captain Heminway's K Company responded and advanced. Crowl described the situation: "They had pushed forward fifty yards without event when the entire cliff on the left of the valley seemed to open up." Nevertheless, Heminway prepared to continue with the attack: "Just as he got up to wave his men forward again he was shot in the head and killed." At least eight other men were killed as well. The troops had to withdraw using a smoke screen. Crowl concluded: "Finally, about 1225, Colonel Mizony brought every weapon he had to bear on the Japanese positions along the cliff and in Hell's Pocket. Under cover of this fire the remainder of Company I was able to crawl and scramble back to the cover of the trees. For the day, casualties in Mizony's 3rd Battalion, 106th alone had amounted to 14 killed and 109 wounded."[16]

The army had little success in Death Valley on 24 June. Howlin' Mad responded with two actions—he removed Ralph Smith from command of the 27th Division and ordered the soldiers to proceed with the same plan the next day—a direct attack into the valley. Before his dismissal, Ralph Smith performed two tasks that Holland Smith had not: he spent most of 24 June with his troops on the front lines in order to investigate the situation firsthand, and he developed an imaginative plan for breaking the stalemate in Death Valley. His plan called for a flanking and encircling operation, with one battalion of the 106th remaining at the southern end of Death Valley to keep the Japanese in place, while the other two battalions of the 106th moved east and then north in order to surround the enemy. While Ralph Smith was being escorted off of Saipan on 25 June, Major General Sanderford Jarman, his replacement, implemented this plan of attack.

On 25 June, while the 2nd Battalion, 106th Regiment, under Major Almerion O'Hara, covered the southern end of Death Valley, the 1st and 3rd Battalions moved east behind the 165th and then north. The plan, which held the possibility of breaking the impasse in Death Valley, was poorly executed due to the caution of Colonel Ayers, commander of the 106th. Rather than follow the route across country that Generals Smith and Jarman had indicated, Ayers allowed his units to remain on roads; when his troops came under fire, they retreated to their point of departure at the beginning of the day. Their efforts at the southern end of Death Valley were therefore unsuccessful, and the offensive ended where it had started. An angry Jarman told Ayers "he had one more chance and if he did not handle his regiment I would relieve him."[17]

On 26 June, Jarman decided to focus on Purple Heart Ridge on the eastern side of Death Valley. This time the 3rd Battalion, 106th Regiment, under Lieutenant Colonel Harold Mizony, and the 2nd Battalion, 165th Regiment, under Lieutenant Colonel John McDonough led the way. While some progress occurred, a disturbing development at the southern end of Death Valley attracted Jarman's attention. Major O'Hara's 2nd Battalion, 106th Regiment, had not made any effort to advance throughout the morning. Ayers, as regimental commander, was held responsible. Jarman fulfilled his promise and replaced Ayers with Colonel Albert Stebbins, the division chief of staff.

Still looking for a way through Death Valley, Jarman implemented a new plan of attack for 27 June. While the 2nd Battalion of the 165th, now under Stebbins, continued its efforts on Purple Heart Ridge, Mizony's 3rd Battalion, 106th Regiment, was ordered to move north along that ridge and then turn left and cut west across Death Valley in the direction of Mt. Tapotchau. At the same time, the 1st Battalion, 106th Regiment, was to assault Hell's Pocket. Following a preparatory artillery barrage against Japanese positions on Purple Heart Ridge, the 3rd Battalion advanced by midmorning. The attack was a success—the battalion secured "Hill King" and was prepared to move west across Death Valley by noon. Crowl described the scene: "The terrain to the battalion front was a steep slope down into the valley proper. The descent would be made through thick, high tufts of grass for most of the way, and then through cane fields into a low ridge line that cut across the valley at that juncture. Directly to the battalion front, about a thousand yard away, were the cliffs of Mount Tapotchau."[18] The troops were subjected to cross fire as soon as they descended into the valley, but nevertheless they held their position despite being low on rations, water, and ammunition. The 2nd Battalion, 106th Regiment, soon joined them, and the units gained ground against the enemy. Jarman expressed his excitement over their progress: "Congratulations on a day's work well done. I have the utmost confidence in our continued success in a vigorous push against the remaining enemy. Keep up the good work."[19]

The promising developments of 27 June were not replicated the next day. When American supply vehicles arrived with food and ammunition, the Japanese used their fortifications on parts of Purple Heart Ridge, especially on "Hill Able," to fire into the valley. As Crowl noted, the vehicles "promptly dropped their supplies and scurried for cover." Company commanders sent patrols to recover the equipment, but an enemy mortar barrage quickly killed seven and wounded twenty-two from I and K Companies (106th Regiment). Casualties mounted in the afternoon when two Japanese tanks opened fire on the 2nd and 3rd Battalions, killing twelve and wounding sixty-one.[20] Private Munka recalled the incident:

> As our platoon moved into the valley, the Japanese opened fire and pinned us down. [Colonel] Mizony communicated to headquarters that his thirty-six men faced an untenable position. General Holland Smith was not complimentary in his response and the platoon was told to hold the line. When the Japanese deployed two tanks into the valley, the 3rd Platoon quickly knocked out both of them. The Japanese crew emerged to withering fire from the soldiers. Despite our success against the Japanese tanks, our platoon was cut off in the valley and trapped for over three hours, and most of the platoon was wiped out. We were in

an open bowl. We were sitting ducks in that bowl. We were pinned down. Finally everyone tried to get out of there and they were cut down. Most of them didn't make it out. Only four or five men of the original thirty-six were not casualties of this battle. We didn't stand a prayer.[21]

Colonel Mizony was not one of the lucky platoon members; he was killed in Death Valley on 28 June.

General Jarman had been a temporary replacement for Ralph Smith, and on 28 June the forty-nine-year-old Major General George Griner of Whitesburg, Georgia, arrived to take command of the 27th Infantry Division.[22] After reporting to Holland Smith, Griner immediately began an assessment of the deployment of his troops. The 3rd Battalion, 106th Regiment, decimated by battle losses, was relieved by the 1st Battalion, 106th Regiment, while the 3rd Battalion, 105th Regiment, was sent to join the 2nd Battalion, 165th Regiment, in the campaign for Purple Heart Ridge.

The 1st and 2nd Battalions of the 106th were now in Death Valley, with the depleted 3rd Battalion moved into reserve. On 29 June the army attacked Japanese positions again, and despite poor intelligence as well as friendly fire that impeded their progress, the troops had regrouped and made significant advances by early afternoon. Before the day ended the 106th Regiment had pushed forward almost a thousand yards, the largest one-day advance since the battle for Death Valley started. Purple Heart Ridge was finally taken the next day, 30 June, when the 2nd Battalion, 165th Regiment, moved toward Hill Able at 0715. The mission was accomplished two and a half hours later. At the same time, the 106th Regiment again made solid progress in the center of Death Valley, and by the end of the day the army had attained most of its objectives.[23] With the army in control of Death Valley and Purple Heart Ridge, the opening between army and marine lines had been closed. The U-shaped gap that worried Holland Smith had been eliminated, and all three divisions were in a line and prepared to complete the conquest of the island.

The 27th Infantry Division's slow progress in Death Valley has been subjected to much criticism. To assess the controversy, however, several factors must be taken into account. Death Valley, Hell's Pocket, and Purple Heart Ridge included some of the most difficult terrain on the island. Sending the soldiers directly into Death Valley, covered on both sides by hills and caves, subjected them to a withering cross fire. Unfortunately, Holland Smith did not develop a plan that accounted for the specifics of this locale. His tactics remained the same regardless of the situation—attack straight toward the enemy. Fortunately, frontline officers, both marine and

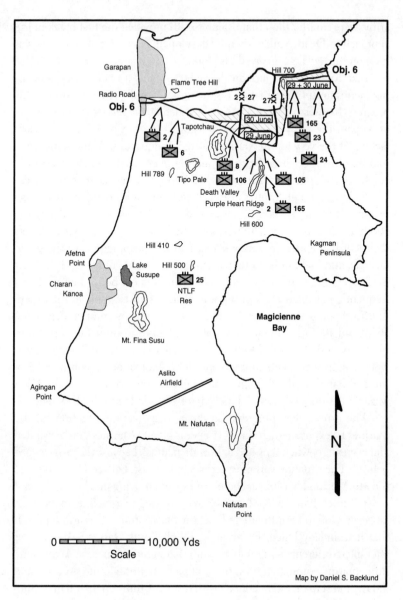

Map 8. Positions on 29–30 June

army, were smarter than that. Ralph Smith provided the first break in the approach to Death Valley when he developed a flanking plan, but he was fired on the day he conceived his plan.

Like Ralph Smith, Jarman showed originality and creativity in devising tactics to suit the situation on the ground, and Griner continued this progress. In assessing the leadership provided by the services in this section of Saipan, the army generals demonstrated the flexibility that was sadly lacking at the very top in Marine Corps headquarters. At the same time, marine officers leading their men along the coasts demonstrated similar creativity and ingenuity, caring for their troops as well as their objectives.

Following Ralph Smith's dismissal, Jarman made an important change in army leadership when he relieved Colonel Ayers, commander of the 106th, on 26 June. This action was justified, as a few companies in Ayers's regiment had appeared demoralized, had not been aggressive the previous day, and had not been prepared to advance that morning. Like their marine counterparts, however, other army officers performed well and frequently put themselves in the line of fire as an example to their men. As Crowl pointed out, "a total of twenty-two company commanders of the 165th and 106th Regiments were either killed or wounded in action during the period."[24] Colonel Kelley, commander of the 165th Regiment, was wounded, as was Lieutenant Colonel John McDonough, commander of the 2nd Battalion, 165th Regiment. Major Gregory Brusseau of the 165th was fatally wounded, and Colonel Mizony was killed in Death Valley.

The army's slow progress did create a dangerous situation for the marines by exposing their flanks to enemy attack. Marines were frustrated and even angry when they had to slow their attack because the army lagged behind. The situation was most serious in the east, between the army and the 4th Marine Division, as the marines were moving quickly up the east coast. Rather than solving the problem by moving marine lines to the west, however, Holland Smith ordered the army to continue the same approach that had already failed. Fortunately, Ralph Smith, Jarman, and Griner attempted different configurations until they achieved success. At the same time, marine commanders on the spot paid attention to the situation and did their best to maintain contact with the army units on their flanks. Sporadic contact between the army and the 2nd Marine Division on the west coast was also a problem, but there the rugged terrain accounted for the separation between the divisions even more than the lack of army progress. Faced with the difficult conquests of Mt. Tipo Pale and Mt. Tapotchau, the 2nd Division was also moving slowly.

Figure 17. Marines firing captured Japanese mountain gun at enemy positions; courtesy of Private Rod Sandburg (USMC).

The battle for Death Valley lasted a week, and the army, while not perfect in its execution of this phase of the campaign, performed well under the difficult circumstances. Simultaneously, the marines on the coasts were continuing to demonstrate their toughness and durability under harsh conditions. The 4th Division cleared Kagman Peninsula while the 2nd Division scaled Mt. Tipo Pale and Mt. Tapotchau. All three divisions fought hard and lost too many men. In one week the American forces lost almost four thousand men (3,987). Losses for each division were high: the 27th Infantry lost 1,465, the 2nd Marine Division suffered 1,016 casualties, and the 4th Marine Division lost 1,506. Each division fought through difficult terrain and faced a determined enemy. Despite the sacrifices of all the troops, Holland Smith credited only the marines with the victory in this area: "Continuous pressure exerted by the Second Division on the left and the Fourth Division on the right enabled the Twenty-seventh to clean up their sector."[25]

Although the Japanese inflicted heavy casualties, they suffered even greater losses themselves. According to American intelligence analysis of captured enemy messages, "the Japanese high command itself realized as early as D plus 5 that without reinforcements and lessening of our complete aerial supremacy their cause was hopeless." On 25 June, Lieutenant General Saito sent a message to Tokyo delineating the difficulties they now faced. In addition to a decrease in available frontline troops, the Japanese confronted serious shortages of food, water, medical supplies, and reserves. Saito's assessment was harsh and realistic:

> The fight on Saipan as things stand now is progressing one-sidedly, since, along with the tremendous power of his barrages, the enemy holds control of sea and air. In daytime even the deployment of units is very difficult, and at night the enemy can make out our movements with ease by using illumination shells. Moreover, our communications are becoming disrupted, and liaison is becoming increasingly difficult. Due to our serious lack of weapons and equipment, activity and control is hindered considerably. Moreover, we are menaced by brazenly low-flying planes, and the enemy blasts at us from all sides with fierce naval and artillery cross-fire. As a result even if we remove units from the front lines and send them to the rear their fighting strength is still cut down every day. Also the enemy attacks with fierce concentration of bombs and artillery. Step by step he comes toward us and concentrates his fire on us as we withdraw, so that wherever we go we're quickly surrounded by fire. . . . The attack of the enemy proceeds ceaselessly, day and night and as they advance with the aid of terrific bombardments it becomes apparent that the northern part of the island for the above-mentioned reasons of (1) water (2) food (3) supply (4) terrain can not be held, with our skeleton strength of 20%.[26]

As the Americans advanced toward his headquarters, Lieutenant General Saito was forced to move several times during the week of 23–30 June, eventually settling about twenty-two hundred yards north of Mt. Tapotchau. While the prospect of a Japanese victory was quickly fading, Saito sent his usual orders to the troops: "Positions are to be defended to the bitter end, and unless he has other orders every soldier must stand his ground."[27] Almost every Japanese soldier followed this command to "the bitter end."

CHAPTER THIRTEEN

GYOKUSAI

The unanticipated length of the Battle of Saipan put a terrible strain on the supply effort. By 1 July as the battle raged, the military was rationing some ammunition, and 81-millimeter mortar ammunition fell to dangerous lows. Fortunately, the troops were able to use captured Japanese mortar shells in American tubes.[1] Despite these shortages, the navy did an incredible job in supplying the troops with food, weapons, and other necessities.

Finally, the Battle of Saipan seemed to be nearing its end. The 4th Marine Division had cleared Kagman Peninsula and continued to move north along the east coast of the island. On 2 July, following an artillery barrage against enemy positions, the 23rd and 24th Marines led a new assault, with the 25th Marines added to the attack the next day. In all areas the American offensive advanced despite strong enemy opposition. As they moved north and then west, the 4th Division captured Hills 721 and 767, with C Company, 23rd Marines, leading the drive against the latter.

Despite their advances, there were times when the marines faced frustration rather than the enemy. The offensive against Hill 767 was a good example. On 3 July, C Company, 1st Battalion, 23rd Marines, was on a ridge on the left flank of the 4th Division, with the 27th Infantry Division to the left of the marines near the center of the island. As the 27th Division moved onto the ridge of the hill to relieve the marines, C Company hiked about two miles toward a gravel road and a promised ten-minute rest. Suddenly the marines were ordered to return to the ridge as quickly as possible.

Figure 18. Marines moving through battle zone, June 1944; courtesy of Private
Paul Schwartz (USMC).

"Because of the urgency of the situation we were alternately double timing
and forced march." Private First Class Orvel Johnson remembered the feeling of exhaustion, trying to move through the vegetation and heat while
carrying his "BAR, ammunition, grenades, machete, K-bar and regular
gear." The marines found several dead and wounded soldiers being tended
to by army medics on the ridge. They were victims of friendly fire: "A mortar barrage had been ordered to clear the areas ahead of the ridge of enemy
soldiers and that these troops had been caught in the open by their own
mortar shells that fell short and along the ridge and not forward of it."

The marines kept watch while the army removed the casualties, and
then C Company was ordered to occupy a hill that overlooked the ridge to
prevent the Japanese from seizing the high ground. Johnson and his squad
worked their way "down the steep bush and vine covered forward slope
from the ridge" and then up the equally dense incline to the nearby Hill
767. "It was necessary to use branches and roots to pull ourselves through
to reach the top," Johnson recalled. He and his buddies spent the night
on Hill 767, but the Japanese never came. The next morning the marines

were ordered off of Hill 767 and back to the original ridge, and Johnson recalled that they were

> relieved of the same position we had been relieved from 24 hours earlier. . . . In the 24 hours starting about noon on the 4th of July, C Company had been relieved from our position on the ridge. We had walked about 2 miles to where we rested for a few minutes. There we were ordered to return to the ridge and we ran most of the way back. We had resumed our defensive position but before nightfall had been ordered to send out a patrol to take and hold high ground beyond a deep jungle ravine. On the morning of the 5th of July, [we] had been ordered to retrace our steps to the ridge, where we were relieved for the second time and finally made our way back to the road where we had stopped for a ten minute break.[2]

The Japanese subsequently reoccupied Hill 767, forcing the 24th Marines to retake it on 5 July.

While the 4th Marine Division pushed north along the east side of the island, the 2nd Division was progressing on the west coast. Just as it had in central Saipan, the terrain played an important role. The 2nd Division had to contend with the mountains and ridges of Mt. Tipo Pale and Mt. Tapotchau. The 6th Marines had occupied Mt. Tipo Pale, and the 8th Marines, with the "bastard battalion" attached, had conquered Mt. Tapotchau. Moving up the coast, the 2nd Marines fought a fierce battle for the city of Garapan, finally taking it in the rain on 4 July. By then naval shelling had largely destroyed Garapan, but fighting within the city was difficult nevertheless.

To mark the approaching victory, General Holland Smith issued a Fourth of July message to the American forces:

> The Commanding General takes pride on this INDEPENDENCE DAY in sending his best wishes to the fighting men on Saipan. Your unflagging gallantry and devotion to duty have been worthy of the highest praise of our country. It is fitting that on this 4th of July you should be extremely proud of your achievements. Your fight is no less important than that waged by our forefathers who gave us the liberty and freedom we have long enjoyed. Your deeds to maintain these principles will not be forgotten. To all hands a sincere well done. My confidence in your ability is unbounded.[3]

Following this pronouncement, Smith ordered the attack to resume at noon on 5 July.

Like the original landing strategy, which envisioned using the 2nd Marine Division as a hinge, the new plan called for the 4th Marine Division and the 27th Infantry to pivot around the 2nd Division and move west across the island and toward the coast north of Garapan. Once the operation had been completed, the 2nd Division would be relieved and placed in reserve for the planned invasion of Tinian. The army, now making much better progress than it had in Death Valley, turned left toward the west coast and met the 2nd Division at Flores Point. The 105th Regiment advanced up the coastal plain, while the 165th Regiment remained in the hilly interior. The 2nd Battalion, 105th Regiment, moved along the beach, checking all the abandoned Japanese defensive positions. When the 2nd Battalion came under enemy fire, soldiers were forced to hold their positions for the night. On their right, the 3rd Battalion, 165th Regiment, was also pinned down by machine-gun fire and could not advance as far as had been hoped. General Griner ordered an attack on 6 July at 0700. He wanted the 105th and 165th to push their lines toward the village of Makunsha by 0900. Mindful of the fate of Ralph Smith and the reputation of his troops, he insisted that "the early advances will be pushed aggressively."[4]

The 4th Division also swung west on 5 July, crossing north of the army and reaching the coast near Tanapag. In the process, the 24th Marines occupied a strategic area around Karaberra Pass, while the 25th Marines were ordered to advance twenty-five hundred yards over difficult ground. "The heat and the humidity were terrific, however, and the long hike resulted in many heat exhaustion casualties."[5] While the marines accomplished their objectives for the day despite these difficulties, they still found themselves only at the O-8 line after twenty days of fighting. Nevertheless, the new troop alignment left the 2nd Division in Garapan, guarding the coast to Flores Point, where the army took over the lines. The 4th Division held the coast north of the army.

On 6 July the planned offensive by the 105th Regiment at 0700 ran into immediate trouble. After skirting a minefield, the soldiers came under attack from Japanese troops hidden in a ditch 150 yards to the north. While a platoon of engineers attempted to disarm or bury the mines, tanks arrived to assist the infantry. One tank caught its tracks on a railroad bed, impeding the progress of all the tanks. Unfortunately, nearby American mortar teams were short of ammunition and their fire could not be deployed.

In midafternoon, three army tanks "in search of a mission" appeared in the vicinity, and Lieutenant Willis K. Dorey from Newton, Kansas, brought the ditch into sight: "Dorey moved to the ditch unhampered by antitank fire and found a tanker's dream target. Japanese soldiers were jammed along the ditch, almost shoulder to shoulder. . . . Using machine guns and

Figure 19. Marines cover advance into Tanapag, July 1944; courtesy of Private Joe DeLeo (USMC).

cannister on the tightly-packed foe, Dorey slaughtered from 100 to 150 as he blasted the ditch from end to end."[6] With the ditch clear, the 105th could again advance. Earlier in the day Dorey had performed a similar service for the 3rd Battalion, 105th Regiment, when it was slowed by enemy fire from a palm grove. Dorey and his fellow tankers had destroyed the two enemy machine guns holding that part of the line as well.

K Company of the 3rd Battalion experienced a frightening event that same afternoon. As the troops of K Company moved forward, Japanese soldiers watching them from above started down from the cliffs. Suddenly the Japanese soldiers began to explode, "hurling Japanese and pieces of Japanese in all direction. The terrific concussion knocked most of the men of Company K off their feet. . . . The most plausible explanation seems to be that the leading Japanese of the counterattack group had blundered upon a mine, detonation of which set off a number of others."[7] Even for battle-hardened soldiers, the sight of body parts flying through the air was difficult to bear. The Japanese troops, running out of officers, probably had not been warned of the location of their own minefield.

Japanese forces faced imminent defeat. Their supply situation was desperate, and they were virtually out of food and water. A Japanese report on 28 June had acknowledged their growing desperation: "In our front line units, the troops have been three days without drinking water but are holding on by chewing the leaves of trees and eating snails." On 30 June, for the sixth time, General Saito was forced to move his command post, this time to a cave in Gokuraku Tani (known to the Americans as Paradise Valley), not far from Makunsha.[8] Clearly, what Saito had called "the bitter end" was approaching, and he was faced with surrender or annihilation. He chose the latter for himself and his remaining seven thousand soldiers.

Saito planned a final mass attack of all remaining Japanese forces on the island. According to the subsequent testimony of a Japanese officer, Saito had not eaten or slept well for a couple of days when he and Vice Admiral Nagumo met on 5 July. By this time, under intense American naval bombardment as well as the threat of imminent attack by marine and army forces, the Japanese leaders knew that "there was no hope for success." The commanding officers held a ceremonial dinner of canned crabmeat and sake and then prepared themselves for death. The next morning all Japanese officers received the following message:

> I am addressing the officers and men of the Imperial Army on Saipan. For more than twenty days since the American Devils attacked, the officers, men and civilian employees of the Imperial Army and Navy on this island have fought well and bravely. Everywhere they have demonstrated the honor and glory of the Imperial forces. I expected that every man would do his duty.
>
> Heaven has not given us an opportunity. We have not been able to utilize fully the terrain. We have fought in unison up to the present time but now we have no materials with which to fight and our artillery for attack has been completely destroyed. Our comrades have fallen one after another. Despite the bitterness of defeat we pledge "seven lives to repay our country."
>
> The barbarous attack of the enemy is being continued. Even though the enemy has occupied only a corner of Saipan, we are dying without avail under the violent shelling and bombing. Whether we attack or whether we stay where we are, there is only death. However, in death there is life. We must utilize this opportunity to exalt true Japanese manhood. I will advance with those who remain to deliver still another blow to the American Devils and leave my bones on Saipan as a bulwark of the Pacific.
>
> As it says in the *Senjinkun* [Battle Ethics], "I will never suffer the disgrace of being taken alive" and "I will offer up the courage of my soul and calmly rejoice in living by the eternal principle."
>
> Here I pray with you for the eternal life of the Emperor and the welfare of the country and I advance to seek out the enemy. Follow me![9]

According to Major Yoshida Kiyoshi, an intelligence officer of Japan's 43rd Division who was captured on 9 July, runners delivered Saito's message to all remaining units at 0800 on 6 July. Japanese soldiers and civilians believed that the order for this mass suicidal attack had come from the emperor, and in such cases the banzai, which could be ordered by a local commander, was transformed into a "Gyokusai" ("To Die with Honor"), which only the emperor could order. While it was unlikely that this command truly originated with Emperor Hirohito, Japanese survivors later confirmed that they had acted with that conviction. The final offensive took on a special meaning for the participants, who were convinced that their sacrifice was in homage to the throne. It was their honor and duty not only to die but also to take seven American lives in the process. Nevertheless, as Lieutenant John Armstrong of the 105th Regiment commented: "If I found myself looking at a large number of enemy troops screaming 'Banzai' while charging my unit, I don't believe I'd care whether it was the Emperor or the local commander who gave the order."[10]

As Major Yoshida reported, Saito felt that "he was too aged and infirm to be of use in the counter-attack" and prepared his own suicide. Seated on a rock and facing east, the general shouted "Tenno Heika! Banzai!" ("Long live the Emperor!") and then cut into an artery with his sword. At that moment his aide shot him in the head. In a nearby cave, Nagumo and Rear Admiral Yano Hideo, his chief of staff, performed the same ritual. Some sources indicate that both Saito and Nagumo committed ritual suicide before being shot, while others suggest that Nagumo simply shot himself. Both bodies were cremated.[11]

While Saito and Nagumo prepared for an honorable death, Japanese soldiers, sailors, and civilians began to gather in the fields, hills, and woods north of the American lines near Makunsha. By nightfall on 6 July all able-bodied Japanese soldiers were moving toward the rendezvous points. According to some reports, anyone who was unable to walk to the assembly grounds was shot or allowed to commit suicide. Some soldiers carried rifles or pistols, but others improvised and armed themselves with knives, swords, grenades, pikes, bamboo poles, and even tree limbs with bayonets attached. Those who started the offensive with crude spears often picked up the rifles of their slain comrades and continued the charge; in some cases they grabbed American weapons and turned those on the U.S. forces. As more and more Japanese gathered, the Americans began to hear the noise and launched artillery shells toward the enemy. The 27th Infantry

Figure 20. Dead Japanese soldier near destroyed tank in June 1944; courtesy of
Private Ralph Browner (USMC).

artillery battalions fired 2,666 shells during the night of 6–7 July. According to army historian Edmund Love, the Gyokusai, originally planned for
2200, had to be postponed for several hours due to the damage caused by
this shelling. Love called the use of army artillery "extremely effective"
and, although "it caused no great casualties after the first few shells, it
completely disorganized the advancing column." Marine Corps historian
Hoffman offered a different view. He praised army artillery for firing 2,666
shells in one hour—more than forty-four rounds per minute—but claimed
that the shelling occurred after the Gyokusai had hit the American lines
early that morning.[12] It is impossible to reconcile these differences in timing, and army and marine witnesses continue to disagree on this and other
details.

During the afternoon of 6 July, 27th Division headquarters ordered
Lieutenant Colonel William J. O'Brien's 1st Battalion, 105th Regiment, to
move out of reserve and toward the front lines. Although O'Brien was concerned that his men would not have enough time to establish a defensible
line before dark, he ordered his troops forward, and his battalion continued
to advance north until early evening, when they dug in for the night to the

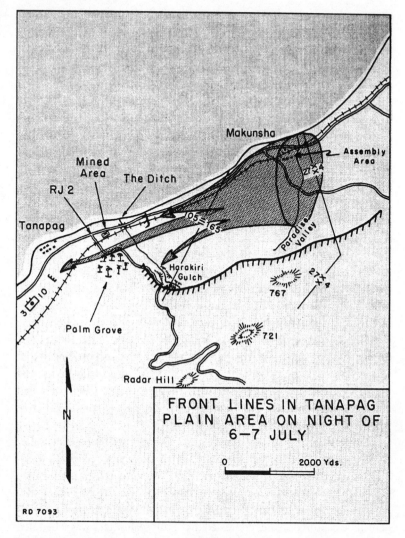

Map 9. Positions at time of Gyokusai, 6–7 July; the location of the 10th Marines (artillery) is disputed by many marine participants.

east of the railroad tracks. At the same time, Major Edward McCarthy's 2nd Battalion, 105th Regiment, also prepared its defensive line for the night. McCarthy was positioned closer to the water, straddling the coast road that ran fifty yards from the beach. Fifty yards farther east were the railroad tracks, and on the other side of those tracks was O'Brien's 1st Battalion.

The 1st and 2nd Battalions of the 105th Regiment were the frontline units on the evening of 6 July. They were deployed approximately twelve hundred yards south of Makunsha, where the Japanese were gathering in force, and fourteen hundred yards north of Tanapag. Four hundred yards south of that town was a creek that ran east for three or four hundred yards. The regimental command post of the 105th was another four hundred yards behind (south of) the creek—called "Bloody Run" by the Americans—and in a location that would play a major role in defending against the Gyokusai. Finally, the 3rd Battalion of the 10th Marines (part of the artillery support for the 2nd Marine Division) was located northeast of the 105th command post a short distance behind the front lines. These marines would also confront the Gyokusai on 7 July.

There is considerable disagreement about how much the army and marines knew about Japanese plans that night. By the evening of 6 July, American forces realized that the enemy was planning an offensive, but the exact nature of that action remained unclear. When O'Brien had led his 1st Battalion forward that afternoon, the supply officer provided them with provisions for a "normal combat situation. No one had any idea at the time that the Japanese were about to launch the biggest Banzai attack ever mounted against American troops in the Pacific campaign."[13] Two officers concurred with this view. Sergeant Frank Cimaszewski of the 106th Field Artillery stated that "before the Banzai charge, we got a report that all that was left was mop-up operations." Similarly, Sergeant Ronald Johnson at the 105th command post asserted that "the intelligence which they had before Banzai attack was that Japanese had been reduced to a small force incapable of withstanding an attack."[14]

Edmund Love, who interviewed most of the survivors immediately after the Gyokusai, indicated that the frontline battalions had received a warning from a captured Japanese prisoner the evening of 6 July. Intelligence Officer (S-2) Luther Hammond of the 1st Battalion, 105th Regiment, also recalled a Japanese prisoner informing his battalion that action was imminent. The captured soldier confessed that a full-scale attack was scheduled for that night, and the soldier and his information were conveyed to 27th Division headquarters.[15] Near the front line, Sergeant Erwin "Mark" Marquardt of the 27th Cavalry Reconnaissance Troop (mechanized) also knew that "something was going to happen."[16] Accordingly, Lieutenant Colonel William M. Van Antwerp at the division command post alerted Brigadier General Ogden J. Ross, assistant division commander, of the prisoner's confession. Van Antwerp alerted Marine Corps headquarters and army division artillery, "followed by notifying each of the infantry regiments, specifically ordering them to alert their battalions. . . . At shortly after 2100, both battalion commanders received the message that they must be ready to repel a counterattack." At 2330 Van Antwerp called Marine Corps headquarters for the second time with an update of the situation and urged that "all units should be particularly alert."[17]

As Love described the situation: "The 1st and 2nd Battalions had already, at this early hour, become aware of excessive enemy activity to their front."[18] The frontline battalions could hear the noise of the gathering Japanese troops. According to First Sergeant Mario Occinerio in the 1st Battalion, "we began to hear this buzz. It was the damnedest noise I ever heard. . . . It kept getting louder and louder."[19] O'Brien and McCarthy discussed the situation, and defenses were tightened between the 1st and 2nd Battalions. O'Brien moved his machine guns toward the railroad tracks. Despite their precautions, however, both commanders knew that gaps existed in their lines. Neither had the manpower to cover either the small openings or the large and dangerous gap of 400–500 yards between O'Brien's 1st Battalion and the 3rd Battalion, 105th, to the east. As Luther Hammond recalled, "normally the battalion established a perimeter defense for the night, with soldiers facing outward in a kind of circle to protect the unit. Nevertheless, there were not enough men to create a solid defense line and the perimeter was not closed on all sides."[20] The Japanese sent patrols to probe the front lines and discovered these gaps in the American defenses. At this time O'Brien called regimental headquarters to ask for reserves, and Lieutenant Colonel Leslie M. Jensen contacted division headquarters and raised the issue. As Love reported, the request was denied: "There were no reserves available. The matter was dropped. It was now 2150."[21]

This denial appears to have been a major error, as the Japanese would penetrate between the 1st and 3rd Battalions and then surround and virtually annihilate the 1st and 2nd Battalions. In practice, however, plugging the gaps after dark would have been difficult if not impossible. All battalions were stretched thin by this time, and the only solutions would have involved swinging the 3rd Battalion, 105th Regiment, toward the 1st Battalion or trying to bring up other army or marine units. The 3rd Battalion was on high ground looking down on the plain, a defensive stronghold that would have been problematic to abandon and a position that ultimately saved this unit during the Gyokusai. Other army and marine battalions were not close enough to move, especially at night. In any case, by this time most American commanders considered the Japanese a defeated force; they preferred to save their troops for future battles.

While American units pondered the meaning of the warnings they had received, the Japanese continued to gather to the north of the American lines. By the early morning of 7 July they were ready to attack in the name of the emperor. According to Major Yoshida, "They knew at the outset they had no hope of succeeding. They simply felt that it was better to die that way and take some of the enemy with them than to be holed up in caves and be killed."[22] Sake was widely distributed. At 0400 thousands of Japanese soldiers moved toward the frontline battalions of the 105th Regiment. By 0445 the Gyokusai had reached the perimeter of the American lines and, as Love noted, "literally ran over the 1st and 2nd battalions." McCarthy described the situation: "These Japs just kept coming and coming and didn't stop. It didn't make any difference if you shot one; five more would take his place. . . . The Japs ran right over us." Another perspective was offered by Technical Sergeant J. F. Polikowski, who observed the onslaught from a distance: "There were so many of them you could just shut your eyes and pull the trigger on your rifle and you'd be bound to hit three or four with the one shot."[23]

The 1st and 2nd Battalions were simply overwhelmed by the number of Japanese attackers. The fighting quickly degenerated into hand-to-hand combat, with each soldier fighting for his life against an enemy willing to sacrifice his own. After only twenty-five minutes, the American troops were suffering from a loss of officers and leadership, a shortage of ammunition, and a depletion of weapons, as rifles of those killed were taken out of the battle or picked up by the attackers. Of course, American soldiers also used the weapons of their fallen comrades, but the situation deteriorated rapidly as organization collapsed. Those who remained alive were forced to seek shelter or cover and began to move back in an attempt to regroup. As soon as they established a new position, however, hundreds of additional Japanese attackers would run over or through them and they would be forced to retreat again looking for defensible ground.

Several hours later, close to 0800, a new perimeter defense was set up in and around Tanapag. McCarthy was one of several officers who helped organize this defensive position, which was subsequently known as the Second Perimeter. Love praised the response of the soldiers: "For the next four hours this group of men put up one of the great defensive fights in American history."[24] The healthy and wounded alike—a total of only a few hundred men remaining from both frontline battalions—participated in the holding action. Desperate for ammunition and medical supplies, McCarthy organized a volunteer unit to make a run for regimental headquarters to seek assistance. Tragically, the entire coastal plain was under observation by American battalions that were too far away to see any details of the ensuing battle. Assuming that whatever moved in the valley below was Japanese, they opened fire on their own soldiers. The marines and army blame each other for this shelling, but for the men caught in the friendly fire the source did not matter. As Hammond noted, "American artillery could not distinguish friend from foe."[25] Love described the result: "The men, panic-stricken and without leadership, stampeded like a herd of cattle. There seemed to be no place else to go and most of them headed for the water." Other American soldiers, seeing this group swimming out to sea, joined them and headed for the reef. About seventy men eventually made it to safety there, where American boats picked them up. Approximately twenty-five other men started into the water and turned back. They established another defensive position near the creek they called Bloody Run, later called the Little Perimeter, with a group eventually totaling about seventy-five men. Love continued: "The two American perimeters can best be described as islands amidst a sea of Japanese. At all times this sea threatened to engulf the islands."[26]

While McCarthy fell back to Tanapag and valiantly organized the Second Perimeter, Lieutenant Colonel O'Brien tried to hold the 1st Battalion together at the front. A large number of Japanese attackers broke through the five-hundred-yard gap separating O'Brien's men from the 3rd Battalion to his east. Some of the Japanese soldiers then turned, surrounded the 1st Battalion, and attacked from the rear. With bullets and bodies flying everywhere, the battlefield turned chaotic. Hammond fired until he ran out of ammunition; then, realizing that he was badly wounded with a head injury, he walked toward an aid station. After receiving basic medical attention, he returned to the battle. He jumped into a shallow hole where O'Brien was operating a light machine gun. When the gun ran out of ammunition, Hammond drifted across an open field toward the beach. Unfortunately, this field was hit by friendly fire, the source of which remains uncertain. Hammond found another abandoned machine gun, but the feeding mechanism was jammed. Light rain and muddy conditions caused some weapons to fail, sand and dirt making many of them useless. Hammond continued to move, firing any weapon he could get his hands on. Other frontline soldiers helped in any way they could. Sergeant Marquardt drove halftracks loaded with ammunition and water to the soldiers and removed the wounded on his trips to the rear.[27]

On the battlefield, O'Brien tried to call headquarters to apprise them of the situation while simultaneously attempting to rally his troops. When some soldiers retreated to more defensible positions, O'Brien moved forward and urged his battalion to fight on. Carrying a pistol in each hand, he ran back and forth along the front line, serving as an example for all his men. Although seriously wounded by a bullet that penetrated his shoulder, O'Brien refused to leave the battle scene. Even as he was being bandaged he continued to shoot with one hand, and then ordered those around him to run for cover. Shouting "Don't give them a damn inch" as he fired at the enemy,[28] he finally "ran to one of the jeeps parked in the middle of the battalion perimeter, jumped aboard and manned the .50-caliber machine gun mounted on it. By this time he was surrounded by a large group of enemy who were trying to get at him. These he mowed down with his machine gun until it, too, ran completely out of ammunition. Then he grabbed a saber from one of the group of Japanese and continued to stand on the vehicle, flailing away at his assailants until he was literally cut to pieces. Around his body lying beside the jeep, lay thirty dead Japanese."[29] For these and other actions performed during the Battle of Saipan, O'Brien was awarded the Medal of Honor posthumously.

O'Brien was not the only soldier to die heroically that day. Another member of the 1st Battalion, Sergeant Thomas Baker, despite having part of his foot blown off by a Japanese grenade, remained on the front lines and fought until he ran out of ammunition. He used his empty weapon as a club in hand-to-hand combat until another American soldier grabbed him and carried him about 150 yards to the rear for safety. When that soldier was wounded, another one took Baker and moved him thirty more yards toward the railroad tracks. After the second soldier was also wounded, Baker refused to be moved again. He asked to be propped up against a pole and requested a cigarette and a pistol. The gun had eight bullets. "When last seen alive, Sgt. Baker was propped against a tree, pistol in hand, calmly facing the foe. Later Sgt. Baker's body was found in the same position, gun empty, with 8 Japanese lying dead before him."[30] In his other hand was a partially burned cigarette. Baker was awarded the Medal of Honor posthumously.

O'Brien and Baker, one a lieutenant colonel and the other a sergeant, were trained in combat and mentally prepared to sacrifice for their men. Captain Ben Salomon was a dentist from Los Angeles, but in the army he served as a regimental surgeon assigned to the 2nd Battalion on the day of the Gyokusai:

In the first minutes of the attack, approximately 30 wounded soldiers walked, crawled, or were carried into Captain Salomon's aid station, and the small tent soon filled with wounded men. As the perimeter began to be overrun, it became increasingly difficult for Captain Salomon to work on the wounded. He then saw a Japanese soldier bayoneting one of the wounded soldiers lying near the tent. Firing from a squatting position, Captain Salomon quickly killed the enemy soldier. Then, as he turned his attention back to the wounded, two more Japanese soldiers appeared in the front entrance of the tent. As these enemy soldiers were killed, four more crawled under the tent walls. Rushing them, Captain Salomon kicked the knife out of the hand of one, shot another, and bayoneted a third. Captain Salomon butted the fourth enemy soldier in the stomach and a wounded comrade then shot and killed the enemy soldier. Realizing the gravity of the situation, Captain Salomon ordered the wounded to make their way as best they could back to the regimental aid station, while he attempted to hold off the enemy until his patients had made it to safety. Captain Salomon then grabbed a rifle from one of the wounded and rushed out of the tent. After four soldiers were killed while manning a machine gun, Captain Salomon took control of it.

According to reports, Salomon fired the gun so quickly that dead Japanese kept piling up in front of his gun and obstructing his view. He had to move the gun at least four times in order to maintain a field of fire. "When his body was later found, 98 dead enemy soldiers were piled in front of his position."[31] After a long campaign by his fellow soldiers to have his actions recognized by the U.S. government, Salomon was finally awarded the Medal of Honor posthumously in 2002.

It is extraordinary that one regiment, the 105th, produced three Medal of Honor recipients from one battle. Clearly, O'Brien, Baker, and Salomon were not the only heroes of that day. Many soldiers were wounded multiple times and fought on as best they could, often without ammunition. Others, despite being wounded themselves, attempted to carry or drag their wounded comrades to safety. In some cases units of soldiers chose not to seek cover. An eight-man squad from B Company of the 1st Battalion stood their ground even after their ammunition was exhausted. They fought with whatever they had, hand-to-hand, and they all died together, leaving a pile of thirty enemy killed in front of them.[32]

The Gyokusai violated the rules of battle as all lines between combatants disappeared; some soldiers described it as being in the middle of a stampede. The troops of the 1st and 2nd Battalions had to move back as the enemy moved past them, but their actions were not indicative of a headlong retreat. Rather, as Lieutenant Joe Meighan of Troy, New York, remembered, "overwhelming force of enemy running through our perimeter caused our GI's to get up and run with the enemy and fight on the move. I'm sure you can visualize a person in the prone position has no chance, and to run and find comrades is a maneuver to resist enemy and form pockets of resistance at the first opportunity." According to Meighan, "this action was not a wild and unorganized retreat but a maneuver to regroup, resist the attack, and form pockets of resistance as soon as possible."[33]

Soldiers established pockets of resistance in the Second Perimeter and the Little Perimeter. Love called the former "a desperate affair. It was hastily organized. The men had little or no chance to dig in and protect themselves, and it was necessary to use whatever means were readily at hand for cover and concealment." In most cases the men crawled into any shallow ditch they could find and spent most of the day trying to keep the Japanese from breaching their lines. Some men just stood and fought wherever they happened to be at the time. When the Japanese tried to come down the beach to move behind the American defenders, Private First Class Willie Hokoanna from Hawaii set his BAR up in the crotch of a tree and "held his position all day long, firing at the enemy as they came along the water's edge. Altogether he is credited with killing over 140 Japanese by nightfall." Sergeant William Baralis joined Hokoanna in the defense of the beach. Baralis, a pitcher on his army company baseball team, gathered as many grenades as he could find. During the day he threw 150 grenades and killed close to one hundred Japanese attackers. Later that afternoon he was shot and killed.[34]

Baralis was not the only casualty near the Second Perimeter. After extensive interviews with survivors immediately after the Gyokusai ended, Edmund Love estimated that fifty soldiers were killed and two hundred wounded in this area. Many were hit two or three times. To add to this tragedy, another forty Americans were killed by friendly fire in an artillery barrage later that day. At the same time, the 1st and 2nd Battalions of the 105th Regiment killed an estimated 2,295 Japanese soldiers at the front lines and near these secondary perimeters.[35] Out of 1,107 men in the 1st and 2nd Battalions, over four hundred were killed and another five hundred wounded, a casualty rate of more than 80 percent. Marine Corps historian Hoffman paid homage to these army troops: "Almost as soon as the attack was launched, communications to the rear were cut. It was then simply a matter of two isolated battalions of soldiers fighting for their lives. This they did and did well. Some of the soldiers stacked so many dead Japanese forward of their positions that it was necessary to move to get fields of fire."[36] In total, the Japanese lost close to four thousand men in the Gyokusai.

Despite the valiant efforts of the frontline battalions, the Japanese broke through various gaps in the line. After running through and around the 1st and 2nd Battalions, Japanese attackers approached the command post of the 105th Regiment, approximately two thousand yards behind the front line. Lieutenant John Armstrong, intelligence officer for Head-quarters Company of the 105th, recalled that the normal perimeter was in effect as the Gyokusai began. His company was not on special alert; only the frontline battalions had been warned of an impending attack, and the regimental staff in headquarters did not know the number or strength of the enemy involved. Further, they could not foresee that the battalions would be overrun. Responding to the noise of the fighting to the north, Captain John "Jack" Baker told Armstrong to take all available men and establish a line of defense at the north edge of the command post at around 0500. Every available man in Headquarters Company was deployed, including communications technicians, drivers, clerks, cooks, and personnel of the Intelligence-Reconnaissance Platoon. Although these men were not designated as frontline troops, they were well trained and qualified to handle assigned weapons. While Armstrong's defense line ran from a road westward to the beach, Baker established a second section that tied in with Armstrong's right flank at the road and extended to the east. The men of Headquarters Company were fortunate to be able to set up their perimeter in a trench system that afforded a good defensive position. The Japanese had originally built those trenches.

Captain Baker sent Sergeant H. La Dieu and Corporal Edward Red-field from the Intelligence-Reconnaissance Platoon forward to find the Japanese lines, and they returned with only a few minutes to spare to report that the enemy was closing in on the command post. Fortunately, the Japanese had to come across an open area in order to attack, giving Headquarters Company a clear line of fire. Armstrong observed that the enemy "made good targets and they came in sufficient numbers to keep us busy." Armstrong received a Bronze Star for his actions that day. "At one time," his citation reads, "he held the fire of his section until approximately one enemy platoon was within 80 yards whereupon he loosed terrific fire upon the enemy and destroyed them."[37]

Shortly after 1400 on the afternoon of 7 July, with an element of the 106th Regiment on their right flank, the soldiers of Headquarters Com-pany counterattacked northward against the Japanese. The offensive had advanced about thirty yards when Baker came over to consult with Armstrong. They crouched in a trench for protection and were surprised to find a dead Japanese soldier sharing the trench with them. They wondered how he had been able to get so close to the previous night's perimeter, as no report of an attempted infiltration had been received. Too busy to give any further thought to the matter, they proceeded with their conference.[38]

In the ensuing three hours, Headquarters Company moved ahead five hundred yards before being relieved by the 106th Regiment and returning to their command post. Armstrong's Bronze Star citation summarized the situation: "During the attack, Lieutenant Armstrong moved out in front of the lines to head his men, exposing himself to heavy enemy rifle and grenade fire. He maintained this position until ordered to retire." In recognition of their collective efforts, Headquarters Company was awarded the Presidential Unit citation: "Meanwhile, the Japanese drive had carried on to the regimental command post where it was completely stopped and contained by the determined stand of Regimental Headquarters and Special Units. Every available man engaged in the action." While exact figures are impossible to verify, the soldiers of the command post killed at least 650 Japanese during the Gyokusai.[39] According to Marine Corps historian Hoffman, the soldiers of this unit "fought from deserted Japanese positions and exchanged blow for blow, bullet for bullet, with their attackers. Their defense perimeter was never penetrated; and, after several hours of close-in fighting, the battle was over."[40]

While the army's 1st and 2nd Battalions and Headquarters Company of the 105th Regiment fought bravely all day on 7 July, several marine units also engaged the enemy. Most importantly, the Gyokusai reached the position of the 3rd Battalion, 10th Marines, who were directly in the path of the gap between the 1st and 3rd Battalions of the 105th Regiment. The 3rd Battalion, 10th Marines, was an artillery unit made up of four batteries: G, H, I, and H&S (Headquarters and Service). Each battery included four 105-millimeter howitzers, but H Battery was the only one to fire during the Gyokusai because of its location in front of the other units. To survive the Japanese assault, this marine artillery battery was forced to fight hand-to-hand like an infantry platoon.

Two days earlier, the 2nd Marine Division had been relieved of duty and told that the army would finish the battle. Marine artillery moved to the former Japanese seaplane base near Tanapag to rest. Guns were set next to each other wheel to wheel with covers on the tubes. The guns were not aimed (surveyed) as the men relaxed, but the next day they were told to move in direct support of the army. Some marines resented this order, believing that they were reentering the battle because frequent "friendly fire" incidents involving army artillery made the army unreliable. "Their Artillery had been dropping too many shells on their own troops," recalled Private Rod Sandburg.[41] On 6 July the marine artillery battalion moved north up the coast.

Like so many other aspects of the Gyokusai that remain unclear or controversial, the location of the 10th Marines continues to be disputed. According to the marine and army official histories and maps, marine artillery was twelve hundred yards behind army lines and assigned to support the 4th Marine Division on the east side of the island. The marines who served in the artillery, however, strongly disagree with this account. According to Private Sandburg and his comrades in H Battery, they positioned their 105-millimeter howitzers north of Tanapag and "about two city blocks" from the ocean, only six hundred yards behind army front lines: "The official version of the counterattack is false. We were not in support of the 23rd Marines of the 4th Division. We were in support of the 27th Army, and all the men who were there that are still above ground will tell you the same thing." This positioning of the 10th Marines six hundred rather than twelve hundred yards behind the front lines placed the artillery regiment directly in the line of attack of the Gyokusai.[42]

Like the army's 1st and 2nd Battalions, which had arrived at the front too late in the day to establish a solid perimeter, the marine artillery battalion moved into position as night approached on 6 July. "We couldn't dig our guns in because of the late hour, so orders were to hide the guns the best we could," explained Sandburg. Fortunately, the marines were "among a bunch of trees for good air cover," with trenches and trees behind them and a three-acre sugarcane field in front. Unknown to the marines, there was a trench in front of them as well, between their position and the sugarcane field. The railroad tracks ran a few yards to the east of their guns, which were pointed toward Marpi Point on the northwest end of the island.

For a reason that cannot be explained, the marines were not informed of the impending attack. While no one anticipated the scope of the Japanese plan, army headquarters had alerted its frontline battalions to prepare for action. Holland Smith had been telling everyone for several days that the Japanese might attack, but he issued no specific warning that night and had not moved any reserve units into strategic locations. Army headquarters had called Marine Corps headquarters with information gained from its Japanese prisoner, but Marine Corps headquarters had failed to inform its own men in more than a general way. There was no reason for marine artillery to expect anything unusual. "We didn't expect anything to happen that night," recalled Sandburg. "Everyone felt we wouldn't have much to do as the island was all but secured." Believing that the battle was virtually over, the marines "didn't think it would be very rough duty. Because of this we took men in our outfit that were usually left behind when we were firing our Guns. We had the Battery Clerk, the Mess Cooks, and the Quartermaster people so they could experience what it was like to be on the firing line."[43] All of these men would soon become frontline troops.

On 7 July the Japanese ran through the army's 105th Regiment at the front. Directly behind the 105th was H Battery, 3rd Battalion, 10th Marines, in the gap that O'Brien's men had not been able to cover. Just as the sun was coming up, Sandburg was surprised to see "Japs marching five abreast, followed by a tank, another column of Japs and another tank. . . . The Jap tanks gave them away." Gun number 1 immediately fired and knocked out the first tank: "I watched #1 fire a round at the tank. It went through the side and into the belly of the tank, exploded and the tank spun like a top." Suddenly the Japanese soldiers charged the marine artillery. "A contingent of Japs like none of us had ever experienced before was out front of the Battery. . . . Standing at the guns it looked like the Japs were crawling in the cane field and all of a sudden one row after another seemed to stand up and run towards us. We didn't know there was a ditch there because the trees on the other side of the ditch were on the same level as our Guns." The marines started firing as fast as they could: "The guns were given permission to fire at will. They did. Fuses of the guns were set so close that when they exploded, they sprayed our position with shrapnel. The setting was estimated at 4/10 of a second." Despite these extreme and dangerous methods, the marines kept firing and the attackers kept coming. "This didn't even slow down the Japs. Men on the guns couldn't take powder out of the shells or get shells from cloverleafs fast enough. They started to ricochet shells off the ground in front of the gun tubes. This was done to try and keep the fragments of the shell from hitting those on the guns." Sandburg and his comrades worked heroically to stop the Gyokusai, but there were too many of the enemy at this point. "The men in the Battery were dropping like flies, some wounded, others dead." Finally, Lieutenant Arnold Hofstetter ordered the survivors to run for cover: "Get the hell out of here, every man for himself."[44]

Eventually, Hofstetter, Sandburg, and several other marines established a small perimeter in a supply dump protected by some bushes and underbrush. In this vulnerable position, like the soldiers in the Second Perimeter, they fought with the few weapons and limited ammunition they possessed. "We fought all morning, using Jap rifles and ammo. It was a terrifying morning, dead Japs lying all around us." Sandburg volunteered to seek assistance and crawled out of his defensive position hoping to find friendly tanks. Unsuccessful at first, he returned to his comrades and then tried again. This time he was spotted by a group of enemy soldiers who threw grenades at him: "A concussion grenade bounced off my helmet and exploded in my face." Nevertheless, he continued toward American lines. "My ears were ringing and my eyes were blurry when I arrived at the beach road." Sandburg moved south and finally found regimental headquarters, where a relief party was organized. Trucks and ambulances made their way north, where they picked up the battery's abandoned guns and the wounded marines.[45]

Individual marines also moved quickly to aid the wounded. Harold Agerholm of Racine, Wisconsin, served with the 4th Battalion, 10th Marines. Because it was situated behind the other marine emplacements, this artillery battery was unable to fire its guns during the Gyokusai. Nevertheless, after the Japanese attacked Sandburg's unit, Agerholm volunteered to help the wounded. "Locating and appropriating an abandoned ambulance jeep, he repeatedly made extremely perilous trips under heavy rifle and mortar fire and single-handedly loaded and evacuated approximately 45 casualties, working tirelessly and with utter disregard for his own safety during a grueling period of more than 3 hours." He made trip after trip into enemy territory to bring wounded marines out of danger, and he could have stopped at any time. When he saw two more wounded men who needed assistance, he decided to make another run into enemy territory. "Despite intense, persistent enemy fire, he ran out to aid 2 men whom he believed to be wounded marines but was himself mortally wounded by a Japanese sniper while carrying out his hazardous mission." For his "brilliant initiative, great personal valor and self-sacrificing efforts in the face of almost certain death," Agerholm was awarded the Medal of Honor posthumously.[46]

When they finally counted the dead in this one sector, 3rd Battalion, 10th Marines, had lost seventy-five dead and sixty-five wounded in the fifteen-hour battle; 75 percent of H Battery was lost in the Gyokusai.

Any soldier or marine who was close to the Gyokusai retained vivid images of that event. Corporal Joe Ojeda and Private First Class Don

Swindle both served with the 4th Marine Division. Ojeda, with the 24th Marines, was only seventeen years old in October 1943 when he joined the Marine Corps. He considered the Japanese good soldiers: "They killed a lot of us and we killed a lot of them." His company had been warned that the Japanese might attack on 7 July, so they remained "aware and alert." In the middle of the night "they came all at once hollering and screaming. We caught them in crossfire. It was raining and it was all very scary." Swindle, with the 23rd Marines, supported Ojeda's assessment: "I was on a hill overlooking the valley and recall firing at least eight hundred rounds of ammunition, but I couldn't claim to have got one."[47]

Private Joe Epperson, with the 14th Marines, remembered the emotions experienced during any Japanese attack. "It's kind of scary. They are coming and they have no fear or sense of stopping to save their own lives. But they are coming after you. You either cut them down or suffer the consequences. They were tough individuals. If it's them or me then it's them. I never hated them as human beings but if they didn't want to surrender then I could care less." During the charge on 7 July Epperson was pinned down for more than two hours in a sugarcane furrow. "I got very low and very skinny and hugged the ground."[48]

Despite sustaining heavy losses, the Japanese continued to launch smaller attacks throughout the day on 7 July. Moving out from Paradise Valley, one group ran toward the army's 2nd Battalion, 165th Regiment, while additional thrusts came from "Harakiri Gulch" toward the 1st Battalion, 165th, and the 3rd Battalion, 105th.[49] On this day Private First Class Emmett Scott "Scotty" Prothero of Ogden, Utah, was relatively lucky. Although it was assigned to A Company, 2nd Battalion, 105th Regiment, one of the units that absorbed the brunt of the Japanese attack, Prothero's 102nd Combat Engineers had been ordered to move off the beach and onto a hill with the 3rd Battalion the day before the Gyokusai. Prothero helped man a machine-gun position on the hill overlooking the Tanapag Plain. During the night he and his comrades heard gunfire, but only in the morning could they see movement below: "As it was getting light all hell broke out. From our position we could hear the noise and the squeaky sound of a tank. We could see from our view point waves of the enemy storming south, hundreds of them, extending from the water's edge east to the hill where we were and as far north as we could see." The main Japanese thrust was against the 1st and 2nd Battalions, and "up there on the hill we could see all that was going on; nothing we could do but hold our own position."

From his vantage point Prothero saw soldiers on the plain "using the butt of their rifle and bayonet to ward off an attack." Eventually some Japanese started to advance up the hill toward the 3rd Battalion as well:

> We opened up on them as they came crawling up the hill. This continued for a full day and into the next. Three members of our squad were wounded and two dead. Three Japanese soldiers came into the post with their hands held high and they were yelling loudly as they approached. We assumed they wanted to surrender but later we realized they were giving away our position. A short time later from a higher elevation across a gulch came a barrage of machine gun fire and grenades that hit our position, killing one BAR man who had been trying to narrow his sights to discover where the firing was coming from.

Shortly thereafter, Prothero's unit ran out of water and ammunition and moved in search of fresh supplies. Two hours later they returned to their original positions, only to be greeted by a strange sight: "We saw that the Japs had entered our post and what we found amazed us. They must have been hungry. We had left a block of composition C-2 explosive and there were what looked like teeth mark indentations in it as though someone had taken a bite out of it, perhaps thinking that the sweet-smelling C-2 was candy or some kind of sweet food. Just a few feet below the gun position that I and my buddy had shared, there were five or six bodies of young Japanese soldiers."[50]

The army and marines brought in bulldozers and pushed thousands of Japanese bodies into huge pits. Anyone who witnessed that sight never forgot it. Private Clifford Howe, serving with 1st Battalion, 165th Regiment, was on a hill overlooking the plain where the Gyokusai had occurred. He heard the sounds of the battle and in the morning found a pair of binoculars. As he gazed at the valley, he noticed "huge humps of something that had not been there the day before. As it got lighter, I could see that the mounds were bodies. Later, American bulldozers came in and scooped out long trenches, pushed the bodies into the trenches, and covered them with dirt. They then marked each burial site with a sign that read '479 Japanese buried here,' '278 Japanese buried here,' and on and on until all those that had been killed had been buried."[51] American dead were buried individually.

Sandburg joined a detail sent to collect the bodies of marines killed in the Gyokusai. It was one of the most unpleasant events of his twenty-one years:

A large detail of the remaining men were ordered to go where our position was and pick up our dead. What a traumatic experience this was. Many of the dead could not be recognized. In the intense heat a body would become blown up and its clothes split open to the point where no one, not even a family member, could recognize it. In addition it would have maggots crawling in and out of its mouth, eyes, and ears. They were identified only by their dog tags. Those we saw go down couldn't be recognized without their dog tags, even though we knew them and watched them go down.[52]

Sergeant Mark Marquardt, with the 27th Cavalry Reconnaissance Troop (Mechanized), "saw piles of dead Japanese soldiers everywhere. The island reeked of the terrible odor of death, with maggots coming out of the eyes, noses, and wounds of all the bodies." John Earley of the 106th Regiment was recovering from dengue fever during the Gyokusai, but he visited the scene of the Japanese attack and witnessed "the sight and stench of Jap bodies swarming with maggots piled six to seven high." He remembered both soldiers and marines busy with the "horrible job of separating our own dead for burial." Finally, Sergeant Jerry Wachsmuth called the scene that day "indescribable." With bodies everywhere, "you couldn't take a step without stepping on bodies or body parts."[53]

Once the attack was over, army-marine controversy began to surface again. Without conducting a thorough investigation of the events of 7 July, Holland Smith again condemned the 27th Infantry Division, calling it "the worst division I've ever seen." This time, however, rather than criticizing only the officers, he went on to denounce the soldiers themselves: "They're yellow. They are not aggressive. They've just held up the battle and caused my Marines casualties."[54] It was telling that Smith referred to "my Marines," while a commanding general concerned about all the forces under his command would have considered both the marines and soldiers as "his." Not surprisingly, he reported to Spruance that the Japanese attack had included only "300 enemy supported by two or three tanks."[55] General Griner immediately protested Smith's report of only three hundred Japanese attackers and ordered a careful count of bodies the next day. While the inventory of buried bodies revealed more than four thousand Japanese dead after the Gyokusai, Smith still refused to credit the army with any kills: "When we cleaned up the area in front of the Twenty-seventh's sector and wiped out the scattered groups of Japanese resistance, we counted 4,311 enemy bodies, some of which were obviously long decomposed and could not have been killed during the banzai attack."[56] Howlin' Mad apparently had never gone on burial detail and witnessed how quickly bodies decomposed in the hot sun. He preferred to dismiss the possibility that the army had killed significant numbers of the enemy. While the exact numbers of Japanese attackers and killed will never be known, Smith's dismissal of the sacrifice of the soldiers exacerbated the army-marine dispute and had a negative effect on the morale of the 27th Division.

Once again, Smith's superiors had to inject themselves into the controversy. On 9 July Nimitz asked Spruance to examine the situation. Griner continued to object to Smith's characterization of the 27th Division and its role in the Gyokusai, and on 12 July he filed a letter as part of the investigation:

> In view of press releases and official dispatches indicating the numerical strength of the enemy counterattack on 7 July as between 300 and 500, basic report is forwarded indicating that by actual count, 4,311 enemy soldiers were buried in the area between the farthest advance of the 1st and 2nd Battalions, 105th Infantry, and the farthest advance of the enemy. . . . A further breakdown of enemy dead indicated that 2,295 were killed in the combat area of the 1st and 2nd Battalions, 105th Infantry, and 2,016 in the combat area of the 1st and 2nd Battalions, 106th Infantry, the 3rd Battalion, 6th Marines [sic], and the 3rd Battalion, 105th Infantry. These dead represented the number of enemy that pushed beyond the defensive line of the 1st and 2nd Battalions, 105th Infantry.[57]

Griner, who credited both army and marine battalions with heroic action, wanted a correction of the historical record, and in this regard he continued his protest:

> The assumption that the Japanese dead found on the ground in the area around Tanapag were killed by the action of our air arm and by naval gunfire since the preliminary strikes on this island on 11 June cannot be supported. As the only general officer to visit the scene on 8 July, I must insist that my observations in the case be given credence. I viewed personally upwards of one thousand enemy bodies and nowhere did I find marked decomposition of bodies which would indicate that the enemy had been dead for more than thirty-six to forty-eight hours. I call your attention to the Army field manual on military sanitation and hygiene which states, "At temperatures of 85 degrees Fahrenheit, maggots will begin forming on bodies in approximately forty-eight hours." There were no maggots on these bodies when I viewed them.[58]

In response, Spruance issued a report on 19 July that supported the army and contradicted Holland Smith's estimates by putting the number of attackers in the thousands rather than the hundreds. He did include some criticism of one part of the army response, namely the 3rd Battalion, 105th

Regiment, which he felt could have done more to assist the 1st and 2nd Battalions. Nevertheless, Spruance carefully balanced this comment and asserted that "although the position of the 27th Division was penetrated to a depth of 1000 to 1500 yards, this penetration was always firmly contained. There is no question that our troops fought courageously in this action. The 1st and 2nd Battalions and Headquarters Company, 105th Infantry and the 3rd Battalion, 10th Marines deserve particular mention."[59] Unlike Howlin' Mad, Spruance was fair and reached the correct conclusions.

Although the Gyokusai had devastated the 1st and 2nd Battalions of the army's 105th Regiment, remaining army units were intact and prepared to advance on 8 July. Nevertheless, Smith, disgusted with the 27th Division, decided to move the rested 2nd Marine Division through army lines and allow the marines to complete the mopping-up operations. On 8 July Smith ordered the marines to "attack, mop up and destroy enemy elements," and they proceeded to complete that task against the remnants of a defeated, bedraggled, and suicidal Japanese force.[60] Despite their diminished capacity as an organized fighting force, the Japanese remained dangerous because each soldier was willing to sacrifice himself and take American lives at the same time.

Marines went from cave to cave flushing out or sealing up the enemy forces. Sergeant Grant Frederick Timmerman served as a tank commander with the 2nd Tank Battalion in support of the 6th Marines. On 8 July Timmerman was "advancing with his tank a few yards ahead of the infantry in support of a vigorous attack on hostile positions." As he fired steadily, his progress was halted by enemy trenches and pillboxes. "Observing a target of opportunity, he immediately ordered the tank stopped and, mindful of the danger from the muzzle blast as he prepared to open fire with the 75mm., fearlessly stood up in the exposed turret and ordered the infantry to hit the deck." At that moment a Japanese soldier threw a grenade that would have dropped through the open turret into the tank. Timmerman "unhesitatingly blocked the opening with his body, holding the grenade against his chest and taking the brunt of the explosion." His action saved the rest of his crew, but he sacrificed his own life in the process. He was awarded the Medal of Honor posthumously.[61]

Other marines also performed heroically. Private First Class Ralph Browner, born in Oklahoma and raised in southern California, was only sixteen years old, five feet, six inches tall, and about 125 pounds when he joined the marines. A veteran of "Bloody Tarawa," Browner landed

on Saipan with A Company, 1st Battalion, 2nd Marines, to the north of
Charan Kanoa. From 15 June until early July his regiment fought its way
north with the rest of the 2nd Division. In the aftermath of the Gyokusai,
the Japanese attempted to move men through Karaberra Pass on 8–9 July
in order to prepare for another attack. Warned that the Japanese were coming, Browner's A Company established a defensive position and waited for
the charge. "Our company was too far in front of the rest of our men," he
recalled. "A piper cub flew over and dropped a message that warned us that
300–500 Japs were right ahead of us." Japanese soldiers would "get liquored
up with sake" before the charge and then run at the Americans. At about
2100 on 8 July they attacked and "we were killing them right and left."
Browner recalled that as they charged, several Japanese soldiers screamed
"Babe Ruth no good," "Japanese drink Marine blood," and "Roosevelt son
of bitch." Some marines shouted "Hirohito eats shit" or "Tōjō eats shit"
in response.

Although Browner and his fellow marines had killed many of the
attackers, they worried that some Japanese might try to circle behind them.
Browner volunteered to go down to the beach and set up a defensive position west of Karaberra Pass to cover a trail that the enemy used to move
into the cliffs above. "I was all alone on a beach with the ocean about two
yards to my left, the cliff five yards to my right, and the beach behind me
about twenty yards deep." Browner had his .30-caliber machine gun, his
carbine, and several grenades. After digging a foxhole—not an easy task in
the coral sand—he remained alone in that position throughout the night,
watching toward the tree line ahead. He remained ready for action when
suddenly he heard a dripping noise behind him. As a Japanese attacker
stood up, water dripped off his loincloth and the sound alerted Browner.
He turned toward the water and saw three Japanese soldiers emerging from
the ocean brandishing knives. Firing his carbine, he quickly shot each of
them in the head. A fourth soldier lunged at him, and Browner swung his
carbine and caught the attacker in the chest. He then turned toward the
front just in time for the main attack. Firing the machine gun "free hand"
so he could shoot faster, Browning simultaneously pulled the pins on a
couple of grenades and lobbed those with his other hand. He fired all night,
and when the gun jammed he field-stripped it, reassembled it in nineteen
seconds, and continued to fire. The battle raged throughout the night, with
Browner fighting both the enemy and his body's high temperature brought
on by dengue fever. In the morning he heard a loud buzzing sound that

he could not identify until he saw "billions of flies all over the dead Japs." When the battle was over, Browner had killed approximately forty of the enemy, an act that won him the Navy Cross.[62]

On 8 and 9 July the marines pushed toward Marpi Point, the northernmost section of the island. Originally the American objective for day nine, Marpi Point was finally achieved after more than three weeks of battle. On the afternoon of 9 July, Admiral Turner and General Holland Smith declared the island secure. Rather than surrender, Japanese soldiers and civilians committed mass suicide.

The Americans spent another week cleaning out caves and enemy resisters. In the process, they found the remains of Saito and Nagumo. The enemy commanders were buried in Charan Kanoa with full military honors. Nevertheless, Spruance, mindful of Nagumo's role at Pearl Harbor, savored his victory: "One thing that has appealed to me most in this operation was the end of the Saipan commander, Vice Admiral Nagumo. He is the gentleman who commanded the Jap Fleet on December 7th, 1941 and again at Midway. After Midway he went ashore to Sasebo and then came here in May. Three strikes and out."[63]

CHAPTER FOURTEEN

SUICIDE CLIFF AND BANZAI CLIFF

Following the Gyokusai, marines prepared to move north toward Marpi Point: the final sweep to clean out all pockets of Japanese resistance. Fighting remained intense, with enemy soldiers either flushed out of caves and other hidden locations or killed inside caves by flamethrowers, grenades, and satchel charges. If there were civilians in the caves the Americans would try to persuade them to surrender, but those entreaties were often answered with the sounds of grenades as the Japanese committed suicide. As corpsman Chester Szech remembered: "We rarely saw live Japanese. Every time we saw Japanese they were already dead. When we approached a cave, we would tell them to come out, and then turn the flame-thrower on them and that was the end of it. One guy came out in flames and someone shot him and put him out of his misery."[1]

Gunnery Sergeant Keith Renstrom of the 25th Marines recalled one occasion when a marine moved down a hill to save a baby in front of a cave, only to be shot and killed by a woman hiding behind the rocks. The marines then opened fire, killing the woman and her child.[2] Private Don Swindle of the 23rd Marines recalled a similar experience when his platoon discovered some enemy soldiers in a bunker. Sergeant Vern Lees "wanted to try and talk them into giving up. So he laid his carbine down and this Jap officer shot him in the chest." The marines responded with a flamethrower, cleaning out the bunker. Swindle remembered one Japanese soldier on fire, running out of the bunker: "You could see his skin split and turn yel-

Figure 21. Marines using demolition charge to eliminate Japanese defensive position, June 1944; courtesy of Private Rod Sandburg (USMC).

low—someone shot him." Despite heroic efforts to save him, Sergeant Lees did not make it.[3] As a result of experiences such as those encountered by Renstrom and Swindle, American bulldozers were often called in to seal up a cave, leaving the inhabitants to a certain and unpleasant death.

Corporal Frank Britt served as a demolition man assigned to the 24th Marines. He spent time blasting caves along the northern mountains and ridges of Saipan. Toward the end of the battle at Marpi Point a Japanese sniper shot and killed a marine, and Britt and his squad hung over a cliff and swung a sixteen-pound demolition charge into the cave where the sniper had taken refuge. As the Japanese soldier ran from the cave in the direction of the ocean, Britt opened fire with his submachine gun and "shot him before he covered the five or six yards to the water." This sequence of events was captured by a *Life* magazine photographer and was printed in four frames in the 28 August 1944 edition.[4]

Despite such cases of continued resistance, surviving enemy soldiers began to surrender in large numbers for the first time after the collapse of the Gyokusai attack. Sergeant Renstrom described the "glorious feeling" of saving fifteen or twenty civilians on the verge of starvation. Renstrom put down his Thompson machine gun and poured water into the mouths of the desperate crowd before sending them to a refugee camp.[5]

Another marine who played a major, if somewhat controversial, role in taking Japanese prisoners and sending them to American camps was Private Guy "Gabby" Gabaldon. Gabaldon referred to himself as a Chicano from East Los Angeles. As a boy he became friends with two Japanese American brothers, moved in with their parents, and learned to speak Japanese. Although only seventeen years old and too short for the Marine Corps, the five-foot, four-inch Gabaldon was allowed to enlist because of his language ability, a skill the marines realized might prove useful. Gabaldon eventually became a scout for the 2nd Marines, 2nd Marine Division.

According to interviews with Gabaldon after the war, he had quickly discovered during the battle that he could use his language ability to capture Japanese soldiers and civilians. His method was usually the same—he would position himself outside an enemy cave, yell in that the cave was surrounded, and establish a short deadline for the soldiers to come out or be killed. If he did not receive a response, Gabaldon would throw a couple of grenades into the cave, followed by a smoke grenade that would force out any survivors. The emerging Japanese became his prisoners, and these captured enemy fighters often proved a valuable source of intelligence and information. Gabaldon asserted that his commanding officer, Captain John L. Schwabe, had been impressed and allowed him to operate on his own as a "lone wolf," moving in Japanese-controlled territory to kill or capture the enemy. Gabaldon claimed a remarkable success rate.[6]

Gabaldon's greatest single day was 7 July, immediately following the massive Japanese attack on American forces. Gabaldon captured a few Japanese prisoners and convinced them that they would receive fair treatment from the marines. Some of his new prisoners were then persuaded to return to the caves and encourage other Japanese soldiers to come out. Gabaldon estimated that he brought eight hundred Japanese soldiers to American prisoner camps that day; most of the soldiers and civilians who surrendered were starving and willing to gamble on his promise of food and medicine. Toward the end of the battle, Gabaldon again played a role in convincing some of the enemy that the Americans would treat them well. For this he was awarded a Silver Star, upgraded to a Navy Cross after the 1960 movie *Hell to Eternity* extolled his exploits.[7] For many years thereafter, Gabaldon campaigned to have his Navy Cross upgraded to the Medal of Honor, arguing that he was denied that award because he was of Mexican descent.

Gabaldon elaborated on his exploits in an interview with the *Fresno Bee* in 2000. "I captured more Japanese by myself than two or three divisions combined," he claimed. "I'd go out and kill and capture Japanese every day and I know I got 800 prisoners on one day." Gabaldon asserted that he captured more than fifteen hundred Japanese soldiers altogether.[8] Nevertheless, he never developed the respect for the enemy that other marines had: "I never ceased to be amazed at the stupid carelessness of the Japanese. Time after time, whenever I got the drop on them, they had left themselves completely exposed. The first time it happened I suspected a trap, but later I realized that they were just plain 'baka' [stupid]. Good soldiers, hell—they lost every battle against the Marines whether it was at Guadalcanal, Tarawa, the Marshalls, Iwo Jima, and later even on their home turf, Okinawa."[9]

Gabaldon's story remains controversial to this day. Other marines question his claim that he was allowed to operate alone and separate from his company while the battle for Saipan raged around him. In addition, many marines dispute Gabaldon's statement that he captured as many as fifteen hundred prisoners, placing the estimate at about half that number. Finally, some marines point out that most of Gabaldon's captures occurred after the failed Gyokusai, when the Japanese left alive on the island were mostly the walking wounded, desperate to surrender in exchange for food and water. At that point it was not difficult to round up willing prisoners, and all marines could claim responsibility for such actions. While some of the prisoners were Japanese soldiers, many more were civilians, either Chamorros or Okinawans, anxious to receive American aid.

Sergeant David Dowdakin, who served with I Company, 3rd Battalion, 2nd Marines, questioned Gabaldon's assertions. He recalled finding scores of civilians as the battle came to a conclusion, although he did not expect a medal for having done so: "I believe they were Okinawans. They were sitting here and there and were trying to eat or drink some water. There were also on the road a number of strangers, marines with noticeable cleaner clothes, cleaner faces and lightly armed. These marines had formed up a column of civilians, now numbering in the hundreds and were slowly marching them southward. Could this be a part of the hundreds of prisoners that Guy Gabaldon captured?"

Dowdakin discussed the Gabaldon controversy with Sergeant Donald Williams, who served in K Company, 3rd Battalion, 2nd Marines. Williams remembered Gabaldon at the scene the day after the Gyokusai, but the sergeant remembered Gabaldon shouting in Japanese and abusing a prisoner. Dowdakin admitted that Gabaldon had his defenders, but he added that "the rest of us think he is an importuning glory seeker who is playing the race card. But, then, the two traits often go together: bravery and glory seeking."

Dowdakin described the bloody events at the northern end of island in the aftermath of the Gyokusai:

> We dug in a double line on either side of the road—one facing toward the cliff and one facing toward the sea. We were keeping our normal watch on, watch off, at night so that half of us would be awake at any time. After 25 days of this routine we were suffering badly from sleep deprivation. . . . The first night I awoke to find a Japanese soldier crouched behind me. I shot him as he cracked the fuse on a grenade. Back to sleep accompanied by the cries of women and children nearby. The second night we all awoke at once to find ourselves under seeming attack. I opened fire and cut down a man who seemed to be struggling with smaller people. I got him and his daughter. He was killing his children with a knife. A figure in a skirt leaped over the double concertina wire and kept running full tilt to the cliffs and leapt over. Another burst of fire from the BAR man next to me and he got a teenaged boy in the head. At dawn we sat eating our C rations calmly in the midst of what could truthfully be described as a slaughterhouse. Two women and several children sat among us. We gave them a gauze compress to put on the head of the boy. We gave them C rations but they wouldn't eat them. They drank all our water.[10]

On 9 July at 1615, Admiral Spruance and General Smith declared Saipan "secured." Spruance and Holland Smith had decided that organized resistance had ended. The announcement did not make the island safe for all troops, however. The 23rd Marines had been moved into a reserve role by the end of the battle. Corporal Roland Lewis described the tragedy suffered by C Company, 1st Battalion. As they were only a few hundred yards from the beach on the west side of the island, company commander Captain Fred Eberhardt directed the men toward the water for a swim. On their way to the ocean the marines approached some heavy underbrush and came under fire. Private First Class Gene Dominguez was killed, as was Private First Class Ed Day when he stood up to try to retrieve Dominguez. The issue was resolved when a mortar crew "lobbed a few rounds into the area"; nevertheless, Eberhardt canceled the swim plans.[11]

On 10 July, the day after Spruance declared Saipan secure, Privates Alva Perry and Paul Scanelon of A Company, 24th Marines, decided to head for the ocean and wash off. Like most other marines, neither one had bathed or changed clothes for nearly four weeks. As they approached the beach near Marpi Point on the northern end of the island, a Japanese family that included elderly parents, a teenage girl, and a six-year-old boy walked out from behind a rock. The girl, sick from drinking seawater, pointed to Perry's canteen. When Perry offered her a drink, a long line of Japanese survivors emerged from behind the rocks and queued up for a drink. Perry and Scanelon tried to ration the amount each person took, and finally Scanelon left to try to find more water. He returned with two five-gallon cans, and an even longer line formed. At the same time, Perry noticed at least fifty Japanese in the water: "They were too far out to make it back to shore. They had to be swimming out to drown themselves." Soon more Americans arrived on the beach, but they were newly arrived occupation troops, not veterans of the battle. The marines in new dungarees started to shoot at the heads moving out in the ocean. Perry objected and asked that the Japanese be allowed to "die with some dignity. They ignored me and kept shooting. One of the Marines said something about getting a Japanese before he had to go home."[12]

Despite the callous attitude of a few marines, most American troops watched in horror as the Japanese committed mass suicide at the end of the battle. Rather than surrender, hundreds of Japanese soldiers killed themselves with grenades. Some were afraid to surrender, having been taught that American recruits had to shoot their own mothers and fathers in order to become marines.[13] These American beasts would surely kill all the captors they could find. In order to avoid this imagined fate, Japanese soldiers would often push women and children off the cliffs before jumping themselves. Some of them shot their family members before taking their own lives; in other cases entire families jumped off either Suicide Cliff, about 800 feet high, or Banzai Cliff, about 265 feet above the ocean. While those on Banzai Cliff aimed for the water, they often landed on protruding rocks. Marines watched as groups of Japanese, men, women, children, and soldiers would gather in a circle and detonate a grenade. In some cases Japanese officers shot soldiers who hesitated or thought about surrender; the officers then killed themselves.

Sergeant Bill More witnessed the suicides of hundreds of Japanese soldiers and civilians. "We could see them a hundred or two hundred yards away. There would be a group of people, women and kids with a guy in the middle. A grenade would go off and the whole family was gone." More also remembered seeing men throwing women and children off the cliffs before jumping after them.[14]

Figure 22. Marine talks with Chamorro woman, July 1944; courtesy of Private Rod Sandburg (USMC).

Lieutenant Frederic Stott, writing immediately after these events, summarized the process:

> Suddenly a waving flag of the Rising Sun was unfurled. Movement grew more agitated, men started leaping into the sea, and the chanting gave way to startled cries, and with them the popping sound of detonating grenades. It was the handful of soldiers, determined to prevent the surrender or escape of their kinfolks, who tossed grenades into the milling throng of men, women, and children, and then dived into the sea from which escape was impossible. The exploding grenades cut up the mob into patches of dead, dying, and wounded, and for the first time we actually saw water that ran red with human blood.[15]

Corporal John "Jack" Rempke watched as the Japanese committed mass suicide at the northern end of Saipan. The Americans set up loudspeakers, using prisoners to call out in Japanese for the soldiers and civilians to surrender. The navy also sent boats into the nearby waters, broadcasting in Japanese to convince the remaining soldiers and civilians to surrender. Many of those who chose death were wearing few clothes, and it was impossible to tell if they were soldiers or civilians. Despite such efforts to stop the suicides, the voluntary death continued. Some Japanese jumped off the cliffs, and "some of them just walked out into the water and disappeared."[16]

The efforts of the 2nd Marine Division to discourage suicides were ultimately unsuccessful. Corporals Steve Judd and Jim Montgomery saw soldiers throw children off the cliffs: "They threw kids off. Americans with PA systems were right below the cliffs trying to get them to stop." According to corpsman Chester Szech: "There was not anything the Americans could do about this terrible situation. We had an LST in the water asking them not to jump. We were down below and just sat there and watched them. There were a lot of women and kids. They were Japanese nationals stationed on Saipan and they just committed suicide. They would throw the kids, then the wife would jump and then he would jump."[17]

The scene was grisly even for battle veterans, and many marines and soldiers were haunted by the memories. Corporal Joe Ojeda was in the front lines of the marines at Marpi Point and had a clear view of the suicides: "All these women and young children killing themselves. You'd hear an explosion and see body parts flying all over." Ojeda was assigned to go down to the ocean, where he saw a Japanese man facedown in the water: "He moved and I shot him. To this day I see that all the time. I have a guilt feeling about that." Private Clifford Howe shared similar feelings: "We saw hundreds of bodies, washing in the surf or lying dead on the rocks below. It made even the most hardened American soldiers sick to see this." Some troops grudgingly accepted the scene as the logical culmination of the bloody battle. While Corporal M. F. Leggett did not see anyone jump, he did view some of the bodies later on the rocks and shrugged it off: "You get hard when you're in combat." By the time the suicides ended, the areas below Suicide Cliff and Banzai Cliff were "red with blood."[18]

Although the Battle of Saipan was officially over, pockets of Japanese resisters remained hidden in caves, and their presence posed a threat to the construction workers who were turning Saipan into a base for bombing runs and a future invasion of Japan. Holland Smith ordered the two marine divisions, with the 165th Infantry attached, to "mop up" on the island. This action continued for a few days, when the marines were relieved in order to recuperate and prepare for the invasion of Tinian.

Deprived of their swim a few days earlier, the 23rd Marines were able to enjoy a week of rest on the southern end of the island. "When I took my

Figure 23. Japanese drawing of a soldier, captured on Saipan in July 1944; courtesy of Corporal William Dodson Smith (USMC).

shoes off for the first time since D-Day, 25 days ago, there were only a few threads of my socks left," recalled Private John Seymour. "I'm sure we all smelled rather ripe, but we were all in the same fix so no one noticed!"[19]

After 16 July, Smith ordered the 105th Infantry to continue the mop-up phase to eliminate snipers and stragglers, and on 30 July he assigned all of the 27th Division to this task. As Lieutenant John Armstrong commented, this contradicted Smith's vow that "he would never use the division again."[20] In the period between the battle's official end on 9 July and the evacuation of the 27th Division on 4 October, the army killed nearly two thousand more enemy soldiers and captured more than three thousand civilians.[21] Then in December a new element was introduced when the 24th Infantry Regiment, consisting of African American soldiers with white officers, was deployed on this mission. By the following summer, these troops had killed or captured more than seven hundred Japanese soldiers, suffering over thirty casualties of their own.[22]

Despite these efforts, Japanese forces continued to operate on Saipan. The most notorious case involved Captain Oba Sakae, who disappeared into the hills surrounding Mt. Tapotchau with 350 soldiers as the battle ended. Oba spent several months organizing his men as well as securing and stealing supplies to keep them alive. Despite marine sweeps through the area, he continued to elude capture. Nevertheless, his forces suffered from hunger and from attrition as a result of hit-and-run encounters with Americans. The situation remained unresolved for more than a year, but after Japan's official surrender on 2 September 1945, the Americans sent other Japanese officers to persuade Oba that the war had ended. Three months after Japan's surrender, Oba led his remaining forty-six men out of the mountains of Saipan.[23]

CHAPTER FIFTEEN

TŌJŌ AND TINIAN

It was appropriate that General Tōjō Hideki resigned after the Battle of Saipan, as Japan's chances for victory ended with the loss of the Mariana Islands. Tōjō, who entered the cabinet in 1940, was a prime mover in the decision to go to war with the United States and the symbol of Japanese militarism. As prime minister he exemplified the Japanese people's commitment to diligence and self-sacrifice and their belief in ultimate victory. Despite the increasingly bad news from both the Pacific and European fronts throughout 1943, Tōjō continued to believe that hard work and unity could defeat the Allied powers.

There was, however, no way for Tōjō to escape the consequences of the fall of Saipan. At first he intended to reconstitute his cabinet while remaining in office, but other powerful individuals in Japan, including elder statesmen and former prime ministers, had turned against his leadership. In a radio address on 18 July, he told the Japanese people of the loss of Saipan and then presented his resignation to Emperor Hirohito.[1]

When Tōjō went into retirement, the bravado that he represented, and which had been evident in Japanese forces at the beginning of the war, was replaced by a year-long attrition of Japanese soldiers who fought on despite the desperation of their military mission. The illusion that victory was still possible had been ripped away. From that moment on, Japan fought only to slow the American advance by inflicting massive casualties on the enemy, with some Japanese officials willing to fight to the death and others hoping that the United States might seek a negotiated settlement. In reality, the only remaining questions were when the United States would win the war and what sacrifices Japan would be willing to endure in its own inevitable defeat. In the end, Japan would pay a very high price.

Following Tōjō's resignation, the news for Japan grew steadily worse as the United States extended the battle to the other islands in the Mariana chain. The Battle of Saipan officially ended on 9 July, but American forces involved in that bloody struggle were given little time to relax. Spruance, Turner, and Smith intended to invade and occupy Tinian as soon as possible after Saipan was secure. The reasons were obvious: Tinian was only three and a half miles from Saipan, and Japanese forces there posed a continuing threat to the American presence on Saipan. In addition, Tinian possessed an excellent airstrip, longer than the one at Aslito Airfield. A major reason for the American offensive in the Marianas was the desire to secure forward air bases for the B-29 Superfortress bomber. There was never any doubt that Tinian was a primary target after Saipan.

Even as the battle for Saipan raged, American artillery forces moved to the southern end of the island and fired at Japanese installations on Tinian. The army's XXIV Corps Artillery played a major role in this bombardment, firing more than seventy-five hundred rounds at the island. Unfortunately, the rainy season started in July. As J. William "Bill" Winter, a member of the 532nd Field Artillery, recalled, that rain was more of a nuisance than an impediment: "Rain is just one more enemy to contend with in combat. As for heavy artillery, the weapon itself is not particularly bothered by rain, as long as the optics and directional controls used for orientation are protected. However, in a prolonged period of rain, it was usually necessary to pull the guns (which weighed in at 13-tons) out of position, lay down a timbered bed over the gun position, and roll the guns back into position over the timbered beds." Winter participated in the support fire for the Tinian invasion and celebrated the effectiveness of the artillery shelling: "With the range of our guns, it was easy for us to protect U.S. forces going ashore on the designated landing beaches of Tinian."[2]

Simultaneously, battleships kept up a steady barrage on the small island while P-47 Thunderbolts strafed and bombed at will. While these efforts did not destroy the Japanese positions, they kept the enemy pinned down and prevented the reinforcement of defensive emplacements. American superiority on the sea and in the air helped soften the enemy for the weary marines preparing for another amphibious landing.

Admirals Spruance and Harry Hill, in consultation with Generals Smith and Harry Schmidt, decided to land on Tinian's northwest coast,

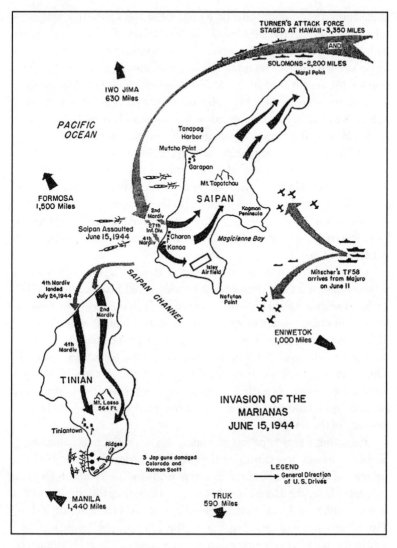

Map 10. Saipan and Tinian

or designated White beaches. The Japanese had aimed most of their guns toward the southwest, where the widest and most likely landing beaches existed. Rather than attack directly against the primary Japanese defenses, the American landing would outflank the defenders and take a chance on a narrower beach.

The invasion began six days after Tōjō's resignation. The marines landed only a few minutes after their designated time on the morning of 24 July, three days after the 3rd Marine Division had invaded Guam. Although their battalions now averaged approximately 565 men rather than the regulation strength of 950, tired but determined marines from the 4th Division led the assault. The 24th and 25th Marines quickly established their presence on the beach and began the drive forward. Resistance was much lighter than had been encountered on Saipan on D-Day, and the marines started to bring their heavy equipment ashore almost immediately.

At the same time, American shelling continued from Saipan. Private Joe Epperson's artillery battery fired toward Japanese outposts in the vicinity of the 23rd Marines: "We had some miscommunication and a few shells landed short and we got a few of our own people. Then they told us on radio to raise our elevation. Nothing you can do about that."[3] Despite these few errors, artillery shelling damaged Japanese positions and kept the defenders pinned down.

Consistent with their usual offensive tactics, the Japanese launched a series of banzai attacks the first night and suffered heavy casualties. On 25 July the 2nd Marine Division arrived on Tinian, and from then on the marines made steady progress. The most difficult battles occurred on 31 July and 1 August, as Japanese soldiers were pushed back to their last defensive position on a cliff on the southern end of the island. Although Tinian was declared secure on 1 August, Japanese resistance continued for one more week. Nevertheless, Spruance, Turner, and Smith were very pleased and considered Tinian one of the most successful amphibious landings of the war.

Following the occupation of Tinian, navy construction battalions— Seabees—rebuilt and expanded the island's airfields. By early 1945, six runways of eighty-five hundred feet were ready for use by the B-29s. The sixty-ton plane, the largest bomber in service during the war, carried a larger number of lethal payloads than any plane previously in history. The fifteen-hundred-mile flight from the Marianas to Japan was well within the plane's five-thousand-mile range, and the B-29s commenced sustained bombing of the Japanese home islands as soon as the runways were complete.

In early 1945, General Curtis LeMay took personal command of the 20th and 21st Bomber Commands, soon combined to create the 20th Air Force. Because the B-29s had difficulty hitting specific targets from thirty thousand feet, LeMay advocated fire-bombing enemy targets. Tokyo was first on his list. On 10 March more than three hundred B-29s dropped incendiary bombs on Japan's capital, destroying sixteen square miles of the city and killing approximately one hundred thousand people. Over the course of the next ten days similar—though not as destructive—attacks were made on Nagoya, Ōsaka, and Kōbe.

Despite the damage brought to the home islands, the Japanese fought on. While Japan was pounded from the air, the U.S. Navy continued to move across the Pacific toward Japan. The major battles of 1945, at Iwo Jima in February and Okinawa in April, were incredibly bloody. The ferocious Japanese resistance on both islands suggested to the United States that the war in the Pacific would not end until Japan had been totally destroyed.

Early on the morning of 6 August 1945, a B-29 named the *Enola Gay* took off from Tinian. The plane carried a single two-ton bomb of a new type. The long runways on Tinian were necessary for the plane, which carried seven thousand gallons of fuel in addition to the bomb. Five hours after takeoff, pilot Paul Tibbets received a favorable weather report over his primary target, and one hour later, at 0815 local time, he flew over Hiroshima. Japan surrendered a little over a week later.

In response to Japan's surrender, Tōjō shot himself in the chest. He survived his suicide attempt and was placed on trial before the International Military Tribunal for the Far East (Tokyo War Crimes Trials). Found guilty of war crimes and crimes against humanity, he was executed by hanging on 23 December 1948.

CONCLUSION

The casualty figures for the Battle of Saipan reveal the intense nature of the conflict: "The toll of American killed and wounded was high. Of the 71,034 officers and men that made up Holland Smith's Northern Troops and Landing Force, it is estimated that 3,674 Army and 10,437 Marine Corps personnel were killed, wounded or missing in action. This total of 14,111 represents about 20 percent of the combat troops committed, or roughly the same percentage of casualties suffered at Tarawa and Peleliu, both of bloody renown." The number of deaths was fairly evenly distributed among the units involved in the invasion: approximately 1,250 killed from the 2nd Marine Division, 1,100 from the 4th Marine Division, and 1,030 from the 27th Infantry Division. Many rifle companies suffered more than 20-percent casualty rates. As Crowl noted, "In exchange, almost the entire Japanese garrison of about 30,000 was wiped out."[1]

Every battle in the Pacific war was difficult and bloody, but the Battle of Saipan included some unique features. The fleet that transported the invasion force to the Marianas was one of the war's most impressive, both in size and firepower. The attack on the Mariana Islands necessitated carrying men, landing vehicles, supplies, food, guns, ammunition, tanks, and other equipment thousands of miles from the nearest naval or land bases. The invasion of Saipan was a logistical challenge that the U.S. Navy brilliantly mastered.

Having learned lessons from previous amphibious landings, the United

States greatly improved its planning and implementation in the Marianas in several areas: better use of intelligence gathering, including both photo and underwater reconnaissance; improved knowledge of reef configuration and tides; increased quality and quantity of landing vehicles (only 125 at Tarawa, but more than 700 at Saipan); use of submarines to interdict enemy reinforcements; and deployment of Task Force 58 to destroy Japanese land-based planes before the battle.

The battle plan itself was straightforward, massing American naval and airpower and placing sufficient marines on the beach to overwhelm the enemy. Given the difficulty of launching an amphibious operation on that scale, and despite unavoidable problems such as crowding on the beach, the first phase of the attack went as well as could be expected. By the end of D-Day the navy and army had delivered twenty thousand marines onto the beaches of Saipan, and the marines carried out their mission with the courage and dedication expected of the Corps. Confronted with overwhelming American power, the Japanese were supposed to surrender or be defeated in three days.

Holland Smith, as general in charge of all ground troops, did not have an alternative plan in case the Japanese refused to abide by the three-day time limit. In response to growing marine casualties as well as the imminent confrontation with the Japanese navy, the reasonable decision was made to land the reserve force, the 27th Infantry Division. These troops were deployed without adequate coordination between marine and army commanders, a contributing factor in the controversy between Holland Smith and Ralph Smith.

Another area of controversy involved the Battle of the Philippine Sea, as two of the best admirals in the U.S. Navy, Spruance and Mitscher, bickered over tactics. Mitscher wanted to sail directly toward the Japanese fleet so that he could launch his planes and take the offensive. Spruance, responsible for overall strategy, insisted on remaining relatively close to Saipan to protect the ground troops. In the ensuing confrontation, Japanese planes were forced to take the offensive, allowing American planes and antiaircraft fire to destroy most of them. Despite this decisive victory, Spruance and Mitscher continued to squabble after the war. This was unfortunate, as both had performed brilliantly during the battle. Spruance's defensive plan led to a decisive American victory, while Mitscher's launch schedule decimated Japanese resources. Finally, Mitscher's audacity in turning on all the lights on his ships in order to guide his pilots home surely ranks as one of the great moments in naval history.

In contrast to Admiral King, General MacArthur had insisted that the offensive line proceed through New Guinea toward the Philippines. The compromise between the army and navy, allowing both offensive prongs to advance simultaneously, had its advantages and disadvantages. The plan seemed to violate the military principle of concentration of forces, since it divided American resources and thereby weakened the amount of power that could be focused on any given Japanese target. But in practice, what appeared as a compromise that soothed egos turned out to be a brilliant strategy. The Japanese, already spread thinly over the vast island empire they had conquered, often guessed wrong in their predictions of where the Americans would strike. They were unable to consolidate their forces, as the American attack could emanate from several different directions simultaneously. At the same time, the Japanese military was confronted with the formidable and increasingly impossible job of supplying all of its dispersed units. Due to its tremendous productive capacity, the United States was able to supply MacArthur's offensive across New Guinea, the navy's attack against Japanese island strongholds, and the European war concurrently. The Japanese were unable to compete in this war of production; when they attempted to send supplies to island outposts, American submarines increasingly decimated their forces.

While MacArthur might not have acknowledged it, the Battle of Saipan and the Battle of the Philippine Sea laid the foundation for his victory. Japanese aircraft carriers lost many of their best planes and pilots as a result of the Battle of Saipan and the Great Marianas Turkey Shoot. Once Japan's carrier force was neutralized, the preconditions for the American victory at the Battle of Leyte Gulf in October were established.

Despite these quarrels among American military leaders, the progress of the battle was not seriously impeded, because the quality of individual marines and soldiers was excellent. After the Gyokusai, three posthumous Medals of Honor were awarded to soldiers. No one, not even Holland Smith, should have ever questioned the bravery of Lieutenant Colonel William J. O'Brien, Sergeant Thomas A. Baker, Captain Benjamin L. Salomon, and many other soldiers.

Similarly, three marines were awarded Medals of Honor posthumously, and many marines received other well-deserved medals and citations. Marines took great pride in being members of a special unit, the Corps, and were willing to make tremendous sacrifices for each other. If an officer was wounded or taken out of action, another marine would step up and take his place, allowing the platoon or company to continue on its mission.

Marines felt a bond to each other and to the Corps itself that helped them endure and conquer.

The Battle of Saipan pitted the marines' toughness against that of the Japanese soldiers. Both sides were totally dedicated and determined to win. Because the Japanese were committed to an offensive strategy that forced them to abandon their secure defensive positions, however, they wasted men, tanks, and resources in fruitless assaults. After the first few days, their only hope was the intervention of the Imperial Navy, but that possibility was eliminated at the Battle of the Philippine Sea. Without the prospect of fresh supplies or reinforcements, the Japanese had no choice but to surrender or fight to the death. Their culture led the vast majority of them to choose the latter course. Approximately a thousand surrendered while thousands more committed suicide.

Japanese soldiers displayed spirit and dedication. While it was not surprising that they lost the battle, the ferocity and length of the struggle must be credited to the toughness and tenacity of the individual Japanese warrior. In the end, even American marines saluted their fighting skills. While some marines called the Japanese sneaky or wasteful of life, many others expressed respect for them as fighters. Pharmacist's Mate Chester Szech paid the Japanese an ironic compliment: "They were good soldiers—about as crazy as marines." Private First Class Ralph Browner, a highly decorated marine, also compared the enemy with the Corps: "They were outstanding—as good as marines." Finally, Private Joe Epperson attributed to the Japanese traits held in high regard by marines: "They had guts—they were tough."[2] Although they failed in their goal to hold Saipan, the Japanese succeeded in their secondary objective of inflicting a high cost on the invaders. The Japanese fought fiercely in a hopeless cause. At the same time, they earned the grudging respect of their adversaries.

The Battle of Saipan was essential to American victory in the Pacific. The Americans broke through Japan's inner defense perimeter; disrupted Japanese shipping, communications, and supply lines to the rest of its forces in the Pacific; won a major sea battle; and captured essential forward air bases for the bombing of Japan. From these secure bases for the new B-29s, U.S. air forces were within striking distance of every city in Japan. Admiral King had hoped for and predicted all of these consequences.

The conquest of Saipan and Tinian made American victory in the Pacific inevitable. Until that moment, the Japanese government continued to believe that success, or at least an honorable settlement that left Japan in control of several of its possessions, remained possible. While Japan had suffered serious setbacks in 1942 and 1943 and throughout the first half of 1944, Saipan was the first loss of its prewar territory or inner defense line. Despite disheartening battlefield news beginning with the defeat at Midway in 1942 and the fall of Guadalcanal in 1943, Japanese officials maintained a positive view of the war's prospects. Saipan ended that optimism and started the psychological defeat of Japan. From the summer of 1944 on, Japan had to confront the reality that it would lose the war.

June 1944 was the decisive month of World War II. Like its more famous counterpart in France, D-Day on Saipan was won despite numerous problems and errors. In order to carry out this invasion, the U.S. Navy had to project its power thousands of miles from a safe port. In the Pacific as in Europe, the United States brought massive firepower against the enemy. For the rest of the war, both fronts witnessed the Allies' inexorable advance against the Axis powers. Just as the Normandy invasion destroyed Germany's chances for victory in Europe, the Battle of Saipan ended Japan's prospects for victory in the Pacific. The Battle of Saipan ranks in importance with Guadalcanal, Iwo Jima, and Okinawa and deserves to be remembered as one of the crucial battles of World War II.

Moreover, this display of American strength, with two nearly simultaneous D-Day invasions, established the United States as the world's most formidable military power. The 6th and 15th of June 1944 demonstrated America's ability to project a global military presence.

HOLLAND SMITH AND THE ARMY

Ralph Smith was not the only high-ranking officer who was relieved of his command during World War II—at least fourteen other senior officers suffered the same fate. Thirteen of those incidents occurred in the European theater, one in the Aleutians, and one in the Pacific. In only two of those cases were army commanders removed by officers from other services: one in the Aleutians and the other in the Pacific. The only such event in the entire Pacific theater was Holland Smith's dismissal of Ralph Smith from command of the 27th Infantry Division during the fighting for Nafutan Point and central Saipan.

Marine Lieutenant General Holland Smith had the right to relieve army Major General Ralph Smith. As the commander of the Fifth Amphibious Corps, Holland Smith was Ralph Smith's superior officer for the duration of the Battle of Saipan. No one, not even army officers, ever questioned Howlin' Mad's authority according to the chain of command. The issue was whether Ralph Smith's actions warranted the treatment he received. While the details are confusing and intricate, the conclusion reached by Benjamin Persons was that "Smith of the Marines was lying in wait for Smith of the Army. . . . In this case there was absolutely nothing that Ralph Smith could have done differently that would have saved him."[1] Holland Smith had admitted his antipathy to the 27th Division even before soldiers arrived at Saipan: "After my experience with the Twenty-seventh at Makin and Eniwetok, I was reluctant to use them again in the Marianas, but when the operation was planned they were the only troops available in Hawaii and I had to take them."[2] His view was not shared by army command, which considered the 27th a well-trained and experienced battle unit.

As the battle for Saipan progressed, Holland Smith was disturbed by several factors involving the performance of the 27th Division. First, he thought the 105th Regiment was taking too long to annihilate the Nafutan Point resistance. Believing that there were only a few hundred Japanese in the area, he wanted to leave only one battalion in the south. The two marine divisions were prepared to turn north to confront the bulk of the Japanese forces, so he wanted all available resources concentrated on that part of the campaign. As a result of the progress the army had made the day before, on the morning of 21 June Holland Smith ordered one battalion to stay at Nafutan and "mop up remaining enemy detachments." Because increased enemy opposition was encountered on 21 June, however, Ralph Smith called Marine Corps headquarters and asked for an entire regiment (three battalions) to remain in the south to complete that task. The two generals compromised, with two battalions of the 105th dedicated to Nafutan Point and one kept in reserve. The 165th Regiment was withdrawn from the fight for Nafutan and turned northward to assist the marines.

Shortly thereafter, new problems arose between the two Smiths. Based on his telephone conversation with Holland Smith, Ralph Smith issued Order 45A, calling for the 105th Regiment to hold its position until it had reorganized its lines and then resume the offensive. At 0830 on 22 June, Howlin' Mad's message confirming his agreement with Ralph Smith arrived at 27th Division headquarters. Later that day the situation changed again, as Marine Corps headquarters decided that one battalion would be sufficient to complete the takeover of Nafutan. Brigadier General Graves Erskine ordered Ralph Smith to withdraw one of his battalions from the south and move it toward marine lines. Despite Ralph Smith's protest and warning that army lines would be too thin to prevent an enemy breakthrough, the order was issued. Under these new conditions, Ralph Smith felt that his men needed time to adjust to the situation, with only one battalion (2nd Battalion, 105th Regiment) covering the territory that had originally been assigned to four battalions. Ralph Smith's Order 46 told the 2nd Battalion to "continue operations to mop up the remaining enemy detachments in Nafutan Point area. On conclusion of this mission revert to Corps control." Nevertheless, when Marine Corps headquarters issued a similar order two hours later, it mandated that the 105th "continue operations at daylight to mop up remaining enemy detachments." The phrase "at daylight" was added without Ralph Smith's prior knowledge, and by the time the order was received and transmitted it was too late for the 2nd Battalion, in the midst of reorganizing its lines, to carry it out. Its attack did not begin until 1300 the next day.[3]

Notwithstanding the army's difficult position in terms of manpower and hazardous terrain, Holland Smith became increasingly impatient and frustrated with the situation in the south as well as in the center of the island. By the afternoon of 23 June he let army Major General Sanderford Jarman know that he was not pleased. As Jarman recalled, Holland Smith "was very much concerned about the situation which he was presented with in regard to the 27th Div. He outlined to me the many things that had happened with respect to the failure of the 27th Div to advance . . . in his opinion he didn't think they would fight." Howlin' Mad indicated that he would "immediately relieve the division commander and assign someone else," but he hesitated because he knew the army would protest.[4] Jarman subsequently spoke with Ralph Smith about the situation:

> I found that General (Ralph) Smith had been up to the front lines all afternoon and was thoroughly familiar with the situation. I talked to General [Ralph] Smith and explained the situation as I saw it and that I felt from reports from the Corps Commander that his division was not carrying its full share. He immediately replied that such was true; that he was in no way satisfied with what his regimental commanders had done during the day and that he had been with them and had pointed out to them the situation. He further indicated to me that he was going to be present tomorrow, June 24, with this division when it made its jump-off and he would personally see to it that the division went forward. I explained my interest in the matter was that I was senior Army commander present and was anxious to see that the Army did its job as it should be done.[5]

Concerned about the progress of his troops, Ralph Smith planned to be at the front lines himself the next day to oversee the advance.

The next morning Holland Smith sent Ralph Smith the following message: "Commanding general is highly displeased with the failure of the 27th Division on June 23rd to launch its attack as ordered at K [King] Hour [1000] and the lack of offensive action displayed by the Division in its failure to advance . . . when opposed only by small arms and mortar fire."[6] This reprimand was received at 1030, four hours after Ralph Smith and his assistant division commander, Brigadier General Ogden Ross, had left for the front. That morning, as Love reported, Ralph Smith "went over every foot of ground with the men who were fighting and made a complete survey of the situation. By noon he had worked out a plan of maneuver by which he hoped to outflank the Japanese stronghold."[7] That afternoon the

27th Division began to implement the flanking maneuver. Ralph Smith remained at the front with his troops all day as the new effort was launched, and at the same time he worked on a comprehensive attack plan for the next day. Despite great danger to himself, he remained in that area for several hours. One of his officers, Major Jacob Herzog, later commented: "He showed a tremendous amount of bravery—took charge in reorganizing things, talking to company and battalion commanders, and getting the front organized."[8]

Ralph Smith was unaware that Holland Smith had already made his decision regarding his dismissal. At 1130 on 24 June, only one hour after Ralph Smith had received the note of disapproval, Howlin' Mad was on board Admiral Turner's flagship, the *Rocky Mount*, outlining his case against the army commander. "Terrible" Turner, also known for his temper, supported Smith's view of the 27th Division and suggested that Howlin' Mad had full authority to relieve Ralph Smith of command.

Nevertheless, given the potential for controversy generated by a marine general's dismissal of an army general, Turner and Holland Smith sailed to confer with Admiral Spruance aboard the *Indianapolis*. In his report to Spruance, the marine general accused Ralph Smith of several transgressions: giving orders to units at Nafutan Point that were not under his command, countering the order to the 105th at Nafutan to attack with an order to "hold," and endangering the entire operation on Saipan by allowing his troops to be late in relieving the marines on 23 June. "Ralph Smith has shown that he lacks aggressive spirit and his division is slowing our own advance," Holland Smith told Spruance. "He should be relieved."[9] Rear Admiral Charles "Carl" Moore, Spruance's chief of staff, described Howlin' Mad as "very indignant . . . disgusted with the general's performance . . . [and] irritated . . . beyond measure with its [the 27th's] failure to attack."[10] Confronted by Smith and Turner, his two highest commanders in the Saipan operation, Spruance was in a difficult situation. According to the admiral's biographer, "Holland Smith thus forced Spruance to make a distasteful decision with potentially explosive repercussions. . . . Spruance was contemplating the open firing of an Army general by a Navy admiral upon the recommendation of a Marine Corps general. The Army would be humiliated and infuriated." Spruance had only the testimony of his corps commander. "Had Holland Smith possessed a modicum of forbearance, had he promoted harmony rather than provoked antagonism, perhaps the crisis would have been averted. But the inflammatory general—Spruance's personal choice to lead his troops—finally had precipitated an imbroglio that Spruance could no longer evade or smooth over. Unless Spruance could find an alternative solution, he had to support his Marine general and to accept the unpleasant consequences."[11] Moore wrote the order for Ralph Smith's replacement, and Spruance signed it: "You are authorized and directed to relieve Major General Ralph Smith from command of the Twenty-seventh Division, U.S. Army, and place Major General Jarman in command of this division. This action is taken in order that the offensive on Saipan may proceed in accordance with the plans and orders of the Commander, Northern Troops and Landing Force."[12]

At 1500 on 24 June a jeep pulled up near the front lines and the driver handed Ralph Smith a sealed envelope that contained the removal notice. After reading the message, Smith remained at the front for the rest of the day, telling no one of his dismissal and continuing to review the attack plans for that day and the next. At 1700 he returned to headquarters and spent much of the evening outlining the frontline situation with his replacement, General Jarman. Smith offered to stay and assist in any way he could. "I had all my maps there and I showed him [Jarman] what my plans were to push through the areas of the 4th Division on the right and envelope the resistance that was holding us up," he recalled.[13] Jarman implemented Smith's plan the next day. Nevertheless, Howlin' Mad did not want Ralph Smith on Saipan any longer, and that night at 2300 a message from Marine Corps headquarters ordered him off the island before dawn. At 0330 Ralph Smith was on Blue Beach 1, just south of the Charan Kanoa pier, and two hours later he boarded a seaplane for the flight to Eniwetok, where he would stop over on the way to Hawaii.

It is important to review Holland Smith's reasons for removing Ralph Smith. From Howlin' Mad's perspective, the 27th Division was under Marine Corps command, and Ralph Smith did not have the authority to issue his Order 45A. Further, Holland Smith was angered by Order 45A's call for the 105th Regiment to "hold" before it attacked. The Marine Corps commander wanted the 105th to move forward "at daylight" and "mop up" any opposition at Nafutan.

The orders issued by both officers were nearly identical. In reality, the wording of Howlin' Mad's Operation Order 9-44 does not support his contention that all of the 27th Division had been placed under Marine Corps control. Ralph Smith later testified that he had never been told that he did not have tactical command of the 105th Regiment. The final Marine Corps headquarters order inserting the words "at daylight" caught the 105th in the middle of reorganizing its lines to compensate for the redeployment of one of its battalions. Nevertheless, once Howlin' Mad was determined to dismiss Ralph Smith, he used the events at Nafutan Point as an excuse. An examination of the substance of the accusation does not support the marine general.

Another issue involved the marine lines in central Saipan on 23 June. Holland Smith was right to worry about his divisions' flanks as they moved north with the army lagging behind. As overall commander, that was his proper concern. Nevertheless, he was not correct in blaming Ralph Smith for the tardiness of one company of the 106th Regiment that had been ordered to move between marine divisions. Transporting all of the soldiers and their vehicles forward took an hour or two longer than planned in only one sector. When the soldiers arrived at the front, they discovered that they were several hundred yards behind their anticipated jumping-off point. On the first day of battle they recovered much of that territory. That was the same day that Ralph Smith was removed from command, even as his soldiers slowly advanced against strong enemy fire. Ironically, the army plan of attack after Ralph Smith's removal was the one developed by Smith himself, who had spent hours at the front with his men checking the terrain and evaluating various tactical alternatives. The 27th Division was deployed in rugged terrain against targets with nicknames like Hell's Pocket, Death Valley, and Purple Heart Ridge. Ralph Smith should not have been blamed for the week of seeming stalemate in this sector. Indeed, he was dismissed at the beginning of the battle for the center of the island, not after the week-long difficulty. Holland Smith did not visit the front or witness in person the obstacles faced by the army or his own marines. Even a Marine Corps historian has acknowledged that "Holland Smith didn't fully recognize the severity of the opposition."[14]

Military commanders in Washington wanted the Smith controversy buried, but interservice rivalry had been simmering beneath the surface in the war in the Pacific. General MacArthur had lobbied for his vision of an army victory in the Philippines, while Admiral King insisted on the primacy of the navy in a central Pacific attack. Although General George C. Marshall, chairman of the Joint Chiefs, did not want the controversy to fester and possibly damage the long-term cooperation still necessary to win the war, it proved to be impossible to keep the entire story a secret.

After leaving Saipan, Ralph Smith returned to Oahu and was seen at the army headquarters at Fort Shafter. When rumors about his dismissal began to spread through Hawaii, Lieutenant General Robert C. Richardson, commander of army forces in the Pacific, decided to conduct an official inquiry. He convened a board that included several distinguished army officers: Lieutenant General Simon B. Buckner, Major General John R. Hodge, Brigadier General Henry Holmes Jr., and Brigadier General Roy Blount.[15] The Buckner Board met in July, hearing testimony and collecting documents. All of the principals involved in the controversy submitted written statements and documentation. In addition to reports from Holland Smith and Ralph Smith, the board received material from Admiral Spruance, Generals Jarman and Griner, Colonel Kelley of the 165th Regiment, and Colonel Ayers of the 106th Regiment. The board collected and examined all of the orders issued by both Smiths as well as Holland Smith's notes to Spruance and additional material provided by Howlin' Mad.[16]

In its conclusion, the Buckner Board found that both of Holland Smith's charges against Ralph Smith were unfounded. "No part of the evidence points toward any attempt on the part of Major General Ralph C. Smith to 'contravene' orders relative to the action on Nafutan Point," it stated. "It was logical and appropriate that the commanding general, 27th Division, take the necessary steps to insure that the 105th Infantry had a directive."[17] The board also examined the 106th's tardy offensive on 23 June:

> The bulk of the 27th Division was opposed by the enemy's main defensive position, on a difficult piece of terrain, naturally adapted to defense, artificially strengthened, well manned, and heavily covered by fire. Lieutenant General Holland M. Smith was not aware of the strength of this position and expected the 27th Division to overrun it rapidly. The 27th Division, instead of massing its personnel in a frontal attack against the strongest part of the enemy's position, initiated a maneuver to contain and outflank the enemy's resistance. The delay incident to this situation was mistaken by Lieutenant General Holland M. Smith as an indication that the 27th Division was lacking in aggressiveness and that its commander was inefficient.[18]

In addition, the board reached four general conclusions: "(1) That Holland Smith had full authority to relieve Ralph Smith from his command. (2) That Holland Smith was not fully informed regarding conditions in the zone of the 27th Division when he issued orders relieving Ralph Smith. (3) That the relief of Ralph Smith was not justified by facts. (4) That Ralph Smith's official record or future commands should not be adversely affected by his relief."[19]

The board's findings were supposed to be kept secret so that the incident would not attract public attention, but it did not work out that way. Other officers had been relieved of command during the war, but those situations had rarely become the subject of open discussion. This caution partly reflected self-imposed press censorship while the outcome of the war remained uncertain, but as the war progressed and Allied victory seemed inevitable, the discretion exercised by reporters lessened and military operations were increasingly debated and critiqued, especially in newspapers hostile to President Franklin Roosevelt. The controversy between the Smiths, which should have remained a private military matter, entered into public discourse in this same manner. Ralph Smith had nothing to do with the debate, as he maintained public silence on the subject for most of his life. Nevertheless, the anti-Roosevelt newspapers of William Randolph Hearst picked up the story. Hearst supported General MacArthur, both in his demand for more resources for the army in New Guinea and the Philippines and in his incipient presidential aspirations in 1944. As described by Gailey and Potter, the controversy became public on 8 July when the Hearst-controlled *San Francisco Examiner* published a pro-army front-page article on the dismissal of Ralph Smith that also criticized the Marine Corps. Colonel John Lemp, who had served as a War Department observer on Saipan, may have leaked the story. Under the headline "Army General Relieved in Row over Marine Losses," the article went on to charge: "Allegedly excessive loss of life attributed to Marine Corps impetuosity of attack. . . . The controversy hangs upon Marine tactics versus Army tactics, the Marines seeking a swift decision at high cost, while the Army moved more deliberately—at lesser cost." In addition to blaming the Marine Corps and its tactics for "excessive loss of life," the article called for MacArthur's appointment as supreme commander of all forces in the Pacific. The newspaper asserted that MacArthur's "difficult and hazardous military operations . . . have been successfully carried out with little loss of life in most cases." On 17 July the *New York Journal-American*, another Hearst paper, called the loss of American lives on Saipan a "reckless and needless waste" and claimed that "the American people were shocked by the staggering casualties on Saipan. . . . The Army's advocate of more cautious tactics has been relieved of his command."[20] While seemingly a criticism of Holland Smith, this article actually had another objective: defense of the army and criticism of the marines again reflected the Hearst agenda to elevate MacArthur. The articles used the controversy for their own purposes, but nevertheless they brought the debate into the public arena. Other newspapers picked up the story, and several editorials appeared on the progress of the war in the Pacific. Finally, as Love pointed out, bills were introduced in Congress demanding an investigation.[21]

Lieutenant General Richardson in Hawaii had always opposed the concept of a marine general commanding army soldiers, and he had specifically tried to block Holland Smith's appointment to lead the invasion of Saipan. Richardson was angry and upset by the events that transpired on Saipan as well as subsequent newspaper and magazine articles, feeling that they insulted the fighting spirit of the army. In addition to appointing the Buckner Board, Richardson took a number of other actions designed to rehabilitate the army's reputation. After notifying Admiral Nimitz of his plans, he traveled to Saipan, arriving on 12 July, just after the island had been declared secured. Without authorization from Spruance, Turner, or Holland Smith, Richardson held a formal review of the 27th Division and distributed medals and decorations to the soldiers. Spruance realized that Richardson's actions and his lack of courtesy to the navy and marines would lead to another fight between the services. Spruance cautioned Howlin' Mad to keep quiet, and Smith promised his best behavior. When Smith and Major General Harry Schmidt, 4th Marine Division commander, visited Richardson, the army general bluntly told Smith what he thought:

> You had no right to relieve Ralph Smith. The 27th is one of the best trained divisions in the Pacific. I trained it myself. You discriminated against the Army in favor of the marines. I want you to know that you can't push the Army around the way you've been doing. You and your corps commanders aren't as well qualified to lead large bodies of troops as general officers in the Army. We've had more experience in handling troops than you've had, and yet you dare remove one of my generals. . . . You marines are nothing but a bunch of beach runners anyway. What do you know about land warfare?[22]

According to Nimitz's biographer: "To the incredulous amazement of all who heard the story, Howlin' Mad Smith managed to hold his tongue through this torrent of abuse."[23] Even Holland Smith was impressed with his own silence: "For a man with my explosive reputation, I must confess that I conducted myself with admirable restraint under this barrage."[24] Smith had kept his promise to Spruance.

Unluckily for Richardson, Turner, who could be as volatile as Howlin' Mad, had not promised Spruance that he would suffer in silence. When Richardson boarded Turner's flagship, the *Rocky Mount*, the admiral rebuked him for ignoring protocol and the chain of command. As Potter indicated, Richardson claimed that "he was in no way accountable to any officer in the Marianas. At that point, Terrible Turner let loose a blast that caused the visiting general to turn white with anger." Richardson sailed to the *Indianapolis* to complain to Admiral Spruance, who attempted to mollify the general: "That's just Kelly Turner's way and no one takes him seriously."[25]

Holland Smith did not verbally confront Richardson, but he did write a full report on Richardson's behavior. General Schmidt corroborated Smith's version. Terrible Turner submitted his own comments, entitled "Reporting unwarranted assumption of command authority by Lieutenant General R.C. Richardson, Jr., USA." Finally, Richardson wrote a report accusing Turner of "gross discourtesy." All of this paperwork was sent to Admiral Nimitz, who at first "simply disregarded the whole silly dispute."[26]

Although the public controversy slowly abated, the military dealt with the situation in its own way—quietly yet firmly. In order to make the point that the army retained control over its own officers, Richardson had replaced Jarman, Holland Smith's appointee, with Major General George Griner as commander of the 27th Division on 26 June. Jarman, who had relieved Ralph Smith on Saipan but was not responsible for the chain of events, had served only two days in command of the army forces there. As a temporary measure, Richardson gave Ralph Smith command of Griner's 98th Infantry Division on Hawaii.

The Joint Chiefs still had to decide where Ralph Smith would serve on a more permanent basis. On 16 August, Major General Thomas Handy, assistant chief of staff to George C. Marshall in Washington, recommended that "it would be desirable that both Smiths be ordered out of the Pacific Ocean area. While I do not believe we should make a definite recommendation to the Navy for the relief of Holland Smith, I think that positive action should be taken to get Ralph Smith out of the area. His presence undoubtedly tends to aggravate a bad situation between the services." The War Department, noted Potter, moved quickly and, "in order to ease frictions, transferred Ralph Smith out of the Pacific theater and gave him a command in Europe."[27] At the end of the summer of 1944, the Allies were just completing the liberation of France, and Ralph Smith's prewar training included both the French language and French military tactics. Smith's expertise in these areas fit in perfectly with the U.S. Army's needs and the sensitivity of the situation.

The navy faced a similar decision with regard to Holland Smith. In this case, some army officers had such strong views on the subject that they did not want to leave the decision to the navy alone. When the Battle of Saipan ended, several army commanders sent reports to Richardson regarding army-marine relations. In August, Ralph Smith declared that "no Army combat troops should ever again be permitted to serve under the command of Marine Lieutenant General Holland M. Smith." A few days earlier, Brigadier General Redmond F. Kernan, in charge of the 27th Division Artillery on Saipan, had conveyed similar sentiments to Richardson. Griner, who led the 27th Division from 26 June until the Saipan hostilities ended, developed the "firm conviction that he [Holland Smith] is so prejudiced against the Army that no Army Division serving under his command alongside of Marine Divisions can expect that their deeds will receive fair and honest evaluation."[28] During the month of August, while various army officers were sending these comments to Richardson, the controversy faded from public interest. It appeared that the military would be able to resolve the situation quietly.

In September, however, *Time* magazine published an article that revived the case and polarized sentiment on both sides. The article clearly supported Holland Smith's version of the events on Saipan. It included a picture of Smith with his fists clenched, as if he were prepared to knock out the Japanese single-handedly. In contrast to the two-fisted Howlin' Mad, Ralph Smith was described as "handsome and soft-voiced," not exactly the image of a tough, no-nonsense general. The article opened:

> At a Washington press conference, after his return last week from the Marianas, tough Lieut. General Holland M. Smith . . . was asked . . . Was it true that he had fired one of his division commanders, the Army's Major General Ralph Smith? . . . Snorted "Howlin' Mad" Smith: "I knew someone would ask that question. One of the many prerogatives and responsibilities of a commanding officer . . . is the assignment and transfer of officers commanding subordinate elements. . . . Unfortunately, circumstances forced me to exercise one of these prerogatives. I did relieve General Ralph Smith."[29]

At first the article suggested that the controversy was related to differences between army and marine tactics: "Marines tear into battle, trying to win it quickly; soldiers proceed cautiously, to save lives. . . . The Marines believe that their forge-ahead tactics cost less in lives than trying to cut off the enemy's tail by inches." Despite these differences, the article claimed, the argument over tactics was not the essential element of the situation, since the marines were moving forward when

> they had to wait, because two regiments of the 27th Army Division—with battalions faced in three directions, unable even to form a line—were hopelessly bogged down in the center. The third regiment of the 27th meanwhile had failed

dismally to clean out a pocket of Japs in the southeast corner of the island. . . .
Ralph Smith's men froze in their foxholes. For days these men, who lacked confidence in their officers, were held up by handfuls of Japs in caves. . . . From the
Marine point of view, General Ralph Smith's chief fault was that he had long ago
failed to get tough enough to remove incompetent subordinate officers.[30]

These were serious charges, none more so than the accusation that
Smith's men "froze in their foxholes." The article claimed that the performance of the 27th Division improved after Smith's dismissal but that
eventually "its greenest regiment broke and let some 3,000 Japs through in
a suicide charge which a marine artillery battalion finally stopped, at great
cost to itself." Finally, the article blamed the 27th Division for unnecessary
casualties on Saipan: "One thing was clear: when field commanders hesi-
tate to remove subordinates for fear of inter-service contention, battles and
lives will be needlessly lost."[31] In effect, the article suggested that, under
incompetent officers, army soldiers had behaved like cowards.

Journalist Robert Sherrod, who had always been a strong supporter
of the marines and had covered the battle for Saipan in person, wrote
the *Time* article. In his subsequent book on the war in the Pacific, *On to
Westward*, he asserted that he had visited Marine Corps headquarters on
24 June, the day Ralph Smith was removed. According to Sherrod's version
of ensuing events, Howlin' Mad was "nervous and remorseful" about his
decision: "Ralph Smith is my friend but, good God, I've got a duty to my
country. I've lost 7,000 Marines. Can I afford to lose back what they have
gained? To let my Marines die in vain? I know I'm sticking my neck out
. . . but my conscience is clear. I did my duty. When Ralph Smith issued
an order to hold after I had told him to attack, I had no other choice but
to relieve him."[32]

Unfortunately, Sherrod did not question why Howlin' Mad made this
self-serving remark in the presence of journalists. In addition, the writer
did not examine the veracity of the comment itself. The majority of marine
losses had occurred before the army landed. The seven thousand marine
casualties were not the fault of the army, which was fighting in the south
of Saipan and was not committed to the center of the island until the day
before Ralph Smith's removal. At the same time, these losses were not the
fault of the marines, who had the daunting task of taking the beaches and
then moving forward against a determined foe. Japanese defenses, com-
bining small-arms fire, artillery, mortars, and the tenacity of its soldiers,
explained the extent of the American casualties. Nevertheless, even forty-
five years later, in 1990, Sherrod could not overcome his anti-army bias.
He admitted that he had gone "too far in questioning the courage of the

Twenty-seventh Division soldiers" when he wrote that they "froze in their foxholes." But his supposed apology was negated by another stinging insult: "Whatever the weakness of this inept National Guard outfit, I should not have done it and I'm sorry."[33] Again Sherrod dropped an unsubstantiated allegation, this time "inept," without evidence. Although the 27th Division was originally a National Guard unit, it had been federalized in 1940 and by 1944 had been significantly transformed by the draft and war experience. The division served with distinction on Makin, on Saipan, and later on Okinawa.

The *Time* article reopened the public discussion. Coincidentally, yet simultaneously with the publication of that article, Admiral Nimitz submitted required paperwork that evaluated Holland Smith and his performance as a commanding officer. In this "Report on Fitness of Officers of the United States Marine Corps," Nimitz lowered several of Smith's grades from his previous report, which had been filed before Saipan. In response to the question about characteristics that might "adversely affect his efficiency," Nimitz wrote that Smith "sometimes talks indiscreetly." Further, when asked to consider whether he wanted this officer under his command in time of war, Nimitz downgraded Smith from "particularly glad to have him" to "glad to have him." Nimitz's explanation put the situation in perspective: "Except for certain of his temperamental qualities that have caused difficulties in dealing with some contemporary officers, check would have been (a) [that is, 'particularly glad']." Nimitz concluded his evaluation by noting: "This officer has demonstrated to a high degree his capabilities as an organizer, planner, and in combat. His usefulness has been to some extent impaired by wrangles and disharmony that might have been avoided." Smith's overall rating was "excellent rather than outstanding." Nimitz's previous report on Smith, completed prior to the Saipan operation, contained none of these criticisms.[34]

In October 1944 "Richardson forwarded to Admiral Nimitz a complete refutation, accompanied by documents that proved the *Time* article had no basis in fact." Sherrod's article had seriously insulted and hurt the army, and Richardson wanted the navy to "take action to officially remove the stigma attached to the name of the 27th Division."[35] Further, Richardson wanted Sherrod to be stripped of his press credentials. By the end of the month, Nimitz was convinced that the army had presented some reasonable arguments and asked Admiral King to assist with rehabilitating the reputation of the 27th Division. Nimitz, who generally favored compromise, was willing to accommodate the army on this matter in order to maintain the morale of the 27th Division and cordial relations between the navy and army. Attempting to avoid a further deterioration in interservice relations, Nimitz told King that he was sending the materials informally so that they would not mandate an official response or inquiry. "I am particularly not bringing these matters to your official attention because I still have hope of effecting settlements locally. . . . If I forward them to you officially, it may become necessary for you to take the matter up with the War Department, which might result in unpleasant and unnecessary controversy at a time when we need all our energies to win the war."[36]

Despite Nimitz's efforts toward reconciliation, King continued to support Holland Smith, and King and George C. Marshall confronted each other on this issue. Each commander defended his own service. King asserted that "Richardson had no business setting up an all-army board to pass on the decision of a marine officer," while Marshall believed that "Richardson was within his rights since the board had no judicial authority and was set up merely to furnish advice to Richardson."[37] Marshall blamed the controversy on the lack of leadership in the Pacific area, insisting that senior officers should prevent and remedy these situations on their own. Marshall was implicitly criticizing Nimitz, Spruance, and Turner for allowing Holland Smith to act as he did, while King disagreed with the actions of the army and Richardson. Nevertheless, Marshall took no further action. He opposed any exacerbation of the interservice rivalries and felt that the entire issue should be allowed to fade from public memory. As chairman of the Joint Chiefs, Marshall had responsibilities over all branches of the military, and he realized that additional letters from one service to another would only make the prosecution of the war more difficult.

In the end, mild action was taken. The navy moved Holland Smith to Hawaii, placing him in charge of the "newly created Fleet Marine Force, Pacific. This promotion, which was in the works before the fracas, assured that Smith would not again command soldiers. Nor would he be in direct command of any combat units."[38] From the perspective of Holland Smith, however, this change in status was hardly a promotion. In his new capacity he exercised administrative control over the marines in the Pacific, but his combat days were almost over. While officially serving as commanding general at Iwo Jima, in reality he played a reduced role compared to his direct control at Saipan. On Okinawa the commanding general was Lieutenant General Simon Bolivar Buckner of the U.S. Army, chairman of the commission on the Smith affair. Holland Smith grew embittered and expressed his disappointment a few years later in his memoir, *Coral and Brass*.

COMING HOME

Although the Battle of Saipan ended in July 1944 and Japan surrendered in August 1945, the war did not end for some of the veterans of the Pacific battles. Most received treatment for their wounds and physical ailments, but few were treated for the psychological effects of their wartime experiences. Although many marines and soldiers spoke with me or wrote to me over a period of several years, many hesitated at first to discuss the details of their battle experiences. Their reluctance in this area was understandable, as articulating a personal account of battle forces a person to relive and to see the picture again in his mind. Some marines indicated that they tried to forget the battles as soon as the war ended but that this proved impossible. As Sergeant Eugene V. Taylor of A Company, 4th Tank Division, 4th Marine Division, wrote: "I have tried to answer some of your questions as they appear in your email, in that order. As for the rest of your questions, I have tried to forget every subject you asked for the last 58 years. It would do me no good to delve into those subjects now or ever."[1]

When marines or soldiers did share their battle stories with me, they often described friends dying violently. Sometimes death came quickly, but just as often it was slow and difficult. Wounds were ugly, brains and guts were spilled, and men suffered in agony. Dead bodies turned black and bloated in the sun; flies and maggots filled every body cavity. The odor was horrific. No one can blame a veteran for not wanting to remember those scenes. Several times, after a marine left my interview table, his

Figure 24. Bidding farewell to marines killed in action, July 1944; courtesy of Private Rod Sandburg (USMC).

wife of perhaps forty or fifty years would take me aside and ask for details of his experiences. For good reasons, the marines did not want to inflict the pain of their memories on their families. They lived alone with their images of war, only feeling comfortable at reunions where they could share their stories with other marines or soldiers who had been through similar experiences.

Post-traumatic stress syndrome, which is now known to have been in evidence after all wars, was not studied seriously until after the Vietnam War. With all veterans returning from World War II as heroes, the idea that stress might result in nightmares, alcoholism, depression, or other health problems was simply not part of the national discussion in the war's aftermath. Studies have suggested that close to 19 percent of combat troops experience some form of traumatic stress and that about 9 percent suffer from more serious disorders. Many of the veterans discussed here fall into the former category, those who experience short-term stress-related symptoms and then make a full recovery.

World War II veterans had won a great victory; they won the good war.

Although they came home to a welcoming nation, it was never that simple. While they had used many long-distance weapons—naval bombardment, artillery, mortars, and airplane strafing and bombing—much of the fighting was close and personal and nasty. Sometimes it was hand-to-hand combat with knives and bayonets. The troops did a fabulous job under unimaginable circumstances. The vast majority adapted well to civilian life and modestly accepted the accolades of a grateful nation.

Private First Class Walter Bailey of Lynn, Massachusetts, served with C Company, 1st Battalion, 24th Marines. As a BAR man, he was a brave and tough marine. When asked how he endured the heat, hills, and slippery slopes they confronted every day, Bailey's explanation was simple: "We were young, we were in good shape, and we didn't know any better." Before landing on Saipan he had participated in the battle for Roi-Namur, where he witnessed an event that changed his attitude toward the marines. As Bailey and three other marines advanced, a marine tank came up from behind and killed Bailey's buddies. After this incident, Bailey never felt the same about the Corps. In fact, he questioned marine tactics, and he related the story of one of his officers who was killed because he insisted on standing up and charging straight toward enemy machine-gun fire. While on Saipan, Bailey received a head wound and was evacuated off the island. He suspected that he might have been a victim of friendly fire, like his three friends on Roi-Namur. After the war Bailey returned to Massachusetts, where he refused to talk about his war experiences with his family. Bailey found comfort in the Twenty-third Psalm.[2]

Private First Class Ralph Browner, from the Bakersfield, California, area, served with A Company, 1st Battalion, 2nd Marines, and received the Navy Cross for his heroic stand on the beach at Karaberra Pass on the night of 8–9 July. He emerged barely conscious after his ordeal; he was suffering from the ravages of dengue fever. He spent nine days in the hospital, but during that time a Japanese soldier slipped into the hospital tent and cut the throats of three wounded marines. Browner was spared because his cot was on the other side of the tent. Although not fully recovered and without permission, Browner left the hospital and rejoined his company for the invasion of Tinian. At the end of that battle he watched as a Japanese woman killed her daughter and herself rather than surrender, but he also recalled finding a box with a newborn baby that he turned over to a corpsman. By the end of the war, Browner had received two more Navy Crosses. Memories of death and "body parts of babies" kept Browner from discussing his war experiences for thirty years. Attending marine reunions where others shared similar experiences helped break down those barriers. His assessment of his survival was simple: "I had a charmed life."[3]

Corporal Basil Duncan of Cooper, Texas, served with the 3rd Battalion, 25th Marines. He joined the Corps in November 1943 and saw his first action in the Marshall Islands at Kwajalein. He recalled the landing on Saipan on D-Day as "a bloody mess . . . what stands out is every day, mostly the artillery shelling, the strafing attack on the beach, the mortars, the constant mortars and a couple of fire fights that I found myself involved in alone. Seeing my friends get blown to pieces will stay in my memory until the day I pass on. I witnessed hundreds of civilians jumping from the cliffs after first tossing their children over the cliff and on the rocks below. That scene will haunt me forever."[4]

Sergeant Jim Evans of Chicago served with K Company, 3rd Battalion, 6th Marines, and he recalled the landing on D-Day as "horrendous . . . the Japs were waiting for us." His luck ran out on the third day when he was wounded, but he was "patched up" and returned to his unit, only to be hit with shrapnel from a mortar round on the sixth day. Evans was evacuated to a hospital ship. He remembered lying in his own blood and dirty uniform when a nurse objected to his soiling the sheets. Evans just looked up, asked if she was talking to him, and turned over and went back to sleep. He was eventually evacuated to a hospital in Hawaii, but the doctors were never able to remove all the mortar shrapnel from his legs. Commenting on his experiences years later, Evans remarked, "If you're going to do it, you might as well do it right."[5]

Corporal William "Jeff" Jefferies of Richmond, Indiana, served with A Company, 1st Battalion, 6th Marines, and was involved in the fierce tank battles the first two nights on Saipan. Wounded four times, Jefferies kept on fighting: "Didn't want to leave the Marines I had been with since early 1943 in New Zealand." With his buddy, Bob Reed, Jefferies "tried to slip around the side of a Japanese weapons depot to fire a rocket into it when we heard bullets fired at us. I was in front of Bob, and some bullets went through my dungaree jacket without hitting me but one got Bob in the chest. We got him out of there and bandaged him up and sent him back for more treatment. He later wrote from Guadalcanal Hospital and said the bullet collapsed his lung but he was doing alright and was more worried about me." Nearly sixty years later, the memories for Jefferies remained difficult to confront: "It is very hard to write about this—brings back too many memories—but they have always been there in back of my head."[6]

Private First Class Carl "Tubby" Matthews of Hubbard, Texas, served with G Company, 23rd Marines. On 8 July, shortly before Saipan was declared secured, Matthews's commanding officer, Lieutenant James Leary, was killed. Later that day, Matthews was evacuated to the navy hospital ship *Samaritan*. He was suffering from a concussion from an artillery shell blast that had fallen short a few days earlier. Blood vessels in his brain were ruptured, and the seepage of blood had created a condition similar to a stroke. He recovered on board ship and then in hospitals in New Caledonia, San Francisco, and Oakland for more than thirty days. Even sixty years later, Matthews could not recall details of his recovery period: "The time between July 8, 1944 and the fall of that year, even today, is not clearly remembered. I remember regaining consciousness for a brief time on the hospital ship." He did remember sailors lifting weights and that when one of the weights dropped onto the steel deck, "the explosive-like sound so unnerved me that I began to tremble and vomit." His recovery time in New Caledonia "is still a blank," and he acknowledged that his "deteriorated emotional state continued for months and months." Weighing only 110 pounds when he left the Marianas, Matthews put on fifteen pounds before being released from the hospital. After leaving Oakland Navy Hospital, he took a train to San Diego and then hitchhiked home to Texas. For the rest of his life, Matthews considered Leary his dearest friend, naming his son in honor of his fallen lieutenant.[7]

Corporal Jim Montgomery of Inkster, North Dakota, served with an 81-millimeter mortar platoon attached to the 3rd Battalion, 6th Marines. He saw action on Tarawa, Saipan, Tinian, and Okinawa and received the Navy and Marine Corps Medal for "putting out a fire in a pile of 81-millimeter mortar shells." Although never wounded, Montgomery suffered from the effects of various tropical diseases: "I was evacuated and put in a hospital because I had dengue fever and malaria. When my 81-millimeter mortar platoon came back from Saipan, I rejoined them and we got ready to go to Nagasaki for occupation duty. I served in the Marine Corps for three years and one day. The end."[8]

Like Montgomery, Private Alva Perry, with A Company, 1st Battalion, 24th Marines, was one of the lucky ones. Despite fighting in the battles of Roi-Namur, Saipan, Tinian, and Iwo Jima, he was never wounded. Perry had volunteered when only seventeen years old, and he served as a company scout (point man) and carried a BAR, both dangerous assignments. His Silver Star commendation praised his action on 6 July: "With his company undergoing a severe enemy counterattack, Private First Class Perry fearlessly rose to his feet and walked forward firing his automatic rifle, personally accounting for twenty-seven Japanese soldiers and setting heroic examples for the balance of the platoon, who moved up behind him and broke the enemy counterattack." Only six men out of his original company of 246 in A Company were not casualties. Perry recited the statistics: "I do know that over 650 went through our company in the 16 months we were in combat. Our division left the U.S. with 18,000 and during the 16 months we were in the Pacific over 80,000 went through our division. There was only three ways to get out of the division. Killed, wounded, or cracked up." These numbers weighed heavily on Perry, who remembered a visit to a war cemetery: "As I walked through the 4th Division cemetery and Taps sounded my heart was heavy, we had not won, nobody had. As I looked at the names on the white markers I wondered something I had never wondered before. Had the burial detail put the arms and legs of the men in those wooden boxes or did they have a burial plot for the pieces left over."[9]

Private Rod Sandburg of Minneapolis, Minnesota, served with H Battery, 3rd Battalion, 10th Marines. After the Gyokusai, Sandburg participated with H Battery and its replacement marines in the invasion of Tinian, and he then returned to Saipan for the final sweep of the island to clean out any remaining Japanese. By the end of 1944 he was suffering from headaches and periodic blackouts. While the doctors could not diagnose his problem, they decided that he was not fit for combat as he might "black out at the wrong time." Sandburg was evacuated to Hawaii and sent to a hospital in Oregon. There the doctors discovered that "when the hand grenade exploded in my face, my head was thrown back and my neck was broken." Despite this injury suffered on 7 July, Sandburg had continued to fight on both Saipan and Tinian until the doctors forced him to return to the United States. Nearly sixty years after the Gyokusai, the memories of that day remained with him: "I have lived those fifteen hours of the counterattack every day of my life since it happened. It's something one doesn't forget." Moreover, Sandburg devoted many years to correcting the official version of the Gyokusai, which placed the 10th Marines in the wrong location: "The official version of the counterattack is false. We were not in support of the 23rd Marines of the 4th Division. We were in support of the 27th Army. We did set up about 600 yards behind them, late in the day, on July 6th." Sandburg continued to emphasize the role of the 10th Marines: "This fight was between the 3rd Battalion of Marines and what was left of the Jap fighting force on the Island. One just does not forget such a tremendous trauma. That day to me and those that were there is buried more in our memory then yesterday." Despite his open discussion of these events, Sandburg added: "My children have no idea what I went through in the service as I never would talk about it. They only know that I was injured. In the early eighties we started to have reunions. Here it was easy to reminisce with those that were there and could understand what we went through."[10]

Private First Class Don Swindle, born in Webtown, Tennessee, served with F Company, 2nd Battalion, 23rd Marines. He dealt with his memories by interlacing war stories with amusing incidents, such as the time he and a buddy took refuge in a pile of "chicken shit." He also laughed while recalling how Charles "Tex" Keeshan, who made the mistake of cutting into a dead ox, was sprayed by the swollen animal's water, guts, and "crap." No one would share a foxhole with Tex for several days. Humor remained Swindle's way of coping with some of his memories, because when asked about battle experiences he choked up and moved quickly to lighter moments in his life. It was clear that he had been a good combat marine, exactly the type who exemplified the best of the military. He received his Purple Heart on Iwo Jima, and then spent many years not thinking about the war: "I spent forty-five years trying to forget about the war and the last fifteen years trying to remember." Still, he expressed a surprising emotion: "I don't feel any remorse even though I think I should."[11]

Sergeant Jerry Wachsmuth of Sheboygan, Wisconsin, served with E Company, 2nd Battalion, 6th Marines. He enlisted in the Marine Corps in 1939, just as events were "heating up in Europe." By 1941 he felt that "it was just a matter of time before we would be involved." His assumption soon was reality: "I was on board the USS *Pennsylvania* in Pearl Harbor on December 7, 1941 when the Japanese attack took place." On Saipan, he suffered from exhaustion, malaria, dengue fever, and dysentery. He continued to fight despite the fevers and chills that were associated with these diseases, and it eventually took him eight months to recover in hospitals in Eniwetok, Hawaii, and Seattle. In Wachsmuth's view, "the mortars were the most devastating because you heard the hiss but you didn't know where it would hit." Wachsmuth still heard that sound after the war: "Back in the States if a trolley came down the street I would duck into a doorway." Nevertheless, he had a positive feeling about his service: "I do believe, in fact know, that my service in the United States Marine Corps gave me a discipline and work ethic that have been very positive and followed me and given me a good, from my point of view, fruitful life. The Corps values have never left me."[12]

Lieutenant John Armstrong, executive officer of Headquarters Company of the 105th Regiment, 27th Division, was from Troy, New York. He joined the National Guard in May 1937, when he was fifteen years old. He told the "amused sergeant" that he was eighteen, and from then on his military records listed his age as three years older than he really was. After the war, as he was about to receive a regular commission, Captain Armstrong requested in a letter sent through channels to the War Department that his records be changed to show his true birth date. The correction was made in September 1947; Armstrong became three years younger, with his age reduced from twenty-eight to twenty-five. Armstrong, along with his friend Lieutenant Luke Hammond, devoted many years to rectifying the allegations of army inaction at the time of the Gyokusai:

> The statement to the effect that the 27th Division was overrun is false, as the 105th Regimental Command Post not only stopped the Jap attack but counterattacked. How could a Division be overrun when the attack is stopped at Regiment? Another statement I challenge is that the Japs were armed only with sharpened bamboo sticks. They may have used the sticks on our wounded as has been reported, but the Japs charging at my section of the line had rifles. I know what they had—I was there. A statement to the effect that H. M. Smith would not have the 27th under his command again is laughable except for the hurt and damage he and his rear area writer—Sherrod—inflicted on the morale of Army troops.[13]

Sergeant Mark Marquardt served with the 27th Cavalry Reconnaissance Troop (Mechanized). After leaving Saipan, Marquardt and his unit sailed on a Dutch troop transport to Espiritu Santo, where he spent time in the hospital. After recovering he was returned to active duty and saw action on Okinawa. Wounded twice, once on Saipan from a flamethrower and once on Okinawa from a mortar, Marquardt years after the war could still "see the maggots crawling out of the body orifices of the dead."[14]

Lieutenant Joe Meighan of Troy, New York, served with M Company, 105th Regiment. He devoted many years to rehabilitating the reputation of the soldiers after the Gyokusai. Many of his views directly contradicted those of Rod Sandburg. While Sandburg insisted that marine artillery was in support of the 27th Division, Meighan asserted that "the Marine battery behind our lines was set up to support their attacking forces, not ours. They were sleeping in hammocks when the Japs struck." Meighan also lobbied for recognition for Ben Salomon, the regimental dentist who fought to defend his wounded patients and died in the process. Salomon was finally awarded the Medal of Honor in 2002.[15]

Private John Munka of Akron, Ohio, served in the 3rd Battalion, 106th

Regiment, under Lieutenant Colonel Harold Mizony, who was killed in Death Valley. The death of his fellow soldiers, and even of the Japanese, bothered Munka. In relating how he shot an enemy tank driver who stood up in the hatch, Munka declared, "I can still see that scene and I can't forget I killed a human being." Munka knew, however, that the Japanese soldier would have killed him if he had not acted. Because enemy soldiers refused to surrender, American forces had no choice but to blow up caves knowing that there were Japanese inside. More difficult was the sight of so many dead women and children. "It would make you sick," Munka said. By the end of the battle, he stopped caring about being killed: "Just kill me fast if I get shot."[16]

A wife of a marine wrote to me almost sixty years after the battle:

> I am writing for my husband. He was wounded in the leg on the fourth day and has a Purple Heart. He was a private and his weapon was a BAR. He was put back in battle and his company helped take Mt. Tapotchau. He will not say if he actually saw any of the suicides but that he saw where they jumped. He will not write or even talk much about the war and his part in it so I am taking it upon myself to do this. When he came home he said he did not want to talk or ever to think about the war again. So his children grew up only knowing he had been a Marine in the war. He went to one 2nd Marine reunion in Las Vegas after some old buddies started writing and visiting him. He had pushed it so far in the back of his mind that he had trouble remembering some of the events they talked about. After awhile you could see he started remembering. Brought back some of the nightmares when he said he was chasing or stomping Japs.[17]

In June 2004, I planned to visit Saipan for the sixtieth-anniversary commemoration of the battle. Hoping to interview several more veterans, I sent a message to the members of the division associations asking about participation in the events on the island. Two 4th Division marines quickly expressed their regrets: John Stone wrote to say: "I've been to Saipan twice. The first time, I lost a leg and the second time I went back to see if I could find it. NO LUCK! Twice was enough for me." Jack Scalici expressed similar sentiments: "Not for me Mr. Goldberg. I saw all that I ever want to see of Saipan." Nevertheless, many marines did return to the island for the commemoration, and I was fortunate to meet and interview three wonderful veterans: Walter Bailey, Keith Renstrom, and Don Swindle.

While the vast majority of veterans made a smooth transition back into civilian society, all had been transformed by their experiences. They carried within themselves their memories of life-changing events that were difficult to explain even to their closest family members. All had participated in bloody and haunting events, yet at the same time they all knew that they had contributed to the Allied victory over malevolent ideologies.

Admirals King, Nimitz, Spruance, Turner, and Mitscher and marine and army generals Holland Smith, Thomas Watson, Harry Schmidt, Ralph Smith, Sanderford Jarman, and George Griner all deserve the recognition that accrues to military commanders after a successful campaign. Nevertheless, the real credit belongs to the men who fought the battles: navy personnel who brought the troops across the Pacific Ocean, pilots who destroyed enemy planes and secured air supremacy, corpsmen who always responded to the call for help in the midst of battle, and of course the marine and army frontline troops themselves.

PRINCIPAL MILITARY UNITS WITH COMMANDING OFFICERS

UNITED STATES FORCES ON SAIPAN

Navy
Admiral Raymond Spruance—commander U.S. Fifth Fleet
Vice Admiral Richmond Kelly Turner—commander Task Force 51 for Mariana Islands and Task Force 52 for Saipan and Tinian
Vice Admiral Marc Mitscher—commander Task Force 58

Marine Corps
Lieutenant General Holland M. Smith—commander Expeditionary Troops
Brigadier General Graves B. Erskine—Chief of Staff

Infantry Regiments of the 2nd Marine Division
Major General Thomas E. Watson—Division Commander
Brigadier General Merritt A. Edson—Assistant Division Commander

2nd Marines—Colonel Walter J. Stuart
  1st Battalion—Lieutenant Colonel Wood B. Kyle
  2nd Battalion—Lieutenant Colonel Richard C. Nutting
  3rd Battalion—Lieutenant Colonel Arnold F. Johnston (WIA 21 June); Major Harold "K" Throneson (21 June to 4 July); Lieutenant Colonel Arnold F. Johnston (from 5 July)

6th Marines—Colonel James P. Riseley
  1st Battalion—Lieutenant Colonel William K. Jones
  2nd Battalion—Lieutenant Colonel Raymond L. Murray (WIA 15 June); Major LeRoy P. Hunt Jr. (from 15 June)

3rd Battalion—Lieutenant Colonel John W. Easley (WIA 15 June); Major John E. Rentsch (15 June to 2 July); Lieutenant Colonel John W. Easley (from 3 July)

8th Marines—Colonel Clarence R. Wallace
    1st Battalion—Lieutenant Colonel Lawrence C. Hays Jr.
    2nd Battalion—Lieutenant Colonel Henry P. Crowe
    3rd Battalion—Lieutenant Colonel John C. Miller (WIA 15 June); Major Stanley E. Larsen (from 15 June)

29th Marines (1st Battalion attached to 2nd Marine Division)—Lieutenant Colonel Guy E. Tannyhill (WIA 17 June); Lieutenant Colonel Rathvon M. Tompkins (WIA 2 July); Lieutenant Colonel Jack P. Juhan (from 2 July); Major William W. McKinley (from 4 July)

10th Marines (Artillery Regiment)—Colonel Raphael Griffin
    1st Battalion—Colonel Presley M. Rixey (transferred to Regimental Executive Officer on 24 June); Major Wendell H. Best (from 25 June)
    2nd Battalion—Lieutenant Colonel George R. E. Shell (WIA 16 June); Major Kenneth C. Houston (from 16 June)
    3rd Battalion—Major William L. Crouch (KIA 7 July); Major James O. Appleyard (from 8 July)
    4th Battalion—Lieutenant Colonel Kenneth A. Jorgensen

18th Marines—Lieutenant Colonel Russell Lloyd (to 6th Marines on 25 June); Lieutenant Colonel Ewart S. Laue (from 26 June)

Infantry Regiments of the 4th Marine Division
Major General Harry Schmidt—Division Commander
Brigadier General Samuel C. Cumming—Assistant Division Commander

23rd Marines—Colonel Louis R. Jones
    1st Battalion—Lieutenant Colonel Ralph Haas
    2nd Battalion—Lieutenant Colonel Edward J. Dillon
    3rd Battalion—Lieutenant Colonel John J. Cosgrove (WIA 19 June); Major Paul S. Treitel (from 19 June)

24th Marines—Colonel Franklin A. Hart
    1st Battalion—Lieutenant Colonel Maynard C. Schultz (DOW 16 June); Major Robert N. Fricke (16 to 18 June); Lieutenant Colonel Austin R. Brunelli (18 June to 4 July); Lieutenant Colonel Otto Lessing (from 4 July)
    2nd Battalion—Lieutenant Colonel Richard Rothwell
    3rd Battalion—Lieutenant Colonel Alex A. Vandegrift Jr. (WIA 27 June, evacuated 29 June); Lieutenant Colonel Otto Lessing (29 June to 3 July); Lieutenant Colonel Alex A. Vandegrift Jr. (from 3 July)

25th Marines—Colonel Merton J. Batchelder
  1st Battalion—Lieutenant Colonel Hollis U. Mustain
  2nd Battalion—Lieutenant Colonel Lewis C. Hudson Jr.
  3rd Battalion—Lieutenant Colonel Justice M. Chambers (WIA 22 June); Major
    James Taul (22 to 23 June); Lieutenant Colonel Justice M. Chambers (from
    23 June)

14th Marines (Artillery Regiment)—Colonel Louis G. DeHaven
20th Marines—Lieutenant Colonel Nelson K. Brown
10th Amphibian Tractor Battalion—Major Victor J. Croizat

Army
Major General Ralph C. Smith (relieved 24 June); Major General Sanderford Jarman (from 24 June, reverted to Saipan Garrison Force Commander on 28 June);
Major General George W. Griner (from 28 June)—Division Commander
Brigadier General Ogden J. Ross—Assistant Division Commander
Colonel A. C. Stebbins—Chief of Staff

Infantry Regiments of the 27th Infantry Division
105th Regiment—Colonel Leonard A. Bishop
  1st Battalion—Lieutenant Colonel William J. O'Brien (KIA 7 July)
  2nd Battalion—Lieutenant Colonel Leslie Jensen (transferred to Regimental
    Executive Officer); Major Edward McCarthy
  3rd Battalion—Lieutenant Colonel Edward T. Bradt

106th Regiment—Colonel Russell G. Ayers (relieved 26 June); Colonel A. C.
  Stebbins (from 26 June)
  1st Battalion—Lieutenant Colonel Winslow Cornett
  2nd Battalion—Major Almerin C. O'Hara
  3rd Battalion—Lieutenant Colonel Harold I. Mizony (KIA 28 June); Major
    Francis Fisher (from 28 June)

165th Regiment—Colonel Gerard W. Kelley (WIA 28 June); Lieutenant Colonel
  Joseph T. Hart (from 28 June)
  1st Battalion—Major James H. Mahoney
  2nd Battalion—Lieutenant Colonel John F. McDonough (WIA 25 June); Major
    Gregory Brousseau (from 25 June, WIA 27 June); Capt James A. Dooley
    (temporary 27 June); Major Dennis D. Claire (from 27 June)
  3rd Battalion—Major Dennis D. Claire (transferred to 2nd Battalion 27 June);
    Major Martin H. Foery (from 27 June)

XXIV Corps Artillery—Brigadier General Arthur M. Harper

JAPANESE FORCES ON SAIPAN

Lieutenant General Obata Hideyoshi—31st Army Headquarters (on Guam)
Lieutenant General Saito Yoshitsugu—43rd Division Headquarters
Admiral Nagumo Chuichi—Central Pacific Area Fleet Headquarters

Main defensive forces on the island:
43rd Infantry Division, reinforced—under Lieutenant General Saito Yoshitsugi
(total strength 12,139):
  118th Infantry Regiment—Colonel Ito Takeshi
  135th Infantry Regiment (less the 1st Battalion, which was on Tinian)—Colonel
    Suzuki Eisuke
  136th Infantry Regiment—Colonel Ogawa Yukimatsu

47th Independent Mixed Brigade—Colonel Yoshiro Oka (total strength 3,437):
  315th (sent to Pagan in May), 316th (Captain Eto Susumu), 317th (Captain
    Sasaki), 318th (Major Nagashima) Independent Infantry Battalions
  1st and 3rd Battalions of the 3rd Independent Mountain Artillery Regiment
  3rd Battalion, 10th Field Artillery Regiment and 3rd Company, 25th Indepen-
    dent Engineer's Regiment

9th Tank Regiment—Colonel Goto Takashi (total strength 550)
3rd Independent Mountain Artillery Regiment—Lieutenant Colonel Nakashima
  Tsune
7th Independent Engineer Regiment—Colonel Koganezawa Fukujiro (total
  strength 600)
25th Independent AA Regiment—Lieutenant Colonel Niiho Jitsunori (total
  strength 900)
Independent Mortar Battalions—Captain Jinnai Tatsuo and Captain Matsunami
  Hajime
5th Base Force Headquarters—Admiral Tsujimura Takahisa
55th Naval Guard Force—Captain Takashima Sanji (total strength about 2,000)
1st Yokosuka Special Naval Landing Force (SNLF)—Lieutenant Commander
  Karashima Tatsue (total strength about 800)
264th and 278th Independent Vehicle Companies—Captain Iwama Tadaomi and
  Lieutenant Arima Shozo (total strength 240)
9th Expeditionary Force (total strength 900)

NOTES

INTRODUCTION

1. Johnston, *Follow Me*, 175.

1. ADMIRAL KING AND GENERAL MacARTHUR

1. See Manchester, *American Caesar*.

2. Potter, *Nimitz*, 1, 8; Sherrod, *On to Westward*, 299; Smith and Finch, *Coral and Brass*, 75, 80.

3. King and Whitehill, *Fleet Admiral King*, 416–20.

4. Ibid., 438.

5. Ibid., 444.

6. Ibid., 482–89.

7. For details on the marines on Tarawa see Shaw, Nalty, and Turnbladh, *Central Pacific Drive*, 53–102, and Alexander, *Utmost Savagery*; for details on the 165th Regiment on Makin see Love, *27th Infantry Division*, 23–55.

8. Smith and Finch, *Coral and Brass*, 125–26.

9. Ibid., 127, 147.

10. Marshall, *Bringing Up the Rear*, 69.

11. Johnston, *Follow Me*, 158; Love, *27th Infantry Division*, 55; Shaw, Nalty, and Turnbladh, *Central Pacific Drive*, 102.

12. Potter, *Nimitz*, 279–83.

13. For details on 27th Infantry Division on Eniwetok see Love, *27th Infantry Division*, 59–111.

14. King and Whitehill, *Fleet Admiral King*, 536.

15. Forrestel, *Spruance*, 99–118; Potter, *Nimitz*, 278.

16. Taylor, *The Magnificent Mitscher*.

17. The Department of Navy website provides detailed information on these ships: www .history.navy.mil/photos/pers-us/uspers-m/m-mitshr.htm; www.history.navy.mil/photos/ usnshtp/cv/cv9cl.htm; www.history.navy.mil/photos/usnshtp/cv/cv122cl.htm.

18. G-2 Report, p. 3, Box 34, Record Group [RG] 127, Records of U.S. Marine Corps, National Archives [NA], College Park, Md.; Crowl, *Campaign in the Marianas*, 26; Love,

27th Infantry Division, 118; Morison, *New Guinea and the Marianas*, 154–55; Sherrod, *On to Westward*, 86.

19. G-2 Report, p. 5, Box 34, RG 127, NA; Crowl, *Campaign in the Marianas*, 51; Shaw, Nalty, and Turnbladh, *Central Pacific Drive*, 245–46.

20. G-2 Report, pp. 4–5, Box 34, RG 127, NA.

21. King and Whitehill, *Fleet Admiral King*, 538; Potter, *Nimitz*, 291.

22. Manchester, *American Caesar*, 351.

23. Forrestel, *Spruance*, 120–21; U.S. Strategic Bombing Survey, *Campaigns of the Pacific War*, 207, 209.

24. Dyer, *The Amphibians Came to Conquer*, 2:873.

2. THE TARGET

1. G-2 Report, p. 74, Box 34, RG 127, NA; Crowl, *Campaign in the Marianas*, 54; Morison gives the length of the Charan Kanoa runway as 3,875 feet; see *New Guinea and the Marianas*, 168.

2. The submarines *Shark*, *Pintado*, and *Pilotfish* hit the seven-ship convoy; see Morison, *New Guinea and the Marianas*, 17, 167–68. Crowl gives slightly different figures for *Sakito Maru*—1,688 rescued out of 3,080 troops—in *Campaign in the Marianas*, 59.

3. Denfeld, *Japanese World War II Fortifications*, 25.

4. Crowl, *Campaign in the Marianas*, 57; Morison, *New Guinea and the Marianas*, 167.

5. Crowl, *Campaign in the Marianas*, 65, 68, 453. Hoffman provides different figures for the Japanese army (22,700) and navy (6,600) on Saipan; *Saipan*, 10–12, 281–82.

6. Robert Kane, e-mail to author, 28 June 2002.

7. Love, *27th Infantry Division*, 118–19, 127.

8. Denfeld, *Japanese World War II Fortifications*, 27.

9. Love, *27th Infantry Division*, 119; for additional information on Japanese defensive positions see Morison, *New Guinea and the Marianas*, 167–69, and Shaw, Nalty, and Turnbladh, *Central Pacific Drive*, 255–62.

10. Denfeld, *Japanese World War II Fortifications*, 27, 31.

11. G-2 Report, p. 7, Box 34, RG 127, NA.

12. Ibid.

13. Quoted in Crowl, *Campaign in the Marianas*, 63.

3. OPERATION FORAGER

1. Smith and Finch, *Coral and Brass*, 181; U.S. Strategic Bombing Survey, *Campaigns of the Pacific War*, 220.

2. Buell, *Quiet Warrior*, 30; Forrestel, *Spruance*, 7; Potter, *Nimitz*, 228.

3. Buell, *Quiet Warrior*, 255; for Turner's early years and career up to the middle of 1943 see vol. 1 of Dyer, *The Amphibians Came to Conquer*; for the rest of the war and Turner's life after the war see vol. 2; for comments on Turner's personality, see Dyer, *The Amphibians Came to Conquer*, 1:xxi, 150; see also Smith and Finch, *Coral and Brass*, 110.

4. For a description of the development of the Higgins boat, see www.higginsboat .org/.

5. Harlan T. Rosvold in *2nd Armored Amphibian Battalion*, 68.

6. Smith and Finch, *Coral and Brass*, 16–17, 18, 22, 57.

7. Marshall, *Bringing Up the Rear*, 69.

8. Gailey, *Howlin' Mad vs. the Army*, 40–42; Marshall, *Bringing Up the Rear*, 62; Morison, *New Guinea and the Marianas*, 158–60; Shaw, Nalty, and Turnbladh, *Central Pacific Drive*, 239–42.

9. Johnston, *Follow Me*, 158.

10. Ibid., 169, 172.

11. Harry Phillips, interview with author, July 2001.

12. Lane, "G" *Company*, 38–39.

13. Matthews, *G-Company*, 17.

14. Alva Perry, e-mail to author, 19, 27 March 2002.

15. Graf, *Easy Company*, 164.

16. Matthews, *G-Company*, 17.

17. Torok, *Stepping Stones*, 30.

18. Chapin, *Breaching the Marianas*, 7.

19. Hilbert, "Charlie's War," 22–26; Proehl, *Fourth Marine Division*, 120–24.

20. Members of each marine regiment used the term "marines," as in "2nd Marines" rather than "2nd Regiment." In the spring of 1944 the 1st Battalion, 29th Marines, was attached to the 2nd Marine Division. Referred to as the "bastard" battalion, it played a major role in the taking of Mt. Tapotchau.

21. Love, *27th Infantry Division*, 116–17; Morison, *New Guinea and the Marianas*, 186–87; Proehl, *Fourth Marine Division*, 120–25.

22. Lane, "G" *Company*, 35.

23. Potter, *Nimitz*, 284–85; Richardson's official title was commanding general, U.S. Army Forces, Pacific Ocean Areas.

24. Marshall, *Bringing Up the Rear*, 74–78.

25. Dyer, *The Amphibians Came to Conquer*, 2:893; LSTs (Landing Ship, Tank) were 336-foot-long flat-bottomed crafts. A huge area belowdecks held tanks, amphibious landing vehicles, and other equipment. A door on the front of the huge area was lowered into the water when landing vehicles were ready to debark. Smaller LCTs (Landing Craft, Tank) were 114 feet long and could be tied down on the decks of the larger LSTs.

26. Crowl, *Campaign in the Marianas*, 46.

27. Graf, *Easy Company*, 179–80; Lane, "G" *Company*, 45; Matthews, *G-Company*, 22–23.

28. *2nd Armored Amphibian Battalion*, 61, 66, 70.

29. Dyer, *The Amphibians Came to Conquer*, 2:893–95.

30. Morison, *New Guinea and the Marianas*, 164.

31. Dyer, *The Amphibians Came to Conquer*, 2:892. Some sources give Spruance up to eight hundred ships; see Jones, *Oba*, 20; Sherrod, *History of Marine Corps Aviation*, 248. For another total (644) see Karig, Harris, and Manson, *Battle Report*, 224. The number of assault troops also varies. According to Crowl, *Campaign in the Marianas*, 36, "there were 105,859 assault troops assigned to capture the three islands; 66,779 were allocated to Saipan and Tinian and the remaining 39,080 to Guam."

32. Gabaldon, *Saipan*, 67.

33. Jim Evans, interview with author, September 2001.

34. Graf, *Easy Company*, 189,

35. Gabaldon, *Saipan*, 68.

36. Harry Phillips, interviews with author, 2001; Phillips ended his military career with the rank of lieutenant colonel.

37. Because of the American commitment in the Pacific, the British navy provided many of the ships for the Normandy invasion. For more on D-Day in Europe see Eisen-

hower, *Eisenhower's Own Story of the War*, 3–26. Admiral King reported that more than twenty-four hundred American ships and craft participated in the operation; see King, *U.S. Navy at War*, 137.

38. *2nd Armored Amphibian Battalion*, 72–76.

39. Proehl, *Fourth Marine Division*, 58; Proehl names correspondent John Campbell as his source for this citation.

4. "A CONDEMNED MAN'S BREAKFAST"

1. Crowl, *Campaign in the Marianas*, 38, 450; Morison, *New Guinea and the Marianas*, 160.

2. Rod Sandburg, e-mail to author, 2 October 2003.

3. Rear Admiral Richard Conolly commanded the Southern Attack Force (Task Force 53) going to Guam.

4. U.S. Strategic Bombing Survey, *Campaigns of the Pacific War*, 211–12.

5. Ibid., 234; U.S. Strategic Bombing Survey lists twelve cruisers; see also Crowl, *Campaign in the Marianas*, 74–76.

6. Hoffman, *Saipan*, 40.

7. Quoted in Crowl, *Campaign in the Marianas*, 74–75; see also Forrestel, *Spruance*, 129; Shaw, Nalty, and Turnbladh, *Central Pacific Drive*, 253–55.

8. Dyer, *The Amphibians Came to Conquer*, 2:901–2; Hoffman, *Saipan*, 41. Crowl reported two divers killed and fifteen wounded in the operation; see *Campaign in the Marianas*, 77. Sherrod states in *On to Westward* that "Kauffman had 80 men and 24 officers. Only 16 were killed or wounded—which was a miracle" (47).

9. Jim Evans, interview with author, September 2001; Best quoted in Hoffman, *Saipan*, 45.

10. All times in this book will follow the twenty-four-hour clock; e.g., 7:15 AM is 0715, and 10:35 PM is 2235. Roush, *Open Fire*, 399; Platoon Level Log Report, Company D, in *2nd Armored Amphibian Battalion*, 144, indicates 0145, while Dock Riddle says 0400. Riddle, *Dock's Wanderings and Wonderings*, 16.

11. Robert Wollin in *2nd Armored Amphibian Battalion*, 69.

12. William Jefferies, e-mail to author, 9 March 2002.

13. Marshall Harris in *2nd Armored Amphibian Battalion*, 102.

14. Alva R. Perry, e-mail to author, 19 March 2002.

15. Winton W. Carter in *2nd Armored Amphibian Battalion*, 94.

16. Harlan T. Rosvold in *2nd Armored Amphibian Battalion*, 103.

17. U.S. Strategic Bombing Survey, *Campaigns of the Pacific War*, 212.

18. Orvel Johnson, e-mail to author, 18 March 2002.

19. Matthews, *G-Company*, 26.

20. Rod Sandburg, e-mail to author, 1 March 2002.

21. Winton W. Carter in *2nd Armored Amphibian Battalion*, 94.

22. Gene Brenner, e-mail to author, 8 March 2002.

23. Sherrod, *On to Westward*, 45.

24. Orvel Johnson, e-mail to author, 18 March 2002.

25. Matthews, *G-Company*, 27.

26. G-2 Report, p. 10, Box 34, RG 127, NA.

27. Matthews, *G-Company*, 27.

28. Orvel Johnson, e-mail to author, 18 March 2002.

5. THE 2ND MARINE DIVISION LANDS

1. Japanese radio broadcasts employed a variety of female announcers, all nicknamed "Tokyo Rose" by U.S. troops. At the end of the war, one Japanese American woman, Iva Ikuko Toguri, was tried and convicted for participating in those broadcasts. She was sentenced to ten years in prison but served only seven (1949–56). She was granted a full pardon by President Gerald Ford in 1977.

2. James "Al" Scarpo and G. Milton Shirley in *2nd Armored Amphibian Battalion*, 68.

3. Quoted in ibid. 77.

4. Quoted in ibid. 78.

5. Colonel Joseph H. Alexander to author, 23 February 2006.

6. Ibid.; for an excellent description of this intricate maneuver, see Alexander, *Storm Landings*.

7. Roush, *Open Fire*, 399.

8. *2nd Armored Amphibian Battalion*, 12.

9. Alexander to author, 23 February 2006; Alexander, *Storm Landings*, 99.

10. *2nd Armored Amphibian Battalion*, 12.

11. Marshall E. Harris in ibid., 129; Hoffman, *Saipan*, 47.

12. G. Milton Shirley in *2nd Armored Amphibian Battalion*, 105.

13. The 2nd Armored Amphibian Battalion lost more men on 15 June than during the entire Battle of Iwo Jima in 1945. See ibid., 82–84, 88. Other units involved in the invasion included 5th Amphibian Tractor Battalion (Marine), 10th Amphibian Tractor Battalion (Marine), 534th Amphibian Tractor Battalion (Army), 715th Amphibian Tractor Battalion (Army), 773rd Amphibian Tractor Battalion (Army), 2nd Armored Amphibian Tank Battalion (Marine), and 708th Amphibian Tank Battalion (Army).

14. George L. Mazarakos, e-mail to author, 1 May 2002.

15. Battalion Special Action Report in *2nd Armored Amphibian Battalion*, 157.

16. R. J. Lee in ibid., 89.

17. S. A. Balsano in *2nd Armored Amphibian Battalion*, 90, 92; Lieutenant Philo Pease was the platoon leader.

18. Charles D. Porter, e-mail to author, 7 April 2002.

19. L. H. Van Antwerp in *2nd Armored Amphibian Battalion*, 95.

20. Corporal David Kinder, e-mail to author, 25 June 2002.

21. The five were Lieutenant Colonel John C. Miller of 3rd Battalion, 8th Marines; Lieutenant Colonel Henry Crowe of 2nd Battalion, 8th Marines; Lieutenant Colonel John W. Easley of 3rd Battalion, 6th Marines; Lieutenant Colonel Raymond L. Murray of 2nd Battalion, 6th Marines; and Lieutenant Colonel Lawrence C. Hayes Jr. of 1st Battalion, 8th Marines. See Hoffman, *Saipan*, 50–51; Johnston, *Follow Me*, 185–86.

22. Graf, *Easy Company*, 174.

23. M. F. Leggett, interview with author, September 2001.

24. Reginald Dunbar, e-mail to author, 1 March 2002.

25. Jim Evans, interview with author, September 2001.

26. Edward Skrabacz, interview with author, September 2001.

27. Chester Szech, interview with author, September 2001.

28. Bird, leader of 2nd Platoon, E Company, 2nd Battalion, 6th Marines, 2nd Division, was removed to a naval hospital and fitted with an artificial leg. After the war he returned to Oklahoma and reenrolled in college. He became the athletic trainer for football at

Oklahoma State University in 1950, and in 1979 he was admitted into the National Athletic Trainers' Association Hall of Fame. Material on Bird, including various newspaper articles, was sent to the author by e-mail and letter by Sergeant Jerry Wachsmuth, who served with Bird.

29. L. H. Van Antwerp in *2nd Armored Amphibian Battalion*, 96.

30. Gabaldon, *Saipan*, 73.

31. Ralph Browner, interview with author, September 2001.

32. Quoted in *Semper Fidelis*, 50–51.

33. Ralph Browner, interview with author, September 2001.

34. Steve Judd, interview with author, September 2001.

35. Jim Montgomery, interview with author, September 2001.

36. Jerry Wachsmuth, interview with author, September 2001.

37. Hoffman, *Saipan*, 66.

38. G-2 Report, p. 11, Box 34, RG 127, NA.

39. Corporal David Kinder, e-mail to author, 8 March 2002.

40. Dodson Smith, e-mail to author, 12 March 2002.

41. Corporal David Kinder, e-mail to author, 8 March 2002.

42. Jim Monroe, interview with author, September 2001.

43. Robert Groves, e-mail to author, 25 February 2002.

6. THE 4TH MARINE DIVISION LANDS

1. Lane, "*G*" *Company*, 48.

2. Lieutenant Colonel John J. Cosgrove, 3rd Battalion, 23rd Regiment; Lieutenant Colonel Edward J. Dillon, 2nd Battalion, 23rd Regiment; Lieutenant Colonel Lewis C. Hudson, 2nd Battalion, 25th Regiment; and Lieutenant Colonel Hollis U. Mustain, 1st Battalion, 25th Regiment.

3. G-2 Report, p. 10, Box 34, RG 127, NA.

4. Proehl, *Fourth Marine Division*, 59.

5. Earl Guy, e-mail to author, 2 April 2002, and letter to author, 11 May 2004.

6. R. P. Willson, interview with author, 11 November 2002.

7. R. B. Roberts, e-mail to author, 17 May 2002.

8. B. G. (Bill) Taylor, e-mail to author, 19 March 2002.

9. Paul Beverley, e-mail to author, 18 March 2002.

10. Alan Taylor, interview with author, September 2001.

11. See www.c123rd.com/.

12. Marriro did not lose his legs; Carl Matthews, e-mail to author, 12 October 2003.

13. Don Swindle, interview with author, June 2004.

14. Norman Gertz, e-mail to author, 28 March 2002; Bill More, Joe Ojeda, and Jasper Smith, interviews with author, September 2001.

15. Captain William Weinstein, copy of letter to author, 29 August 1944.

16. Torok, *Stepping Stones*, 15.

17. Ibid.

18. Marvin Scott, interview with author, September 2001.

19. Paul Schwartz, e-mail to author, 24 March 2002.

20. Ibid.

21. Bob Verna, interview with author, September 2001.

22. See www.c123rd.com/.

23. See Sherrod, *On to Westward*, 68.

24. Donovan quoted in Chapin, *Breaching the Marianas*, 4.

25. Orvel Johnson, e-mails to author, 18 March, 18 April, 25 June 2002; see also www .c123rd.com/.

26. Ibid.

27. Richard Hertensteiner, e-mail to author, 15 April 2002.

28. Richard G. Pederson in *2nd Armored Amphibian Battalion*, 96.

29. Rod Sandburg, e-mail to author, 2 October 2003.

30. John Dickinson, e-mail to author, 19 March 2002.

31. Pete Cypher, e-mail to author, 19 June 2002.

32. Dave Dowdakin, e-mail to author, 19 June 2002.

33. Raymond Hill, e-mail to author, 8 March 2002.

34. Dodson Smith, e-mail to author, 12 April 2002.

35. John Dickinson, e-mail to author, 19 March 2002.

36. Robert R. Montgomery, e-mail to author, 1 March 2002.

37. Calvin E. Orr in *2nd Armored Amphibian Battalion*, 122.

38. Joe Risener, e-mail to author, 25 March 2002.

39. Chapin, *Breaching the Marianas*, 3.

40. Hoffman, *Saipan*, 73.

41. Stott, *Saipan under Fire*; both Alexander and Hoffman stated that Major Robert N. Fricke replaced Schultz; see Alexander to author, 23 February 2006, and Hoffman, *Saipan*, 82.

42. Dyer, *The Amphibians Came to Conquer*, 2:906.

43. Quoted in Hoffman, *The Beginning of the End*, 71.

44. G-2 Report, pp. 19–20, Box 34, RG 127, NA.

7. THE GREAT MARIANAS TURKEY SHOOT

1. U.S. Strategic Bombing Survey, *Campaigns of the Pacific War*, 226.

2. Ibid., 207.

3. Even after the United States dropped the atomic bombs, Toyoda opposed Japan's surrender. He died in 1957.

4. Morison, *New Guinea and the Marianas*, 178.

5. Potter, *Nimitz*, 298.

6. Buell, *Quiet Warrior*, 262–64.

7. Potter, *Nimitz*, 299.

8. On 15 and 16 June, Rear Admirals William K. Harrill and Joseph "Jocko" Clark led the raids on the air bases on Iwo Jima and Chichi Jima. Forrestel, *Spruance*, 132; U.S. Strategic Bombing Survey, *Campaigns of the Pacific War*, 212.

9. Buell, *Quiet Warrior*, 267.

10. Smith and Finch, *Coral and Brass*, 165.

11. Forrestel, *Spruance*, 135.

12. Dyer, *The Amphibians Came to Conquer*, 2:912–13; Forrestel, *Spruance*, 136.

13. Buell, *Quiet Warrior*, 272–73; Forrestel, *Spruance*, 137.

14. For a description of the organization of Ozawa's fleet see Dull, *Imperial Japanese Navy*, 323; Karig, Harris, and Manson, *Battle Report*, 223–24; see also Morison, *New Guinea and the Marianas*, 216; Potter, *Nimitz*, 299.

15. Forrestel, *Spruance*, 136; Morison, *New Guinea and the Marianas*, 233.

16. Buell, *Quiet Warrior*, 267–69; Dull, *Imperial Japanese Navy*, 315; Potter, *Nimitz*, 299.

17. Forrestel, *Spruance*, 136; Morison, *New Guinea and the Marianas*, 233.

18. U.S. Strategic Bombing Survey, *Campaigns of the Pacific War*, 229.

19. Dull, *Imperial Japanese Navy*, 319.

20. Quoted in Buell, *Quiet Warrior*, 270; Potter, *Nimitz* 299.

21. Dull, *Imperial Japanese Navy*, 317; William Sheehan quoted in Petty, *Voices from the Pacific War*, 48.

22. Ozawa and Spruance quoted in Morison, *New Guinea and the Marianas*, 232–33, 253; see also Dull, *Imperial Japanese Navy*, 317.

23. Taylor, *The Magnificent Mitscher*, 224–25.

24. "Judy" was slang for a Japanese dive-bomber. Quoted in Karig, Harris, and Manson, *Battle Report*, 240.

25. Buell, *Quiet Warrior*, 274; Karig, Harris, and Manson, *Battle Report*, 239–40.

26. Dull, *Imperial Japanese Navy*, 320; Forrestel, *Spruance*, 139; Morison, *New Guinea and the Marianas*, 263–274.

27. Forrestel, *Spruance*, 145; King and Whitehill, *Fleet Admiral King*, 558; Morison, *New Guinea and the Marianas*, 277, 319–21.

28. This name was attributed to Commander Paul D. Buie of Fighter Squadron 16 on USS *Lexington*. See Morison, *New Guinea and the Marianas*, 257.

29. Dull, *Imperial Japanese Navy*, 320–21; Forrestel, *Spruance*, 140; Kossler quoted in Karig, Harris, and Manson, *Battle Report*, 241–42.

30. Buell, *Quiet Warrior*, 276; Forrestel, *Spruance*, 143; Spruance quoted in Morison, *New Guinea and the Marianas*, 284.

31. Taylor, *The Magnificent Mitscher*, 233.

32. Karig, Harris, and Manson, *Battle Report*, 246.

33. Quoted in ibid., 246–48.

34. Quoted in Taylor, *The Magnificent Mitscher*, 234, 235.

35. Forrestel, *Spruance*, 143; King and Whitehill, *Fleet Admiral King*, 558; Morison, *New Guinea and the Marianas*, 301–4; U.S. Strategic Bombing Survey, *Campaigns of the Pacific War*, 215.

36. King and Whitehill, *Fleet Admiral King*, 558; Potter, *Nimitz* 302.

37. For estimates of total Japanese air losses see Morison, *New Guinea and the Marianas*, 319–20; also Karig, Harris, and Manson, *Battle Report*, 242.

38. Taylor, *The Magnificent Mitscher*, 237; see also Potter, *Nimitz*, 303.

39. Taylor, *The Magnificent Mitscher*, 238–39.

40. King and Whitehill, *Fleet Admiral King*, 557–58.

41. Taylor, *The Magnificent Mitscher*, 239–40.

42. Potter, *Nimitz*, 303.

43. Smith and Finch, *Coral and Brass*, 160.

8. THE 2ND MARINE DIVISION MOVES FORWARD

1. Hoffman, *Saipan*, 91.

2. Jim Evans, interview with author, September 2001.

3. G-2 Report, pp. 12, 34, Box 34, RG 127, NA; Johnston, *Follow Me*, 191.

4. M. F. Leggett, interview with author, September 2001.

5. Sherrod, *On to Westward*, 66.

6. William Jefferies, e-mail to author, 9 March 2002.

7. Sherrod, *On to Westward*, 66–67.

8. Quoted in Chapin, *Breaching the Marianas*, 8; Johnston, *Follow Me*, 194.

9. Sherrod, *On to Westward*, 67.

10. Johnston, *Follow Me*, 194.

11. Smith and Finch, *Coral and Brass*, 184.

12. Johnston, *Follow Me*, 195.

13. M. F. Leggett, interview with author, September 2001.

14. Hoffman, *Saipan*, 92–93.

15. Everett, *World War II*, 1.

16. Navy Cross citation quoted in Everett, *World War II*, appendix.

17. Johnston, *Follow Me*, 198.

18. Chester Szech, interview with author, September 2001.

19. Dodson Smith, e-mail to author, 1 September 2002.

20. Jones quoted in Sherrod, *On to Westward*, 52–54.

21. Ibid., 65.

22. Johnston, *Follow Me*, 214.

23. Sherrod, *On to Westward*, 74–75.

24. Jim Montgomery, interview with author, September 2001.

25. Johnston, *Follow Me*, 200–201.

26. Ibid., 202.

27. John Orsock quoted in Everett, *World War II*, 25.

28. Robert D. Parker, e-mail to author, 17 August 2002.

29. Earl Lingerfelt quoted in Everett, *World War II*, 28.

30. M. M. Drake quoted in ibid., 35; Chamberlin took command of the 2nd Battalion when Lieutenant Colonel Henry "Jim" Crowe was wounded on D-Day.

31. Robert D. Parker, e-mail to author, 17 August 2002; Johnston, *Follow Me*, 203.

32. M. M. Drake quoted in Everett, *World War II*, 37.

33. Keene, "The Orphan Battalion," 22.

34. M. M. Drake quoted in Everett, *World War II*, 37.

35. Frank Borta quoted in ibid., 34.

36. Crowl, *Campaign in the Marianas*, 210.

37. Mort Hamilton quoted in Everett, *World War II*, 46; Edson's reputation was made in August 1942 when "Edson's Raiders" landed on Tulagi in the British Solomon Islands and took the island in two days of fierce fighting. In September 1942 Edson and his marines defended Lunga Ridge on Guadalcanal. Edson and eight hundred marines held off more than twenty-five hundred Japanese attackers on this "Bloody Ridge." The marines called it "Edson's Ridge," and Edson was awarded a Medal of Honor for this action.

38. Robert D. Parker, e-mail to author, 17 August 2002.

39. Despite the heroic record of the 29th Marines, a few of its members experienced a dishonorable moment. Eleven men of Company C had deserted and were AWOL "from their stations and duty during battle and remained absent for various periods of time from twelve days to one month twenty-eight days." In the fall of 1944 these marines were court-martialed and sentenced to various punishments from death to ten years in prison. In July 1945 all the sentences were reduced and all eleven men were "restored to duty." With the invasion of Japan pending, this reduction in sentence might have meant an even worse fate for the former prisoners. See letter from General Clifton B. Cates to Senator Homer Ferguson, 7 April 1948, in Everett, *World War II*, appendix.

40. Jones quoted in Sherrod, *On to Westward*, 86.

41. Jerry Wachsmuth and Bob Thatcher, joint interview with author, September 2001.

42. For Epperson's Medal of Honor citation, see www.army.mil/cmh-pg/mohiia1.htm.

43. S. E. Brenner, e-mail to author, 10 September 2003.

44. Ibid.

45. G-2 Report, p. 31, Box 34, RG 127, NA.

46. Chapin, *Breaching the Marianas*, 23.

9. THE 4TH MARINE DIVISION MOVES FORWARD

1. For McCard's Medal of Honor citation, see www.army.mil/cmh-pg/mohiibl.htm.

2. For John Seymour and Orvel Johnson, see www.c123rd.com/.

3. For John Seymour, see www.c123rd.com/.

4. Matthews, *G-Company*, 28.

5. Ibid., 30.

6. John Rempke, interview with author, September 2001.

7. Keith Renstrom, interview with author, June 2004.

8. Sherrod, *On to Westward*, 72.

9. Robert Verna, interview with author, September 2001. Verna missed the rest of the battle but developed ideas about heroism: "There's no such thing as a hero. A guy does what he has to do in the situation. The military has a need to give out medals. But people are doing what they have to do. They are all heroes."

10. Matthews, *Skeebow*, 33.

11. Ibid., 34–35.

12. Matthews, *Wendell Nightengale*, 12.

13. Frank Britt, e-mail to author, 20 June 2002.

14. Chapin, *Breaching the Marianas*, 15.

15. Graf quoted in ibid., 17–18; E Company, 2nd Battalion, 23rd Regiment, was led by Major Lester S. Fought Jr., who was killed on Iwo Jima.

16. Jerry Wachsmuth, interview with author, September 2001.

17. M. F. Leggett, interview with author, September 2001.

18. Quoted in Chapin, *Breaching the Marianas*, 18.

19. Matthews, *G-Company*, 36.

20. Clifford Howe, e-mail to author, 1 March 2002.

21. Steve Judd, interview with author, September 2001.

22. Matthews, *G-Company*, 42.

23. Ibid., 45–46.

24. For Perry see http://home1.gte.net/mfperry/history_of_fourth_division_final.htm.

25. Al Perry, Silver Star Citation, http://home1.gte.net/mfperry/history_of_fourth_division_final.htm.

26. See www.c123rd.com/.

10. MARINES UNDER FIRE

1. Orvel Johnson, e-mail to author, 25 June 2002; see also www.c123rd.com.

2. Alva Perry, e-mail to author, 20 June 2002.

3. Rod Sandburg, e-mails to author, 18 April, 9 June 2002.

4. Raymond Hill, e-mail to author, 8 March 2002.

5. John Rempke, interview with author, September 2001.

6. Paul G. "Jerry" Goforth, e-mail to author, 21 July 2003.

7. Jerome Baron, e-mail to author, 18 March 2002.

8. Gabaldon, *Saipan*, 92.

9. Torok, *Stepping Stones*, 40; for information on military rations, see www.ww2rationtechnologies.com/History.html.

10. Rod Sandburg, e-mail to author, 9 June 2002.

11. Paul Beverly, e-mail to author, 18 March 2002.

12. Chapin, *Breaching the Marianas*, 15.

13. Gabaldon, *Saipan*, 75.

14. John Rempke, interview with author, September 2001.

15. Rod Sandburg, e-mail to author, 7 May 2002.

16. Dodson Smith, e-mail to author, 9 March 2002.

17. Torok, *Stepping Stones*, 24.

18. Sandburg, e-mail to author, 7 May 2002.

19. Dodson Smith, e-mail to author, 9 March 2002.

20. M. Neil Mumford in *2nd Armored Amphibian Battalion*, 115.

21. Herb Cracraft in ibid., 115.

22. Gabaldon, *Saipan*, 92.

23. Torok, *Stepping Stones*, 33.

24. Paul G. "Jerry" Goforth, e-mail to author, 21 July 2003.

25. David E. Kinder, e-mail to author, 25 June 2002.

26. John Dickinson, e-mail to author, 18 June 2002.

27. Dodson Smith, e-mail to author, 19 June 2002.

28. Ibid.

29. David Kinder, e-mail to author, 25 June 2002.

30. George Van Houten, e-mail to author, 18 June 2002.

31. Rod Sandburg, e-mail to author, 7 May 2002.

32. Torok, *Stepping Stones*, 42.

33. Basil Duncan, www.geocities.com/Heartland/Plains/5850/saipan1.html.

34. Marvin Scott, interview with author, September 2001.

35. Jerome Baron, e-mail to author, 18 March 2002; a carbine was a semi-automatic weapon with a clip holding eight .30-caliber shells.

36. Rod Sandburg, e-mail to author, 27 February 2002.

37. Marvin Scott, interview with author, September 2001.

38. Stott, *Saipan under Fire*.

39. Chambers quoted in Chapin, *Breaching the Marianas*, 29.

40. Torok, *Stepping Stones*, 33–35.

41. Keith Renstrom, interview with author, June 2004.

42. Mike Mervosh, interview with author, September 2001.

43. M. F. Leggett, interview with author, September 2001.

44. Chambers quoted in Chapin, *Breaching the Marianas*, 29.

45. Bob Thatcher, interview with author, September 2001.

46. Jerry Wachsmuth, interview with author, September 2001.

47. Gabaldon, *Saipan*, 76, 79.

48. Edward Skrabacz, interview with author, September 2001; Skrabacz was talking about another marine.

49. Gabaldon, *Saipan*, 87–88.

50. Robert Winters, e-mail to author, 10 March 2002.

51. M. F. Leggett, interview with author, September 2001.

11. THE 27th INFANTRY DIVISION ON SOUTHERN SAIPAN

1. The 3rd Battalion, 105th Regiment, had joined the 165th Regiment in the invasion of Makin.

2. Love, *27th Infantry Division*, 120.

3. Crowl, *Campaign in the Marianas*, 41; Love, *27th Infantry Division*, 120; O'Brien, *Battling for Saipan*, 73.

4. Potter, *Nimitz*, 295.

5. Holland Smith quoted in Gailey, *Howlin' Mad vs. the Army*, 124.

6. Ross was born in Troy, New York. He served in World War I, and between the wars he was a member of the New York State Senate and a delegate to the New York State Constitutional Convention in 1938. Crowl, *Campaign in the Marianas*, 99–100.

7. John Earley, letter to author, 5 September 2001; Earley served with the 106th Field Artillery Battalion, which was attached to the 165th Regiment in the initial army landing.

8. Love, *27th Infantry Division*, 130.

9. Ibid., 131.

10. John Earley, letter to author, 5 September 2001; Jack Cotton, e-mail to author, 2 March 2002.

11. Clifford W. Howe, e-mail to author, 1 March 2002.

12. Love, *27th Infantry Division*, 133; on 28 June, Colonel Gerard Kelley, commanding officer of the 165th Regiment, was wounded and was replaced by Hart.

13. Crowl, *Campaign in the Marianas*, 114.

14. Love, *27th Infantry Division*, 137.

15. Denfeld, *Japanese World War II Fortifications*, 28–29.

16. Love, *27th Infantry Division*, 135–56.

17. On 18 June the army changed the name of Aslito Field to Conroy Field in honor of Colonel Gardiner Conroy of the 165th Regiment, who had been killed in the battle for Makin in November 1943. At the end of June 1944, the navy renamed the field in honor of Lieutenant Commander Robert Isely, who was shot down and killed over Aslito on 13 June. Isely Field became official, but members of the army resented the change. John Earley, interview with author, September 2001.

18. U.S. Strategic Bombing Survey, *Campaigns of the Pacific War*, 212.

19. Dolan quoted in O'Brien, *Battling for Saipan*, 91.

20. Giuffre quoted in ibid., 95.

21. Love, *27th Infantry Division*, 157–59.

22. John Armstrong, e-mail to author, 15 June 2002.

23. Hammond quoted in O'Brien, *Battling for Saipan*, 104.

24. Love, *27th Infantry Division*, 166.

25. For Baker's Medal of Honor citation, see http://www.army.mil/cmh-pg/mohiia1.htm.

26. Landing Force Operation Order no. 9-44; Crowl, *Campaign in the Marianas*, 149; Love, *27th Infantry Division*, 187.

27. Love, *27th Infantry Division*, 175.

28. Hammond quoted in O'Brien, *Battling for Saipan*, 118.

29. Love, *27th Infantry Division*, 184.

30. For Baker's Medal of Honor citation, see http://www.army.mil/cmh-pg/mohiia1.htm.

31. Crowl, *Campaign in the Marianas*, 149; Love, *27th Infantry Division*, 188.

32. Crowl, *Campaign in the Marianas*, 147.

33. Love, *27th Infantry Division*, 190; other sources claim that seven men were killed. See Crowl, *Campaign in the Marianas*, 150.

34. Quoted in Crowl, *Campaign in the Marianas*, 150–51, and in Gailey, *Howlin' Mad vs. the Army*, 144–45.

35. Crowl, *Campaign in the Marianas*, 151.

36. Sherrod, *On to Westward*, 82.

37. Love, *27th Infantry Division*, 195.

38. Smith and Finch, *Coral and Brass*, 186.

39. Crowl, *Campaign in the Marianas*, 155–60.

40. Quoted in G-2 Report, p. 34, Box 34, RG 127, NA; see also Crowl, *Campaign in the Marianas*, 159, and O'Brien, *Battling for Saipan*, 147–48.

41. Crowl, *Campaign in the Marianas*, 159–61; Love, *27th Infantry Division*, 219–22; O'Brien, *Battling for Saipan*, 149–50.

42. Smith and Finch, *Coral and Brass*, 187.

43. Crowl, *Campaign in the Marianas*, 160–61.

44. Love, *27th Infantry Division*, 222; the magazine was *Time* from 18 September 1944. The magazine's allegations later became part of a major dispute between the army and marines.

12. INTO DEATH VALLEY

1. Crowl, *Campaign in the Marianas*, 169–70.

2. Love, *27th Infantry Division*, 227–28; in another section of his book Love stated that the marines had retreated between four hundred and six hundred yards. See 660.

3. Ibid., 230, 232.

4. Crowl, *Campaign in the Marianas*, 173.

5. Love, *27th Infantry Division*, 244.

6. John Munka, interview with author, September 2001.

7. Love, *27th Infantry Division*, 230–31.

8. Stebbins quoted in Crowl, *Campaign in the Marianas*, 174.

9. Ayers and Ralph Smith quoted in ibid., 179.

10. Ibid., 177–80; Love, *27th Infantry Division*, 232.

11. Crowl, *Campaign in the Marianas*, 175–76; Love, *27th Infantry Division*, 234–39.

12. Love, *27th Infantry Division*, 660.

13. Ibid., 243.

14. Smith and Finch, *Coral and Brass*, 170.

15. Ibid., 173.

16. Ralph Smith quoted in Crowl, *Campaign in the Marianas*, 184, 186; see also Love, *27th Infantry Division*, 254–58.

17. Jarman quoted in Crowl, *Campaign in the Marianas*, 207; for details on the fighting of each company see Love, *27th Infantry Division*, 263–89.

18. Crowl, *Campaign in the Marianas*, 217.

19. Jarman quoted in ibid., 219; for details on the fighting of each company see Love, *27th Infantry Division*, 299–316.

20. Crowl, *Campaign in the Marianas*, 224; for details on the fighting of each company see Love, *27th Infantry Division*, 316–32.

21. John Munka, interview with author, September 2001.

22. In 1943 George W. Griner commanded the 13th Airborne Division in North Carolina; subsequently he led the 98th Infantry Division on Hawaii.

23. For details on the fighting of each company see Love, *27th Infantry Division*, 332–39.

24. Crowl, *Campaign in the Marianas*, 232.

25. Smith and Finch, *Coral and Brass*, 175.

26. G-2 Report, pp. 64–66, Box 34, RG 127, NA.

27. Quoted in Crowl, *Campaign in the Marianas*, 213.

13. GYOKUSAI

1. Love, *27th Infantry Division*, 119–20.

2. For Orvel Johnson, see www.c123rd.com.

3. Smith quoted in Hoffman, *Saipan*, 207.

4. Griner quoted in ibid., 210.

5. Ibid., 211–12.

6. Ibid., 214.

7. Ibid., 215.

8. G-2 Report, pp. 38, 42, Box 34, RG 127, NA.

9. Ibid., 57–58; Saito died at 1000 the same morning; see Hoffman, *Saipan*, 283–84; Love, *27th Infantry Division*, 433–34.

10. John Armstrong, e-mail to author, 9 February 2002.

11. "Tenno" and "Heika" are both terms for "the Emperor." "Banzai" means "ten thousand years," the lifespan wished for the ruler, and "Gyokusai" means "breaking the jewel." See Love, *27th Infantry Division*, 434, and Morison, *New Guinea and the Marianas*, 337.

12. For the army version see Love, *27th Infantry Division*, 439; for the marine version see Hoffman, *Saipan*, 226.

13. O'Brien, *Battling for Saipan*, 206.

14. Cimaszewski and Johnson quoted in ibid., 221.

15. Luther Hammond, interview with author, February 2002.

16. Mark Marquardt, interview with author, September 2001.

17. Love, *27th Infantry Division*, 435–37.

18. Ibid., 435.

19. Occinerio quoted in ibid., 438.

20. Luther Hammond, interview with author, February 2002.

21. Love, *27th Infantry Division*, 437.

22. G-2 Report, p. 59, Box 34, RG 127, NA.

23. McCarthy and Polikowski quoted in Love, *27th Infantry Division*, 443.

24. Ibid., 446–50.

25. Luther Hammond, interview with author, February 2002.

26. Love, *27th Infantry Division*, 450.

27. Luther Hammond, interview with author, February 2002; Marquardt interview with author, September 2001.

28. O'Brien, *Battling for Saipan*, 239.

29. For O'Brien's Medal of Honor citation see www.army.mil/cmh/mohiib1.htm; see also Love, *27th Infantry Division*, 453.

30. For Baker's Medal of Honor citation, see www.army.mil/cmh/mohiib1.htm.

31. For Salomon's Medal of Honor citation, see www.army.mil/cmh/mohiib1.htm.

32. Love, *27th Infantry Division*, 455.

33. Joseph Meighan, e-mail to author, 18 January 2002.

34. Love, *27th Infantry Division*, 462–65.

35. Ibid., 466, 472.

36. Hoffman, *Saipan*, 223.

37. John Armstrong, e-mails to author, 13 December 2001, 21, 29–31 January, 2, 9 February, 12 March, 8, 10, 23 April, 17, 25 May, 15 June 2002.

38. Ibid.

39. Ibid.

40. Hoffman, *Saipan*, 225–26.

41. Rod Sandburg, e-mails to author, 3, 6 February 2004; army veterans deny the accuracy of this explanation.

42. Rod Sandburg, e-mail to author, 3 February 2004.

43. Rod Sandburg, e-mails to author, 26 February, 7, 9 May 2002, 3, 9 February 2004.

44. Ibid.

45. Ibid.

46. For Agerholm's Medal of Honor citation see www.army.mil/cmh/mohiib1.htm; Corporal Alvin Ferry praised Agerholm's bravery in an e-mail to author, 5 March 2002.

47. Joe Ojeda, interview with author, September 2001; Don Swindle, interview with author, June 2004.

48. Joe Epperson, interview with author, September 2001.

49. "Paradise Valley" was about a thousand yards east of Makunsha. The Japanese called the same area "Hell Valley." "Harakiri Gulch" referred to a canyon near Tanapag and below Hill 721: "sixty enemy soldiers had unaccountably committed suicide in these little houses over a period of a few minutes. This was the incident that gave the valley its name of Hara-Kiri Gulch." Love, *27th Infantry Division*, 398.

50. Emmett Scott Prothero, e-mail to author, 15 May 2004.

51. Clifford Howe, e-mail to author, 27 March, 2002.

52. Sandburg, e-mail to author, 7 May 2002.

53. Marquardt, interview with author, September 2001; Earley, letter to author, 5 February 2002; Wachsmuth, interview with author, September 2001.

54. Smith quoted in Cooper, *A Fighting General*, 188.

55. Love, *27th Infantry Division*, 431.

56. Smith and Finch, *Coral and Brass*, 198.

57. Griner quoted in Hoffman, *The Beginning of the End*, 233; Griner should have listed the 3rd Battalion, 10th Marines.

58. Love, *27th Infantry Division*, 433; for another protest by Griner, see also Hoffman, *Saipan*, 234.

59. Hoffman, *Saipan*, 235.

60. Ibid., 230.

61. For Timmerman's Medal of Honor citation see www.army.mil/cmh/mohiib1.htm.

62. Browner, interview with author, September 2001.

63. Spruance quoted in Buell, *Quiet Warrior*, 289; Sasebo is a naval base in Japan.

14. SUICIDE CLIFF AND BANZAI CLIFF

1. Chester Szech, interview with author, September 2001.

2. Keith Renstrom, interview with author, June 2004.

3. Don Swindle, interview with author, June 2004.

4. Frank Britt, e-mail to author, 20 June 2002; *Life*, 28 August 1944, 77.

5. Keith Renstrom, interview with author, June 2004; Gunnery Sergeant Renstrom served with F Company, 2nd Battalion, 25th Regiment, 4th Division.

6. See *War Times Journal*, September 1998, www.wtj.com/articles/gabaldon/.

7. Gabaldon, *Saipan*; the movie, glorifying the role of Gabaldon, starred the tall, blue-eyed, non-Chicano actor Jeffrey Hunter.

8. "Modesto Man Seeks Medal for WWII Capture Exploits," *Fresno Bee*, 29 May 2000, 1, 9; Gabaldon died in 2006.

9. *War Times Journal*, September 1998, www.wtj.com/articles/gabaldon/.

10. David Dowdakin, e-mail to author, 11 May 2004.

11. Rowland Lewis, www.c123rd.com/.

12. For Alva Perry and Paul Scanelon, see http://home1.gte.net/mfperry/history_of_fourth_division_final.htm.

13. Edward Skrabacz, interview with author, September 2001.

14. Bill More, interview with author, September 2001.

15. Stott, *Saipan under Fire*.

16. John Rempke, interview with author, September 2001.

17. Steve Judd, Jim Montgomery, and Chester Szech, interviews with author, September 2001.

18. Joe Ojeda and M. F. Leggett, interviews with author, September 2001; Clifford Howe, e-mail to author, 1 March 2002.

19. John Seymour, www.c123rd.com/.

20. John Armstrong, e-mail to author, 23 November 2001.

21. Love, *27th Infantry Division*, 518–19.

22. Other African American units also served on Saipan and Tinian: 510th Port Battalion (Tinian), 538th Port Company (Saipan), 539th Port Company (Saipan), 590th Port Company (Saipan), 591st Port Company (Saipan), 627th Quartermaster Battalion (Tinian), 848th Quartermaster Gas Supply Company (Saipan), 3291st Quartermaster Service Company (Tinian), 3697th Quartermaster Truck Company (Saipan), 4013th Quartermaster Truck Company (Saipan), 4070th Quartermaster Service Company (Tinian), 4103rd Quartermaster Truck Company (Saipan), 4209th Quartermaster Service Company (Saipan), 4210th Quartermaster Service Company (Saipan), 536th Salvage Repair Company (Detachment) (Tinian), 715th Signal Company (Tinian), 743rd Signal Company (Saipan).

23. See Jones, *Oba*; Captain Oba was accorded full military honors. He retired to Japan and died in 1997.

15. TŌJŌ AND TINIAN

1. For further information on Tojo see Behr, *Hirohito*; Bix, *Hirohito*; and Browne, *Tojo*.

2. J. William Winter, e-mail to author, 12 May 2002.

3. Joe Epperson, interview with author, September 2001.

CONCLUSION

1. Crowl, *Campaign in the Marianas*, 265–66.

2. Chester Szech, Ralph Browner, and Joe Epperson, interviews with author, September 2001.

APPENDIX A. HOLLAND SMITH AND THE ARMY

1. Persons, *Relieved of Command*, 177–78.

2. Smith and Finch, *Coral and Brass*, 168.

3. Love, *27th Infantry Division*, 657–60.

4. Crowl, *Campaign in the Marianas*, 178–79.

5. Smith and Finch, *Coral and Brass*, 172.

6. Holland Smith quoted in Crowl, *Campaign in the Marianas*, 178.

7. Love, *27th Infantry Division*, 661.

8. Herzog quoted in Gailey, *Howlin' Mad vs. the Army*, 188.

9. Quoted in Smith and Finch, *Coral and Brass*, 173.

10. Quoted in Gailey, *Howlin' Mad vs. the Army*, 181.

11. Buell, *Quiet Warrior*, 283.

12. Quoted in Smith and Finch, *Coral and Brass*, 173; see also Love, *27th Infantry Division*, 662; Potter, *Nimitz*, 305.

13. Ralph Smith quoted in Gailey, *Howlin' Mad vs. the Army*, 191.

14. Chapin, *Breaching the Marianas*, 14.

15. In 1943, General Buckner joined in the decision of Rear Admiral Thomas C. Kinkaid and Lieutenant General John L. DeWitt to remove Major General Albert E. Brown from command on the island of Attu; the reason was Brown's slow advance against Japanese forces.

16. Gailey, *Howlin' Mad vs. the Army*, 222.

17. Love, *27th Infantry Division*, 665.

18. Ibid., 667.

19. Ibid.

20. Potter, *Nimitz*, 307; Gailey, *Howlin' Mad vs. the Army*, 4–5.

21. Love, *27th Infantry Division*, 652.

22. Richardson quoted in Potter, *Nimitz*, 308.

23. Ibid.

24. Smith and Finch, *Coral and Brass*, 177.

25. Spruance quoted in Potter, *Nimitz*, 308.

26. Ibid., 308; see also Smith and Finch, *Coral and Brass*, 178.

27. Handy quoted in Gailey, *Howlin' Mad vs. the Army*, 231; Potter, *Nimitz*, 309.

28. Ralph Smith and Griner quoted in Crowl, *Campaign in the Marianas*, 192–93.

29. *Time*, 18 September 1944, 66, 68.

30. Ibid.

31. Ibid.

32. Sherrod, *On to Westward*, 89.

33. Ibid., 299.

34. Fitness reports for Holland McTyeire Smith, 1 April and 19 September 1944, copies in the author's possession.

35. Love, *27th Infantry Division*, 669.

36. Nimitz quoted in Potter, *Nimitz*, 309.

37. Ibid.

38. Ibid.

APPENDIX B. COMING HOME

1. Eugene V. Taylor, e-mail to author, 27 April 2002.

2. Walter Bailey, interview with author, June 2004.

3. Ralph Browner, interview with author, September 2001.

4. Basil Duncan, e-mail to author, 18 March 2002.

5. Jim Evans, interview with author, September 2001.

6. William Jefferies, e-mail to author, 9 March 2002.

7. Carl Matthews, e-mail to author, 21 November 2003.

8. Jim Montgomery, interview with author, September 2001.

9. Alva Perry, e-mail to author, 24 July 2003; www.home1.gte.net/mfperry.

10. Rod Sandburg, e-mails to author, 26 February, 20 April, 7, 9 May 2002, 13 August 2003, 1 February 2004.

11. Don Swindle, interview with author, June 2004.

12. Jerry Wachsmuth, interview with author, September 2001; e-mails to author, 5 February 2002, 26 May 2004.

13. John Armstrong, e-mails to author, 23 November 2001, 21 January 2002.

14. Mark Marquardt, interview with author, September 2001.

15. Joseph Meighan, e-mails to author, 5 November, 4, 7, 30 December 2001, 18, 20 January, 26 April, 4, 18, 19, 22 May 2002.

16. John Munka, interview with author, September 2001.

17. E-mail to author, 24 November 2002.

BIBLIOGRAPHY

INTERVIEWS

Walter Bailey (USMC), June 2004
Enzio Brandolini (USMC), September 2001
Ralph Browner (USMC), September 2001
Joseph Diamond (US Army), September 2001
John Earley (US Army), September 2001
Joseph Epperson (USMC), September 2001
James Evans (USMC), September 2001
Luther Hammond (US Army), February 2002
Steve Judd (USMC), September 2001
Gerald Kelleher (USMC), September 2001
Daniel Koshansky (US Army), September 2001
M. F. Leggett (USMC), September 2001
Erwin Mark Marquardt (US Army), September 2001
Mike Mervosh (USMC), September 2001
James Monroe (USMC), September 2001
James Montgomery (USMC), September 2001
William More (USMC), September 2001
John Munka (US Army), September 2001
John Murach (USMC), September 2001
Joe Ojeda (USMC), September 2001
Harry Phillips (USMC), July 2001
John Rempke (USMC), September 2001
Keith Renstrom (USMC), June 2004
Marvin Scott (USMC), September 2001
Edward Skrabacz (USMC), September 2001
Jasper Smith (USMC), September 2001
Arnold Stanek (USMC), September 2001
Don Swindle (USMC), June 2004
Chester Szech (USMC), September 2001
Joseph Tamulis (USMC), September 2001

Alan Taylor (USMC), September 2001
Robert Thatcher (USMC), September 2001
Victor Varanay (USMC), September 2001
Robert Verna (USMC), September 2001
Jerry Wachsmuth (USMC), September 2001
R. P. Willson (USMC), November 2002

BOOKS AND ARTICLES

Adams, Henry H. *Witness to Power: The Life of Fleet Admiral William D. Leahy.* Annapolis,
    Md.: Naval Institute Press, 1985.
Alexander, Joseph H. *Storm Landings: Epic Amphibious Battles in the Central Pacific.*
    Annapolis, Md.: Naval Institute Press, 1997.
———. *Utmost Savagery: The Three Days of Tarawa.* New York: Ivy Books, 1995.
Behr, Edward. *Hirohito: Behind the Myth.* New York: Villard Books, 1989.
Bix, Herbert P. *Hirohito and the Making of Modern Japan.* New York: HarperCollins,
    2000.
Browne, Courtney. *Tojo: The Last Banzai.* New York: Holt, Rinehart and Winston, 1967.
Buell, Thomas B. *The Quiet Warrior: A Biography of Admiral Raymond A. Spruance.*
    Boston: Little, Brown, 1974.
Cant, Gilbert. *The Great Pacific Victory.* New York: John Day, 1946.
Chapin, John C. *Breaching the Marianas: The Battle for Saipan.* Washington, D.C.: His-
    tory and Museums Division, Headquarters, U.S. Marine Corps, 1994.
———. *The 4th Marine Division in World War II.* 1945. Reprint, Washington, D.C.: History
    and Museums Division, Headquarters, U.S. Marine Corps, 1974.
Cole, Bernard D. "Struggle for the Marianas." *Joint Force Quarterly,* no. 7 (Spring 1995):
    86–93.
Cooper, Norman V. *A Fighting General: The Biography of Gen. Holland M. "Howlin' Mad"
    Smith.* Quantico, Va.: Marine Corps Association, 1987.
Costello, John. *The Pacific War, 1941–1945.* New York: Quill, 1981.
Croizat, Victor J. *Across the Reef: The Amphibious Tracked Vehicle at War.* Quantico, Va.:
    Marine Corps Association, 1989.
Crowl, Philip A. *Campaign in the Marianas: The War in the Pacific.* Washington, D.C.:
    Center of Military History, United States Army, 1993.
Denfeld, D. Colt. *Japanese World War II Fortifications and Other Military Structures in
    the Central Pacific.* Commonwealth of the Northern Mariana Islands: Division of
    Historic Preservation, 2002.
Dull, Paul S. *A Battle History of the Imperial Japanese Navy (1941–1945).* Annapolis, Md.:
    Naval Institute Press, 1978.
Dyer, George Carroll. *The Amphibians Came to Conquer: The Story of Admiral Richmond
    Kelly Turner.* 2 vols. Washington, D.C.: Department of the Navy, 1972.
Eisenhower, Dwight D. *Eisenhower's Own Story of the War.* New York: Arco, 1946.
Everett, Robert E., Sr. *World War II: Battle of Saipan.* Self-published, 1996.
Faquin, Arthur C. *A Walk Down Memory Lane with a Former Marine.* Self-published,
    1997.
Forrestel, E. P. *Admiral Raymond A. Spruance, USN: A Study in Command.* Washington,
    D.C.: Department of the Navy, 1966.
Fought, Jeffrey R. *Major Lester S. Fought Jr.: 23rd Marines, World War II.* Bellevue, Wash.:
    self-published, 1999.

Fuller, Richard. *Shokan: Hirohito's Samurai*. London: Arms and Armour, 1992.

Gabaldon, Guy. *Saipan: Suicide Island*. Saipan: self-published, 1990.

Gailey, Harry A. *Howlin' Mad vs. the Army: Conflict in Command Saipan 1944*. Novato, Calif.: Presidio, 1986.

———. *The War in the Pacific: From Pearl Harbor to Tokyo Bay*. Novato, Calif.: Presidio, 1995.

Gibney, Frank, ed. *Senso: The Japanese Remember the Pacific War*. Armonk, N.Y.: M. E. Sharpe, 1995.

Gilbert, Oscar E. *Marine Tank Battles in the Pacific*. Conshohocken, Pa.: Combined Publishing, 2001.

Graf, Robert. *Easy Company: My Life in the United States Marine Corps during World War II*. Self-published, 1986.

Harwood, Richard. *A Close Encounter: The Marine Landing on Tinian*. Washington, D.C.: History and Museums Division, Headquarters, U.S. Marine Corps, 1994.

Hayashi, Saburo, and Alvin D. Coox, *Kogun: The Japanese Army in the Pacific War*. Quantico, Va.: Marine Corps Association, 1959.

Hilbert, Charles Roy. *"Charlie's War": Memoirs of World War II*. Self-published, 1999.

Hoffman, Carl W. *Saipan: The Beginning of the End*. Nashville, Tenn.: Battery, 1950.

Hough, Frank O. *The Island War: The United States Marine Corps in the Pacific*. Philadelphia: Lippincott, 1947.

Hoyt, Edwin P. *How They Won the War in the Pacific: Nimitz and His Admirals*. New York: Lyons, 2000.

———. *Japan's War: The Great Pacific Conflict*. New York: Da Capo, 1986.

———. *To the Marianas: War in the Central Pacific: 1944*. New York: Van Nostrand Reinhold, 1980.

Johnston, Richard W. *Follow Me! The Story of the Second Marine Division in World War II*. Nashville, Tenn.: Battery, 1987.

Jones, Don. *Oba: The Last Samurai*. Novato, Calif.: Presidio, 1986.

Karig, Walter, Russell L. Harris, and Frank A. Manson. *Battle Report: The End of an Empire*. New York: Rinehart, 1948.

Keene, R. R. "The Orphan Battalion That Took Mount Tapotchau." *Leatherneck*, June 1994, 20–23.

Kido, Koichi. *The Diary of Marquis Kido, 1931–1945*. Frederick, Md.: University Publications of America, 1984.

King, Ernest J. *U.S. Navy at War, 1941–1945: Official Reports to the Secretary of the Navy*. Washington, D.C.: United States Navy Department, 1946.

King, Ernest J., and Walter Muir Whitehill. *Fleet Admiral King: A Naval Record*. New York: Norton, 1952.

Ladd, Dean. *Faithful Warriors: The Second Marine Division*. Spokane, Wash.: Ladd Communications, 1994.

Lane, John E. *This Here Is "G" Company*. New York: Brightlights Publications, 1997.

Levine, Alan J. *The Pacific War: Japan versus the Allies*. Westport, Conn.: Praeger, 1995.

Lodge, O. R. *The Recapture of Guam*. Washington, D.C.: Historical Branch, G-3 Division, Headquarters, U.S. Marine Corps, 1954.

Love, Edmund G. *The 27th Infantry Division in World War II*. 1949. Nashville, Tenn.: Battery, 2001.

Manchester, William. *American Caesar: Douglas MacArthur, 1880–1964*. Boston: Little, Brown, 1978.

Marshall, S. L. A. *Bringing Up the Rear: A Memoir*. San Rafael, Calif.: Presidio, 1979.

Matthews, Carl. *G-Company.* Self-published.

———. *Skeebow: A Pacific Journey.* Self-published.

———. *Wendell Nightengale.* Self-published.

Miller, Nathan. *War at Sea: A Naval History of World War II.* New York: Oxford University Press, 1995.

Morison, Samuel Eliot. *New Guinea and the Marianas, March 1944–August 1944.* Boston: Little, Brown, 1953.

O'Brien, Cyril J. *Liberation: Marines in the Recapture of Guam.* Washington, D.C.: History and Museums Division, Headquarters, U.S. Marine Corps, 1994.

O'Brien, Francis A. *Battling for Saipan.* New York: Ballantine Books, 2003.

Persons, Benjamin S. *Relieved of Command.* Manhattan, Kans.: Sunflower University Press, 1997.

Petty, Bruce M. *Saipan: Oral Histories of the Pacific War.* Jefferson, N.C.: McFarland, 2002.

———. *Voices from the Pacific War.* Annapolis, Md.: Naval Institute Press, 2004.

Potter, E. B. *Nimitz.* Annapolis, Md.: Naval Institute Press, 1976.

Potter, E. B., and Chester W. Nimitz. *The Great Sea War: The Story of Naval Action in World War II.* New York: Bramhall House, 1960.

Pratt, Fletcher. *The Marines' War: An Account of the Struggle for the Pacific from Both American and Japanese Sources.* New York: William Sloane Associates, 1948.

———. "Spruance: Picture of the Admiral." *Harper's Magazine,* August 1946, 144–57.

Proehl, Carl W. *The Fourth Marine Division in World War II.* Nashville, Tenn.: Battery, 1988.

Rees, David. *The Defeat of Japan.* Westport, Conn.: Praeger, 1997.

Riddle, Dock. *Dock's Wanderings and Wonderings: May 24, 1941 thru June 15, 1996.* Self-published, 1999.

Rottman, Gordon L. *Saipan and Tinian 1944: Piercing the Japanese Empire.* Oxford, U.K.: Osprey Publishing, 2004.

Roush, Roy William. *Open Fire!* Apache Junction, Ariz.: Front Line Press, 2003.

Schrijvers, Peter. *The GI War against Japan: American Soldiers in Asia and the Pacific during World War II.* New York: New York University Press, 2002.

2nd Armored Amphibian Battalion USMC WWII: Saipan, Tinian, Iwo Jima. 2nd Armored Amphibian Battalion Association, 1991.

Semper Fidelis: The U.S. Marines in the Pacific—1942–1945. New York: William Sloane Associates, 1947.

Shaw, Henry I., Jr., Bernard C. Nalty, and Edwin T. Turnbladh. *Central Pacific Drive: History of the U.S. Marine Corps Operations in World War II.* Washington, D.C.: Historical Branch, G-3 Division, Headquarters, U.S. Marine Corps, 1966.

Sherrod, Robert. *History of Marine Corps Aviation in World War II.* Washington, D.C.: Combat Forces Press, 1952.

———. *On to Westward: War in the Central Pacific.* New York: Duell, Sloan and Pearce, 1945.

Smith, Holland M., and Percy Finch. *Coral and Brass.* New York: Scribner, 1949.

Spector, Ronald H. *The Eagle against the Sun: The American War with Japan.* New York: Free Press, 1985.

Stott, Frederic A. *Saipan under Fire.* Self-published, 1945.

Taylor, Theodore. *The Magnificent Mitscher.* New York: Norton, 1954.

Torok, Tibor. *Stepping Stones across the Pacific: A Collection of Short Stories from the Pacific War.* New York: Vantage, 1999.

U.S. Strategic Bombing Survey (Pacific). *The Campaigns of the Pacific War.* Washington, D.C.: Government Printing Office, 1946.

Van der Vat, Dan. *The Pacific Campaign: The U.S.-Japanese Naval War, 1941–1945.* New York: Simon & Schuster, 1991.

Wells, Arthur W. *The Quack Corps: A Marine's War—Pearl Harbor to Okinawa.* Chico, Calif.: DolArt, 1999–2001.

Willmott, H. P. *The War with Japan: The Period of Balance, May 1942–October 1943.* Wilmington, Del.: Scholarly Resources, 2002.

INDEX

Photograph page numbers are shown in italics. Maps and caption information are identified by the suffix "f" (e.g. 15f).

HAROLD J. GOLDBERG is Professor of History at the
University of the South, Sewanee.